COLLECTOR'S
REFERENCE GUIDE

Antique American
Tractor and Crawler
Value Guide

Terry Dean & Larry L. Swenson

with photography by Randy Leffingwell

MBI Publishing Company

First published in 2001 by MBI Publishing Company, 729 Prospect Avenue, PO Box 1, Osceola, WI 54020-0001 USA

The information in this book is true and complete to the best of our knowledge. All recommendations are made without any guarantee on the part of the author or Publisher, who also disclaim any liability incurred in connection with the use of this data or specific details.

We recognize that some words, model names and designations, for example, mentioned herein are the property of the trademark holder. We use them for identification purposes only. This is not an official publication.

The photographs in this book are for identification purposes only. This book does not intend to place any values on any specific pieces of equipment pictured.

MBI Publishing Company books are also available at discounts in bulk quantity for industrial or sales-promotional use. For details write to Special Sales Manager at Motorbooks International Wholesalers & Distributors, 729 Prospect Avenue, PO Box 1, Osceola, WI 54020-0001 USA.

Library of Congress Cataloging-in-Publication Data
Dean, Terry.
    Antique American tractor & crawler value guide / Terry Dean & Larry L. Swenson; photography by Randy Leffingwell.
      p. cm.—(Collectors' reference guide)
  Includes index.
  ISBN 0-7603-0976-0 (pbk. : alk. paper)
    1. Antique and classic tractors—Collectors and collecting—United States. 2. Antique and classic tractors—Prices—United States. I. Title: Antique American tractor and crawler value guide. II. Swenson, Larry L. III. Title. IV. Series.

TL233.25.DE43 2001
631.3'72'075—dc21   00-050000

On the front cover: Tractor collecting grew from the enthusiasm of the scattered fancier into a highly respectable pastime with well-organized clubs and thousands of zealous hobbyists. Barns across the countryside harbor treasures such as the Case and International tractors shown here, and people everywhere cherish these wonderful pieces of agricultural history.

On the back cover: The values of the John Deere High-Crops are through the roof! The fortunate collectors who purchased a High-Crop ten to twenty years ago have found values multiplied greatly since then. This rare 1959 630H was not considered collectable 20 years ago; now it ranks high on the want-list of many collectors.

All photos by Randy Leffingwell, unless otherwise noted.
Edited by John Adams-Graf

Printed in the United States of America

CONTENTS

II. CRAWLER TRACTORS

ACKNOWLEDGMENTS

GALLERY OF DISTINGUISHED ADVISORS

Placing accurate values on antique tractors is an arduous task. To make this book as useful (and honest) as we possibly could, we solicited help from many advisors. We selected them for their in-depth knowledge of values for specific brands of tractors as well as for their personal integrity. The dollar amounts in this book resulted from a group effort. Auction results alone could distort values, so we combined that data with our advisors' knowledge of private sales. The enthusiasm and helpful attitudes of the advisors listed below impressed us greatly. One of the finest characteristics of antique tractor collecting is the friendly and honest atmosphere generated by people like these. We want to express deep gratitude for the efforts and expertise of these distinguished advisors.

Dave Baas	Floyds Knobs, IN	Gibson
Clayton P. Badgley	Kinde, MI	Eagle
Dennis Baker	Richwood, OH	Oliver
Bill Black	Melbourne, FL	John Deere (Dubuque)
Richard Bockwoldt	Dixon, IA	Rock Island, Heider
Keith V. Clark	Spokane, WA	Caterpillar, Best, Holt
Roger E. Culbert	Fillmore, NY	Allis-Chalmers
Bart C. Cushing	Gilsum (Keene), NH	John Deere
Darrell Darst	Moscow Mills, MO	International Harvester
John W. Davis	Maplewood, OH	Case
Craig Detwiler	Goshen, IN	Banting
John Dudkewitz	Landenberg, PA	Massey-Harris
Jess G. Enns	Kearney, NE	Graham-Bradley
Chris Epping	Funk, NE	Rumely, Aultman-Taylor
Rod Epping	Funk, NE	Rumely, Aultman-Taylor
Lavon H. Fred	Rochester, IN	Co-Op, Silver King, Bradley, Graham Bradley
Wayne Gamm	Bowling Green, MO	Case
Ron Goller	Defiance, OH	B.F. Avery, M-M Avery, Wards Twin Row
Tom "DC" Graverson	Bremen, IN	Case (D-series)
A. K. "JR" Gyger	Lebanon, IN	Case
Carl Hering	Cayuga, NY	Empire
Ray E. Hoffman	Blanchard, IA	Case
Leslie M. Holte	Dalton, MN	Massey-Harris
Maurice Horn	Rochester, IN	John Deere
Jeff Huff	Honeoye, NY	Caterpillar, Cletrac, rare brand crawlers
Jack F. Johnson	Bellingham, WA	Gibson
Kent Kaster	Shelbyville, IN	John Deere
Cork Lemmon	Camden, MI	B.F. Avery, M-M Avery, Wards Twin Row

Gary Love ....Canandaigua, NY .... International Harvester
Paul Lowry ....Francesville, IN ...... Minneapolis-Moline
Richard Lowry .....Francesville, IN ...... Minneapolis-Moline
Larry Maasdam .....Clarion, IA .... Caterpillar, Best, Holt
Steve Malecha ......Northfield, MN ..... Massey-Harris
Rick Mannen ......Lynden, Ontario ..... Eagle, Sawyer-Massey,
                                           Goold, Shapley & Muir
Arthur A. May .....York, PA .... Graham-Bradley
Keith A. McClure ...Big Prairie, OH ..... Cockshutt, Co-op
Larry Meservey .....Trenton, MO .... International Harvester
Russel Miner ......Pleasant Plains, IL .... Custom, Lehr, Rockol,
                                           Lowther, Wards, Simpson,
                                           Earthmaster
Larry Moit ....Evansville, IN .... John Deere
James R. Owensby ..Cochranville, PA ..... Monarch Neverslip,
                                           rare crawlers
Dan Perry ....Osceola, WI .... Centaur, Le Roi
Charles Plott ....Southington, OH .... Ferguson
Dave Preuhs ....LeCenter, MN ...... Hart-Parr
Ed Purvis ....South Whitley, IN ... Cockshutt
Neil A. Reitmeyer ...Shohola, PA .... Ford N series, Earthmaster
Marlo Remme .....Dennison, MN ...... Fordson, Ford
Jake Rens ....Boring, OR .... John Deere
Rufus M. Roberts ...Cortland, OH ...... Ford Motor Co.
Brian Rukes ....Weatherford, OK .... Minneapolis-Moline
Al Schubert ....Republic, OH .... Huber
Bernard Scott ......Cocoa, FL .... John Deere (Dubuque)
Earl Scott ....Marysville, OH ..... Global
Harold Sherron .....Boaz, KY .... Gibson
Richard Smith .....Ouaquaga, NY ...... John Deere
Gary Spitznogle ....Wapello, IA .... Cletrac, Hart-Parr, Oliver
Charles Stanton ....Kinde, MI .... Eagle
Richard C. Sterner ..Chambersburg, PA ... Sheppard
Dick Stoyell ....Moravia, NY .... International Harvester
Mark Strusz ....Goodhue, MN ...... Various brands
Benjamin Swart ....Fort Atkinson, WI ... American Tractor Corp.
                                           (Terratrac)
Larry Swenson .....Easton, MN .... Allis-Chalmers
Popeye Thompson ..Alexandria, OH ..... Eagle
Bob Vanderploeg ...Bellingham, WA ..... Allis-Chalmers
Bernard M. Wade ...Whitney Point, NY ... Sheppard
Ed Welters ....Verona, MO .... Minneapolis-Moline
Norm Westervelt ...Nichols, NY .... Fate-Root-Heath
                                           (Silver King)
Charles A. Widlund .Palmer, IA .... Allis-Chalmers (British)
Larry Widner ......Auburn, IN .... Oliver
Wayne Withers .....Newark, IL .... International Harvester
John Wythe ....Miniota, Manitoba ... International Harvester
                                           crawlers

We wish to thank Steve Krna of Whitney Point, New York, for the time and advice that he gave while we were working on this book. We also wish to acknowledge the advisors who helped so much yet preferred not to be mentioned. Your assistance was vital and we sincerely thank you for your help.

PHOTOGRAPHY ACKNOWLEDGMENTS

The beautiful photographs by Randy Leffingwell were taken from several different locations with the pleasant cooperation of some wonderful people. A special thanks to:

Allen and Cheryl Anderson	Arlington, OR
Mike and Linda Androvich	Bowling Green, OH
Frank and Evelyn Bettancourt	Vernalis, CA
The late Tiny Blom	Manila, IL
John Boehm	Woodland, CA
Herc and Betty Bouris	Sun City, CA
Paul Brecheisen	Helena, OH
Dr. Richard Collison	Carroll, IA
Paul Cook	Yakima, WA
Laurence Darrach	Nicolaus, CA
Dwight and Katie Emstrom	Galesburg, IL
Ray and Dorothy Erret	Harlan, IA
Palmer and Harriett Fossum	Northfield, MN
Dale Gerken	Fort Dodge, IA
Jack and Barbara Gustafson	Byron, IL
Ellen Hector and the late Robert Hector	LaGrande, OR
Edith Heidrick and the late Joe Heidrick Collection	
Fred Heidrick	Woodland, CA
Duane and Carolyn Helman	Rosewood, OH
Bob and Jeannete Hinds	Rio Linda, CA
Joan Hollenitsch	Garden Grove, CA
Don Hunter	Pomona, CA
John Jonas	Wahoo, NE
Travis and Shirley Jorde	Rochester, MN
Wendell and Mary Kelch	Bethel, OH
Bruce and Judy Keller	Kaukauna, WI
Walter and Lois Keller	Forrest Junction, WI
Paul Kirsch	St. Paul, OR
Harland Layher	Grand Island, NE
Kenny Layher	Grand Island, NE
Lester Layher	Wood River, NE
David and Suella Loory	Platteville, WI
Wendell and Carolyn Lundberg	Richvale, CA
Larry and Melanie Maasdam	Clarion, IA
Clyde and Jeannette McCullough	Dennison, IA
Mike McGaarity	Pinon Hills, CA
Doug Norman	Montevideo, MN
Bob and Mary Pollock	Dennison, IA
Bill and Barbara Peterson	Lowell, IN
Bill (Jr.) and Kim Peterson	Lowell, IN
Carlton Sather	Northfield, MN
Eugene Schmidt	Bluffton, OH
Raynard and Ruth Schmidt	Dennison, IA
F. P. Smith	Suisun, CA
The late Roland Spenst	Alsen, ND
Gary Spitznogel	Wapelo, IA
Wes and Bonnie Stoelk	Westside, IA
Case-New Holland Historical Collection	
University of Nebraska Tractor Test Museum	
Antique Steam and Gas Engine Museum	Vista, CA
University of California, Davis	Davis, CA
Antique Agriculture Equipment Collection	

ABOUT THIS BOOK

A s tractor collecting has flourished in the last several years, the demand for a collectible tractor value guide has grown intense. One of the most common inquiries at a tractor show is, How much is that tractor worth? Often, potential tractor sales are ruined because an owner has priced his tractor unrealistically high. On the other hand, someone might sell his or her tractor only to find out later that it was worth much more. We hope this book will help collectors feel more confident in their dealings.

Let's say that you were a bit uncertain about the asking price of an antique tractor. Wouldn't it be wonderful if you could ask the advice of an experienced collector? The honest opinion of experienced collectors is what this book is about. The collectors who have contributed information have extensive knowledge of certain brands. This impressive massing of minds includes tractor book, magazine, and website authors; full-time antique tractor and parts dealers; well-known major collectors; museum curators; and tractor club founders. They are well aware of rare and desirable variations and for what price particular models in any condition would sell. Many of the rarest tractors in existence are owned by these collectors. Without their cooperation, the high degree of accuracy in this book would not have been possible.

This book is, without a doubt, one of opinions. The values assigned are to be used as guidelines and are not meant to be inflexible or to replace one's own judgment. Regional interest in certain types of tractors may cause escalation or reduction of the average prices. This book is not intended to establish accurate values but to give ballpark prices. The prices are our estimates of values based on information provided by our advisors plus auction results and private sales. We wish to make it clear that tractor prices are based on demands that can change suddenly. This book is not to be used for actual appraisals or to determine actual value. The publisher, authors, and anyone else associated with this book do not assume any liability in any way whatsoever and shall not be held liable for any damages of any kind regardless of whether incidental or consequential or in any other way in addition to business damages and/or profit losses brought about by any use whatsoever of this value guide.

In the last six years, many tractors that the collector community thought were unique actually turned out to have a twin that was also believed to be unique. Prices for extremely rare models are listed in all five categories of condition even though it is unclear whether some of them exist.

Values in this book are intended for tractors and crawlers with standard factory features unless stated otherwise. Alterations of equipment such as rubber tire conversions from the original steel wheels (cutoffs) will detrimentaly affect tractor values from that of this book. Tractor values assume no mounted implements or significant options such as three-point hitch, added wheel weights, or special shielding unless specified. All crawler values assume no mounted equipment such as dozer blades, bucket loaders, cranes, or winches.

THE RATING SYSTEM

The rating system uses five levels based on the overall condition of the tractor. Broken castings, missing parts, lost serial number tags, mends, and tire wear are just a few of many factors that may downgrade the condition of the tractor. Certain parts missing on an extremely rare model may be more detrimental to its rating than they would be on a high-production model. In some cases, restorers have brought the condition of a tractor to a state that is better than new. Other tractors are in a phenomenal original condition, which commands much more interest than a highly restored version. These special exceptions may exceed the bounds of this rating system and command prices that cannot be determined by any book. The following is an explanation of each rating:

(5) IMPECCABLE CONDITION

A tractor must be next to new and in an exquisite state of restored condition to be considered a five. Popular model tractors should have almost all original parts and only very few indistinguishable reproduction parts. Rare models may have a limited number of professionally reproduced parts. Rubber tires, steel wheels, and crawler tracks should be matched and be the proper style and size for that particular model. There should be no appearance of wear or pitting on any part except on the exposed gearing of early tractor models and crawlers, which can show only very minor wear. Paint and trim should be of a professional quality and appear fresh. The overall condition will draw special attention at shows and will get nods of approval from the most hard to please critics. Very few tractors are a grade five.

(4) EXCELLENT CONDITION

These tractors are restored to a high state of originality. Popular models may have a limited number of high-quality replacement parts, while more replacement parts can be present on rare tractors. Rubber tires, steel wheels, and crawler tracks should be the proper style and size for the original equipment. No major restoration repairs should be visible. Paint and trim should look professional and may show only a hint of wear or fading. The overall condition should impress the average passerby at a show, and only the trained eye will find trivial flaws.

(3) VERY GOOD CONDITION

Grade three tractors are in sound mechanical condition, perhaps needing only minor work to run like new. They should be usable and not appear shabby. Only minor parts may need replacing. The paint and trim might be professionally done, but may show fading or chipping. Rare models may have some major parts that show moderate wear and have very few minor parts that are missing or ruined. A fair amount of effort may be needed to locate or fabricate these minor parts. Popular model tractors should have the major parts in good condition and may need several minor parts to complete an admirable restoration. The overall condition should appear presentable although probably not impressive. Restoration to the next higher grade should not be a huge undertaking.

(2) GOOD CONDITION

Rare tractors may have a few substantial parts broken or missing and may require several small replacement parts. A fair amount of effort and expense will be required to elevate a grade two tractor to the level of a four or five. There may be some noticeable repairs to major castings or frame members. Popular models may need some internal mechanical work. A good-sized list of small parts for replacement may be required for proper restoration. Crawlers may need a few undercarriage parts and tracks may need the pins turned or replaced. The overall condition appears complete but not necessarily attractive.

(1) RESTORABLE CONDITION

These machines are on the edge of being "parts tractors," but they are complete enough to be eligible for restoration. Rare models may need parts fabricated. They would require a major effort to bring them up to a four or five rating. Popular models may need some major parts replaced along with numerous small parts. Excessive wear from time and hard use will make restoration a significant effort. The overall condition may appear poor, but most of the tractor's mechanical integrity is intact.

WHERE ARE THESE VALUES GOING?

The interest in antique tractors is growing fast. Finding an unrestored tractor sitting in a hedgerow for fifty dollars was not uncommon five years ago, but is a rare occurrence today. Just as collectors and profit-seeking opportunists have grabbed up antique cars, antique tractors are disappearing from behind barns, out of fence rows, and off the back forties. As the supply is limited and the demand increases, values will continue to go up and up. Tractors from the 1960s have caught the eye of many as being nostalgic and even some 1970s tractors are becoming collectable.

Many people over forty wish they had the toys today that they had as children. A piece of wisdom might be to learn from our thoughts of wishing we had kept things from long ago and saved them for today. The tractors of today will most likely become collectable in several years. One might learn to collect current literature, advertising, and even the tractors themselves. A low-production tractor from the 1970s may be overlooked by collectors today, but be suddenly in demand in perhaps another five or ten years.

One thing we must learn is that we cannot control the destiny of tractor collecting. Some of the charm and casualness is sapped out when the little guy gets pushed out of the way. Men who once proudly brought tractors to a show are becoming more and more intimidated and embarrassed by the power restorations that overshadow their pride and joy. Collectors with deep pockets are hoarding rare models and leaving the little guy just crumbs to sweep up. The trend is not intentional, but unfortunately somewhat natural. Antique cars went there first. The only thing that we might be able to do is try not to fan the flames and make the best of it.

The authors, Terry Dean and Larry Swenson, have been involved with antique tractors for years. Dean has collected tractors for over fifteen years and has authored several magazine articles as well as the *Allis-Chalmers Farm Tractor and Crawler Data Book.* Larry Swenson is a well-known supplier of antique Allis-Chalmers tractors and parts. Neither man has any intention of robbing the charm that this hobby offers. We wish only to relay values of antique tractors as accurately as possible. If any reader has information of private sales and auctions of antique tractors, we would be pleased to be informed. The model, condition, and selling price of tractors will help us in future revisions of this book. Constructive information is very welcome.

Terry Dean
3 Dings Hollow Road
Whitney Point, NY 13862
Mccorm1809@aol.com

Larry Swenson
48127 235th Street
Easton, MN 56025
lswenson@bevcomm.net

CHAPTER 1

WHEEL TRACTORS

Acme Harvesting Machine Company, Peoria, Illinois
Acme 12-25 (1918–1919)
(1) $14,000 (2) $20,000 (3) $26,000 (4) $32,000 (5) $42,000

The magnificent Rumelys were the kings of the prairie tractors. Hardly any other tractor in its day had the high reputation of quality and service that the Rumely enjoyed; and this feeling is carried on to today's tractor collectors, which helps empower the values.

Advance-Rumely Thresher Company, LaPorte, Indiana

Rumely sold its first OilPull tractor in 1910. As one of the finest tractors of its day, the OilPull tractor has a powerful collector attraction. Due to a major crop failure in Canada during 1914, hundreds of farmers were unable to pay Rumely for financed tractors and threshing machines. The company was forced into receivership and reformed into the Advance-Rumely Thresher Co. Gaar Scott, Minneapolis Threshing Machine, and Aultman-Taylor were taken over by this reformed company. In 1924, as the age of the prairie giants was coming to a close, the company introduced newer lightweight models. The DoAll and Rumely 6A models were the last two tractors introduced before Allis-Chalmers took over the Advance-Rumely operations in 1931 and quickly phased out the Rumely tractor line. A-C employees assembled the remaining DoAll and Model 6A parts into tractors sold with both companies' names in the advertisements. Because of this, these models have a certain amount of appeal to Allis-Chalmers collectors as well as Rumely enthusiasts. Most tractor collectors would love to own an enormous Model E 30-60. One can expect all these "blue chip" Rumely tractor models to steadily increase in value.

This is a Rumely 14-28. A 16-30 (rerated version of the 14-28) sold for $16,000 at auction in 1998. A similar 14-28 sold for $8,900 in 1991. The values of the Rumely tractors have been like a blue-chip stock as they increase at an almost predictable rate that is perhaps a bit more elevated than the inflation rate. The most volatile values tend to be on later-year tractors such as the rare models from different brands during the 1950s and 1960s.

Kerosene Annie 25-45 (1910)
(1) $35,000 (2) $50,000   (3) $70,000   (4) $90,000 (5) $100,000

Gaspull 20-40 (rerated 15-30, 1912–1915)
(1) $7,000   (2) $10,000   (3) $15,000   (4) $20,000 (5) $25,000

OilPull B 25-40 (1910–1912)
(1) $22,500 (2) $37,500   (3) $40,000   (4) $50,000 (5) $60,000

OilPull E 30-60 (1910–1923)
(1) $22,500 (2) $37,500   (3) $40,000   (4) $50,000 (5) $60,000

OilPull F 15-30 (rerated 18-35, 1911–1918)
(1) $15,000 (2) $22,000   (3) $25,000   (4) $28,000 (5) $32,500

OilPull 14-28 (rerated 16-30, 1917–1918)
(1) $6,000   (2) $12,000   (3) $15,000   (4) $17,000 (5) $20,000

OilPull G 20-40 (1918–1924)
(1) $6,000   (2) $12,000   (3) $15,000   (4) $17,000 (5) $20,000

OilPull H 16-30 (1917–1924)
(1) $3,500   (2) $7,000   (3) $10,000   (4) $12,000 (5) $14,000

OilPull K 12-20 (1918–1924)
(1) $4,500   (2) $8,000   (3) $11,000   (4) $12,500 (5) $14,000

Rumely Rein-Drive (two known to exist, 1921)
(1) $13,000 (2) $22,500   (3) $28,000   (4) $35,000 (5) $45,000

OilPull L 15-25 (1924–1927)
(1) $2,500   (2) $4,500   (3) $6,000   (4) $7,000   (5) $8,500

OilPull M 20-35 (1924–1927)
(1) $2,000   (2) $3,500   (3) $5,000   (4) $6,000   (5) $8,000

OilPull R 25-45 (1924–1927)
(1) $3,000   (2) $5,000   (3) $7,000   (4) $9,000   (5) $11,000

OilPull S 30-60 (1924–1928)
(1) $7,000   (2) $10,000   (3) $12,500   (4) $15,000 (5) $17,000

OilPull W 20-30 (1928–1930)
(1) $2,000   (2) $4,000   (3) $6,000   (4) $7,000   (5) $8,000

OilPull X 25-40 (1928–1930)
(1) $2,500   (2) $5,500   (3) $7,000   (4) $8,000   (5) $10,000

OilPull Y 30-50 (1929)
(1) $4,500   (2) $8,000   (3) $11,000   (4) $12,500 (5) $14,000

OilPull Z 40-60 (1929, not converted S models)
(1) $13,000 (2) $22,500 (3) $28,000 (4) $35,000 (5) $45,000

Do-All (1928–1931)
(1) $1,900   (2) $3,300   (3) $4,800   (4) $6,400   (5) $9,000

Rumely 6A (1930–1931)
(1) $1,750   (2) $3,000   (3) $4,550   (4) $6,000   (5) $8,500

Agrimotor Tractor Company, Wichita, Kansas
Mid-West 9-18 (1921–1924)
(1) $3,600   (2) $8,000   (3) $12,000 (4) $15,250 (5) $18,000

S. L. Allen & Company, Philadelphia, Pennsylvania
Planet Jr. (front-wheel drive, 1920-approx. 1922)
(1) $2,900   (2) $4,800   (3) $6,250   (4) $7,500   (5) $9,200

Allis-Chalmers Company, Milwaukee, Wisconsin
In 1861, Edward P. Allis bought the languishing Decker and Seville Reliance Works, makers of French burr millstones. As his renamed Edward P. Allis and Company grew, steam power became its main industry. By the 1880s, Allis was a leader in the manufacturing of huge expansion and centrifugal pumps. In 1901, E. P. Allis Company merged with Fraser and Chalmers, Gates Iron Works, and Dickson Manufacturing Company, and the name was changed to the Allis-Chalmers Company. Allis-Chalmers expanded into a multimillion dollar company that became a commercial leader in steam, turbines, electrical equipment, and mining machinery. By 1911 the company was in financial trouble because of excessive expansion and succumbed to a reorganization. General Otto Falk became the new president in 1913 and the only true crusader on the board of directors who wanted Allis-Chalmers to produce farm tractors. Because of Falk's persistence and tremendous influence, the company jumped into the tractor business and invested over three million dollars in the first few years. Allis-Chalmers built its first production tractor in 1914; others followed. The brutal competition of the time almost put Allis-Chalmers out of the tractor business entirely. But in 1927 a reworked version of its Model 25-35 began to turn a profit for the tractor division for the first time, and plans to end tractor production were dropped. By the 1930s this company became one of the tractor production giants. Advance-Rumely and Monarch Tractor Company were two of Allis-Chalmers' greatest acquisitions. Allis-Chalmers has a very loyal following of collectors. Prices for the scarcer models have been booming in the last three years. The trend is comparable to the boom in John Deere prices about six and seven years ago.

Model 10-18 (1914–1923)
(1) $12,750 (2) $16,500 (3) $21,750 (4) $27,500 (5) $33,750

Model 6-12 (1919–1926)
(1) $5,250 (2) $8,000 (3) $11,500 (4) $15,250 (5) $18,750

Model E 15-30 (rerated 18-30) (1918–1921)
(1) $1,850 (2) $4,000 (3) $6,600 (4) $8,000 (5) $12,500

Model E 20-35 (long fenders) (1923–1926)
(1) $1,500 (2) $3,000 (3) $5,500 (4) $7,000 (5) $11,000

Model E 20-35 Special Road (long fenders, road wheels, 1923–1926)
(1) $2,000 (2) $3,500 (3) $6,000 (4) $7,500 (5) $11,500

Model E 20-35 Thresherman Special (long fenders, steel wheels, 1923–1926)
(1) $2,250 (2) $4,000 (3) $6,500 (4) $8,000 (5) $12,500

Model E 20-35 (short fenders, steel wheels, 1927–1930)
(1) $750 (2) $2,050 (3) $3,200 (4) $5,500 (5) $7,200

Model E 25-40 (steel wheels, 1930–1936)
(1) $1,500 (2) $2,500 (3) $3,500 (4) $6,000 (5) $8,500

Model E 25-40 (rubber tires, standard bore, 1930–1936)
(1) $2,500 (2) $4,000 (3) $5,000 (4) $7,500 (5) $10,000

Model E 25-40 (rubber tires, 5.25-inch bore, 1930–1936)
(1) $2,500 (2) $4,050 (3) $5,250 (4) $8,000 (5) $10,750

Model L 12-20 (1920–1921)
(1) $2,850 (2) $5,500 (3) $7,000 (4) $8,500 (5) $13,000

Model L 15-25 (1922–1927)
(1) $1,850 (2) $2,500 (3) $4,000 (4) $5,000 (5) $9,000

Model L 15-25 Road Tractor (1924–1927)
(1) $2,100 (2) $3,200 (3) $5,000 (4) $6,000 (5) $10,500

Model L 15-25 Orchard (1924–1927)
(1) $3,600 (2) $6,200 (3) $7,800 (4) $9,400 (5) $14,000

Model U (Continental engine, steel wheels; some also labeled "United," 1929–1932)
(1) $965 (2) $1,425 (3) $2,175 (4) $3,500 (5) $4,400

Model U (Continental engine, rubber tires; some also labeled "United," 1929–1932)
(1) $435 (2) $875 (3) $2,075 (4) $2,975 (5) $3,775

Model U (Allis-Chalmers engine, steel wheels, 1932–1952)
(1) $965 (2) $1,400 (3) $2,000 (4) $3,175 (5) $4,000

Allis-Chalmers built 7,404 Model U tractors with the Continental brand engine. This Model U is shown at the Nebraska Tractor Test track where a very similar tractor was tested in 1935. Many collectors place a high value on these flat-head Model U tractors.

Model U (Allis-Chalmers engine, rubber tires, 1932–1952)
(1) $300　(2) $775　(3) $1,400　(4) $2,600　(5) $3,475

Model UC (Continental engine, steel wheels, 1930–1933)
(1) $2,250　(2) $3,850　(3) $5,500　(4) $7,500　(5) $8,850

Model UC (Continental engine, rubber tires, 1930–1933)
(1) $700　(2) $1,550　(3) $3,000　(4) $5,000　(5) $6,000

Model UC (Allis-Chalmers engine, steel wheels, 1933–1943)
(1) $1,700　(2) $2,250　(3) $4,000　(4) $6,000　(5) $7,000

Model UC (Allis-Chalmers engine, rubber tires, 1933–1943)
(1) $500　(2) $1,000　(3) $2,500　(4) $4,500　(5) $6,000

Model UC Cane (high-clearance, rubber tires, 1937–1953)
(1) $900　(2) $1,500　(3) $3,800　(4) $5,800　(5) $9,000

Model WC Nonstreamlined (Waukesha engine, steel wheels, 1933)
(1) $7,000　(2) $10,000　(3) $15,000　(4) $22,000　(5) $28,500

Model WC Nonstreamlined (steel wheels, dual narrow front, 1934–1938)
(1) $700　(2) $1,050　(3) $1,825　(4) $2,825　(5) $3,500

Model WC Nonstreamlined (rubber tires, dual narrow front, 1934–1938)
(1) $225　(2) $675　(3) $1,500　(4) $2,275　(5) $3,200

Model WC Nonstreamlined (steel wheels, single front wheel, 1934–1938)
(1) $375　(2) $800　(3) $1,600　(4) $2,400　(5) $3,275

Model WC Nonstreamlined (rubber tires, single front wheel, 1934–1938)
(1) $1,100　(2) $1,400　(3) $2,200　(4) $2,725　(5) $4,275

Model WC Nonstreamlined (steel wheels, wide-front, 1934–1938)
(1) $975　(2) $1,300　(3) $2,125　(4) $2,625　(5) $4,125

Model WC Nonstreamlined (rubber tires, wide-front, 1934–1938)
(1) $975   (2) $1,300   (3) $2,150   (4) $2,725   (5) $4,225

Model WC Streamlined (rubber tires, dual narrow front, 1938–1948)
(1) $250   (2) $575   (3) $1,025   (4) $2,275   (5) $2,775

Model WC Streamlined (steel wheels, dual narrow front, 1938–1948)
(1) $575   (2) $775   (3) $1,450   (4) $2,425   (5) $3,125

Model WC Streamlined (rubber tires, single front wheel, 1938–1948)
(1) $375   (2) $675   (3) $1,175   (4) $2,375   (5) $2,975

Model WC Streamlined (rubber tires, wide-front, 1938–1948)
(1) $975   (2) $1,275   (3) $1,775   (4) $2,400   (5) $3,275

Model WF Nonstreamlined (rubber tires, 1937–1940)
(1) $975   (2) $1,550   (3) $2,525   (4) $4,075   (5) $5,275

Model WF Nonstreamlined (steel wheels, 1937–1940)
(1) $1,675   (2) $2,500   (3) $3,275   (4) $4,800   (5) $6,000

Model WF Streamlined (rubber tires, 1940–1951)
(1) $1,000   (2) $1,775   (3) $2,475   (4) $3,925   (5) $5,275

Model WF Streamlined (steel wheels, 1940–1951)
(1) $1,675   (2) $2,425   (3) $3,200   (4) $4,600   (5) $5,925

Model TW SpeedAce (1935–1937)
(1) $2,000   (2) $2,800   (3) $4,000   (4) $8,000   (5) $11,500

Model A (steel wheels, 1936–1938; prior to serial no. 26526)
(1) $3,000   (2) $6,000   (3) $7,500   (4) $10,000   (5) $14,000

Model A (rubber tires, 1936–1938; prior to serial no. 26526)
(1) $1,000   (2) $4,000   (3) $5,500   (4) $8,000   (5) $12,000

Model A (rubber tires, 1938–1942; serial no. 26526 and up)
(1) $2,000   (2) $5,000   (3) $6,500   (4) $9,000   (5) $13,000

Model B (Waukesha engine, 1937; prior to serial no. 100)
(1) $2,000   (2) $3,000   (3) $4,250   (4) $5,500   (5) $7,500

Model B (steel wheels, 1938–1957)
(1) $800   (2) $1,625   (3) $2,325   (4) $3,100   (5) $3,850

Model B (rubber tires, 1938–1957)
(1) $225   (2) $1,025   (3) $1,650   (4) $2,500   (5) $3,250

Model B Asparagus Special (rubber tires, 1944–1957)
(1) $500   (2) $2,000   (3) $3,500   (4) $4,500   (5) $5,500

Model B Potato Special (rubber tires, 1944–1957)
(1) $600   (2) $2,100   (3) $3,500   (4) $4,400   (5) $5,300

Model IB (rubber tires, 1939–1958)
(1) $600   (2) $1,700   (3) $2,475   (4) $3,500   (5) $4,800

Model RC (steel wheels, 1939–1941)
(1) $750   (2) $1,450   (3) $2,150   (4) $3,725   (5) $5,325

Model RC (rubber tires, 1939–1941)
(1) $350   (2) $1,100   (3) $1,825   (4) $3,325   (5) $4,925

Model C (steel wheels, dual narrow front, 1940–1950)
(1) $800   (2) $1,125   (3) $1,825   (4) $2,625   (5) $3,150

Model C (rubber tires, dual narrow front, 1940–1950)
(1) $225   (2) $525   (3) $1,250   (4) $2,050   (5) $2,600

Model C (rubber tires, single front wheel, 1940–1950)
(1) $475   (2) $700   (3) $1,425   (4) $2,300   (5) $2,800

Model C (rubber tires, adjustable wide-front, 1940–1950)
(1) $550   (2) $825   (3) $1,600   (4) $2,500   (5) $3,025

Model G (no options, 1948–1955)
(1) $700   (2) $1,500   (3) $2,500   (4) $2,800   (5) $3,500

Model G (hydraulic lift, 1948–1955)
(1) $1,200   (2) $2,000   (3) $3,000   (4) $3,300   (5) $4,000

Model WD (dual narrow front, 1948–1953)
(1) $425   (2) $800   (3) $1,400   (4) $2,250   (5) $3,500

The Allis-Chalmers Model C doesn't usually command a high price when sold, but with a rare full set of steel wheels, this example is worth considerably more than the normal rubber-tire versions. During World War II, rubber tires were hard to come by and steel wheels were used to complete orders for desperately needed tractors.

The little 3/4-ton Allis-Chalmers Model G is a prize for any serious collector. When new in 1949, the G sold for about $760, but today a nicely restored copy will bring five or six times that amount. The G in this picture sports a very desirable set of dual rear wheels.

Model WD (single front wheel, 1948–1953)
(1) $625   (2) $1,000   (3) $1,600   (4) $2,450   (5) $3,725

Model WD (wide-front, 1948–1953)
(1) $700   (2) $1,325   (3) $2,100   (4) $2,800   (5) $4,200

Model WD (cane, 1948–1953)
(1) $1,100   (2) $2,000   (3) $2,800   (4) $3,500   (5) $5,000

Model CA (dual narrow front, 1950–1958)
(1) $475   (2) $1,300   (3) $1,825   (4) $3,300   (5) $4,825

Model CA (single front wheel, 1950–1958)
(1) $550   (2) $1,450   (3) $2,000   (4) $3,500   (5) $5,050

Model CA (wide-front, 1950–1958)
(1) $600   (2) $1,550   (3) $2,150   (4) $3,635   (5) $5,325

Model CA (cane, 1953–1958)
(1) $1,300   (2) $2,400   (3) $3,500   (4) $5,500   (5) $6,900

Model WD-45 (gasoline, dual narrow front, 1953–1957)
(1) $625   (2) $1,500   (3) $2,000   (4) $3,925   (5) $5,000

Model WD-45 (gasoline, single front wheel, 1953–1957)
(1) $650   (2) $1,650   (3) $2,325   (4) $4,150   (5) $5,425

Model WD-45 (gasoline, wide-front, power steering, 1953–1957)
(1) $625   (2) $1,450   (3) $2,500   (4) $4,325   (5) $5,650

Model WD-45 (diesel, dual narrow front, 1954–1957)
(1) $900   (2) $2,450   (3) $4,250   (4) $5,500   (5) $6,825

Model WD-45 (diesel, single front wheel, 1954–1957)
(1) $1,125   (2) $2,650   (3) $4,500   (4) $5,750   (5) $7,025

Model WD-45 (diesel, wide-front, 1954–1957)
(1) $1,125   (2) $2,825   (3) $4,650   (4) $6,000   (5) $7,325

Model WD-45 (LPG, dual narrow front, 1953–1957)
(1) $1,100   (2) $2,650   (3) $4,550   (4) $5,800   (5) $7,225

The Allis-Chalmers WD-45 Diesel had a total production of 6,509 units, just a mere fraction of the more than 90,000 WD-45 tractors built. With the wide-front axle, this tractor is probably worth about $1,600 more than the more common gasoline version. The interest in Allis-Chalmers tractors has been intense in recent years. Values for lower-production versions have been surprisingly high.

Model WD-45 (LPG, single front wheel, 1953–1957)
(1) $1,325   (2) $2,850   (3) $4,800   (4) $6,050   (5) $7,425

Model WD-45 (LPG, wide-front, 1953–1957)
(1) $1,325   (2) $3,025   (3) $4,950   (4) $6,300   (5) $7,725

Model WD-45 Orchard (after-market conversion, 1953–1957)
(1) $2,500   (2) $4,300   (3) $6,000   (4) $7,500   (5) $9,500

Model D-14 (gasoline, dual narrow front, 1957–1960)
(1) $700   (2) $1,750   (3) $2,250   (4) $3,000   (5) $3,800

Model D-14 (gasoline, single front wheel, 1958–1960)
(1) $875   (2) $1,975   (3) $2,625   (4) $3,125   (5) $4,025

Model D-14 (gasoline, wide-front, 1957–1960)
(1) $925   (2) $2,050   (3) $2,750   (4) $3,250   (5) $4,150

Model D-14 (LPG, dual narrow front, 1957–1960)
(1) $750   (2) $1,900   (3) $2,550   (4) $3,100   (5) $4,000

Model D-17 (gasoline, Series I, Series II, Series III, dual narrow front, 1957–1964)
(1) $1,025   (2) $2,000   (3) $2,900   (4) $3,900   (5) $5,150

Model D-17 (gasoline, Series I, Series II, Series III, wide-front, 1957–1964)
(1) $1,150   (2) $2,500   (3) $3,350   (4) $4,250   (5) $5,550

Model D-17 (diesel, Series I, Series II, Series III, wide-front, 1957–1964)
(1) $1,150   (2) $2,600   (3) $3,550   (4) $4,250   (5) $5,600

Model D-17 (LPG, Series I, Series II, Series III, dual narrow front, 1957–1964)
(1) $1,325   (2) $2,300   (3) $3,150   (4) $4,100   (5) $5,350

Model D-17 (LPG, Series I, Series II, Series III, wide-front, 1957–1964)
(1) $1,450   (2) $2,800   (3) $3,600   (4) $4,450   (5) $5,750

Model D-17 (gasoline, Series IV, wide-front, Snap-Coupler, 1964–1967)
(1) $2,050   (2) $3,150   (3) $4,150   (4) $5,250   (5) $6,000

Model D-17 (gasoline, Series IV, wide-front, 3-point hitch, 1964–1967)
(1) $2,550   (2) $5,150   (3) $6,150   (4) $7,250   (5) $8,000

Model D-17 (gasoline, Series IV, dual narrow front, Snap-Coupler, 1964–1967)
(1) $1,800   (2) $2,900   (3) $3,750   (4) $4,750   (5) $5,500

Model D-17 (gasoline, Series IV, dual narrow front, 3-point hitch, 1964–1967)
(1) $2,800   (2) $4,900   (3) $5,750   (4) $6,750   (5) $7,500

Model D-17 (diesel, Series IV, wide-front, Snap-Coupler, 1964–1967)
(1) $2,400   (2) $4,250   (3) $5,250   (4) $6,400   (5) $7,250

Model D-17 (diesel, Series IV, wide-front, 3-point hitch, 1964–1967)
(1) $2,400   (2) $4,750   (3) $5,750   (4) $6,900   (5) $7,750

Model D-17 (LPG, Series IV, wide-front, Snap-Coupler, 1964–1967)
(1) $2,050   (2) $3,150   (3) $4,150   (4) $5,750   (5) $6,500

Model D-17 High-clearance (all series, 1960–1967)
(1) $3,400   (2) $5,700   (3) $7,050   (4) $8,350   (5) $9,350

Model D-17 Orchard (full citrus fenders, gasoline, Series I, II, III, 1957–1964)
(1) $3,200   (2) $5,250   (3) $7,000   (4) $9,250   (5) $12,000

Model D-17 Orchard (full citrus fenders, gasoline, Series IV, 1964–1967)
(1) $3,300   (2) $5,400   (3) $7,500   (4) $9,750   (5) $13,000

Model D-17 Grove (gasoline, series I, II, III, 1957–1964)
(1) $2,500   (2) $3,500   (3) $4,500   (4) $6,000   (5) $8,000

Model D-17 Grove (gasoline, series IV, 1964-57)
(1) $2,900   (2) $4,000   (3) $5,000   (4) $6,500   (5) $8,500

Model D-17 Wheatland (gasoline, ca. 1959)
(1) $2,650   (2) $4,550   (3) $5,450   (4) $6,750   (5) $8,500

Model D-17 Wheatland (diesel, ca. 1959)
(1) $2,750   (2) $4,850   (3) $5,950   (4) $7,150   (5) $9,000

Model D-17 Wheatland (LPG, ca. 1959)
(1) $3,200   (2) $5,400   (3) $7,000   (4) $8,150   (5) $10,000

Model D-17 Rice Series I, II, III (1957–1964)
(1) $2,350   (2) $3,500   (3) $4,500   (4) $5,700   (5) $6,800

Model D-17 Rice Series IV (1964–1967)
(1) $2,400   (2) $3,850   (3) $4,750   (4) $6,100   (5) $7,250

Model D-10 Series I (black-bar grille, serial nos. 1001–1950, 1959)
(1) $1,750   (2) $3,050   (3) $4,550   (4) $5,300   (5) $6,000

Model D-10 Series I (after serial no. 1950) and Series II (1960–1965)
(1) $1,750   (2) $3,050   (3) $4,550   (4) $5,300   (5) $6,000

Model D-10 Series III (4-speed, 1965–1968)
(1) $2,000   (2) $3,650   (3) $5,250   (4) $5,950   (5) $6,700

Model D-10 Series III (8-speed, 1965–1968)
(1) $2,250   (2) $3,900   (3) $5,500   (4) $6,200   (5) $6,950

Model D-10 High-clearance Series I and II (1959–1964)
(1) $2,550   (2) $4,000   (3) $5,850   (4) $6,700   (5) $8,600

Model D-10 High-clearance Series III (1964–1968)
(1) $3,050   (2) $4,900   (3) $6,800   (4) $7,600   (5) $9,550

Model D-10 Industrial (without mounted equipment; all series, 1959–1964)
(1) $1,250   (2) $2,600   (3) $4,150   (4) $4,950   (5) $5,700

Model D-12 Series I (black-bar grille, serial nos. 1001–1950, 1959–1960)
(1) $1,750   (2) $3,050   (3) $4,550   (4) $5,300   (5) $6,000

Model D-12 Series I (after serial no. 1950) and Series II (1960–1965)
(1) $1,750   (2) $3,050   (3) $4,550   (4) $5,300   (5) $6,000

Model D-12 Series III (4-speed, 1965–1968)
(1) $2,000   (2) $3,650   (3) $5,250   (4) $5,950   (5) $6,700

Model D-12 Series III (8-speed, 1965–1968)
(1) $2,250   (2) $3,900   (3) $5,500   (4) $6,200   (5) $6,950

Model D-12 High-clearance (Series I and II, 1959–1964)
(1) $2,550   (2) $4,000   (3) $5,850   (4) $6,700   (5) $8,600

Model D-12 High-clearance (Series III, 1964–1968)
(1) $3,050   (2) $4,900   (3) $6,800   (4) $7,600   (5) $9,550

Model D-12 Industrial (without mounted equipment; all series, 1959–1964)
(1) $1,250   (2) $2,600   (3) $4,150   (4) $4,950   (5) $5,700

Model I-40 Industrial (without mounted equipment, 1964–1966)
(1) $2,000   (2) $3,500   (3) $4,500   (4) $5,500   (5) $6,400

Model I-400 Industrial (without mounted equipment, 1966–1968)
(1) $1,800   (2) $2,800   (3) $3,700   (4) $4,600   (5) $5,500

Model I-400 Industrial (without mounted equipment; 3-point hitch, 1966–1968)
(1) $2,000   (2) $3,600   (3) $4,800   (4) $6,000   (5) $6,800

Model D-15 Series I (gasoline, wide-front, 1960–1962)
(1) $1,600   (2) $2,650   (3) $3,450   (4) $4,400   (5) $5,350

Model D-15 Series I (gasoline, dual narrow front, 1960–1962)
(1) $1,400   (2) $2,300   (3) $3,200   (4) $4,150   (5) $5,100

Model D-15 Series I (gasoline, single front wheel, 1960–1962)
(1) $1,600   (2) $2,550   (3) $3,375   (4) $4,325   (5) $5,325

Model D-15 Series I (diesel, wide-front, 1960–1962)
(1) $1,750   (2) $3,000   (3) $4,450   (4) $4,950   (5) $5,700

Model D-15 Series I (diesel, dual narrow front1960–1962)
(1) $1,600   (2) $2,550   (3) $4,000   (4) $4,700   (5) $5,450

Model D-15 Series I (diesel, single front wheel, 1960–1962)
(1) $1,725   (2) $2,775   (3) $4,175   (4) $4,875   (5) $5,675

Model D-15 Series I (LPG, wide-front, 1960–1962)
(1) $1,525   (2) $2,875   (3) $4,250   (4) $4,975   (5) $5,850

Model D-15 Series I Grove (with full citrus fenders, 1961–1962)
(1) $3,000   (2) $4,250   (3) $5,500   (4) $7,000   (5) $9,000

Model D-15 Series I High-clearance (wide-front, 1960–1962)
(1) $1,750   (2) $3,000   (3) $4,450   (4) $4,950   (5) $5,700

The D-15 Allis-Chalmers was produced from 1960 to 1968. The headlights were fender-mounted and the muffler was an oval black-type on the Series II unlike the first series shown here. Collector value has seemed to surpass the high practical value of this tractor in the last few years.

Model D-15 Series II (gasoline, wide-front, 1963–1968)
(1) $1,850   (2) $3,650   (3) $4,750   (4) $5,500   (5) $6,250

Model D-15 Series II (gasoline, dual narrow front, 1963–1968)
(1) $1,600   (2) $3,400   (3) $4,450   (4) $5,150   (5) $5,850

Model D-15 Series II (gasoline, single front wheel, 1963–1968)
(1) $1,725   (2) $3,525   (3) $4,675   (4) $5,475   (5) $6,275

Model D-15 Series II (diesel, wide-front, 1963–1968)
(1) $1,750   (2) $3,650   (3) $4,750   (4) $5,500   (5) $6,250

Model D-15 Series II (diesel, wide-front, 3-point hitch, 1963–1968)
(1) $2,750   (2) $5,150   (3) $6,250   (4) $7,000   (5) $7,750

Model D-15 Series II (diesel, dual narrow front, 1963–1968)
(1) $1,600   (2) $3,300   (3) $4,450   (4) $5,200   (5) $5,950

Model D-15 Series II (diesel, single front wheel, 1963–1968)
(1) $1,750   (2) $3,275   (3) $4,425   (4) $5,225   (5) $5,925

Model D-15 Series II (diesel, single front wheel, 3-point hitch, 1963–1968)
(1) $1,850   (2) $4,775   (3) $5,925   (4) $6,735   (5) $7,425

Model D-15 Series II (LPG, wide-front, 1963–1968)
(1) $1,750   (2) $3,075   (3) $4,400   (4) $5,425   (5) $6,125

Model D-15 Series II Grove (diesel, with full cage, 1963–1968)
(1) $4,000   (2) $5,800   (3) $7,800   (4) $9,500   (5) $11,500

Model D-15 Series II High-clearance (wide-front, 1963–1968)
(1) $3,100   (2) $4,500   (3) $5,500   (4) $6,800   (5) $8,200

Model I-60 Industrial (without mounted equipment, 1965–1966)
(1) $2,100   (2) $2,950   (3) $4,400   (4) $5,100   (5) $5,700

Model I-600 Industrial (without mounted equipment, 1966–1968)
(1) $1,700   (2) $2,750   (3) $3,650   (4) $4,450   (5) $5,400

Model D-19 (gasoline, dual narrow front, 1961–1964)
(1) $1,400   (2) $2,650   (3) $3,400   (4) $4,250   (5) $5,000

Model D-19 (gasoline, dual narrow front, 3-point hitch, 1961–1964)
(1) $2,400   (2) $4,150   (3) $4,900   (4) $5,750   (5) $6,500

Model D-19 (gasoline, single front wheel, 1961–1964)
(1) $1,600   (2) $2,850   (3) $3,600   (4) $4,450   (5) $5,200

Model D-19 (gasoline, single front wheel, 3-point hitch, 1961–1964)
(1) $2,600   (2) $4,350   (3) $5,100   (4) $5,950   (5) $6,700

Model D-19 (gasoline, wide-front, 1961–1964)
(1) $1,500   (2) $2,500   (3) $3,600   (4) $4,450   (5) $5,250

Model D-19 (gasoline, wide-front, 3-point hitch, 1961–1964)
(1) $2,500   (2) $4,000   (3) $5,100   (4) $5,950   (5) $6,750

Model D-19 (diesel, wide-front, 1961–1964)
(1) $1,350   (2) $2,900   (3) $4,100   (4) $5,000   (5) $5,900

Model D-19 (diesel, wide-front, 3-point hitch, 1961–1964)
(1) $2,350   (2) $4,400   (3) $5,600   (4) $6,500   (5) $7,400

Model D-19 High-clearance (gasoline, 1961–1964)
(1) $3,200   (2) $5,000   (3) $6,100   (4) $6,750   (5) $7,700

Model D-19 High-clearance (diesel, 1961–1964)
(1) $3,200   (2) $5,000   (3) $6,100   (4) $6,750   (5) $7,700

Model D-21 Series I (3-point hitch, 1963–1965)
(1) $2,150   (2) $3,200   (3) $6,000   (4) $6,900   (5) $8,400

Model D-21 Series II (3-point hitch, 1965–1969)
(1) $2,150   (2) $3,200   (3) $6,000   (4) $6,900   (5) $8,400

The Allis-Chalmers D-19 is a powerful tractor with 62-drawbar horsepower in this diesel version. As a collectible, the D-19 is beginning to draw more attention. This 1961 version was made in the first year of the four-year production run of 10,597 total units built.

Model D-21 Industrial Series I and Series II (no 3-point hitch, 1963–1969)
(1) $1,750   (2) $2,500   (3) $4,150   (4) $5,000   (5) $6,750

Model ED-40 (United Kingdom,1960–1966)
(1) $1,400   (2) $2,350   (3) $3,500   (4) $4,100   (5) $5,200

Model D-272 (United Kingdom, 1957–1963)
(1) $1,500   (2) $2,500   (3) $3,500   (4) $5,000   (5) $7,000

Model D-272 High-clearance (United Kingdom, 1958–1963)
(1) $1,850   (2) $2,900   (3) $4,200   (4) $5,900   (5) $8,100

Model Two-Twenty (no 3-point hitch, 1969–1972)
(1) $1,500   (2) $2,200   (3) $4,800   (4) $6,000   (5) $9,000

Model Two-Twenty (3-point hitch, 1969–1972)
(1) $2,000   (2) $4,500   (3) $6,500   (4) $8,000   (5) $10,500

Model Two-Twenty (front-wheel assist, 3-point hitch, 1970)
(1) $4,000   (2) $6,500   (3) $9,500   (4) $11,500   (5) $14,000

Model Two-Ten (1970–1972)
(1) $2,500   (2) $5,500   (3) $8,500   (4) $10,500   (5) $12,500

American-Abell Engine and Thresher Company, Toronto, Ontario

The Universal Farm Motor tractor was the forerunner of the famous Rumely GasPull tractor.

Universal Farm Motor (1911)
(1) $7,000   (2) $10,000   (3) $15,000   (4) $20,000   (5) $25,000

American Engine and Tractor Co. (renamed American Tractor and Foundry Co.), Charles City, Iowa
American 15-30 (1918–1920)
(1) $6,000   (2) $9,750   (3) $13,000   (4) $16,000   (5) $21,000

American Gas Engine Company (renamed Weber Engine Co.), Kansas City, Missouri
Weber (35 horsepower, 1914)
(1) $6,500   (2) $9,500   (3) $12,000   (4) $14,000   (5) $17,000

American Steel Tractor Corporation, Canton, Ohio
American Model 226 (ca. 1947)
(1) $6,000   (2) $9,500   (3) $13,000   (4) $15,750   (5) $18,000

American Tractor Corporation, Peoria, Illinois
American (1918)
(1) $7,500   (2) $10,000   (3) $15,000   (4) $18,000   (5) $22,000

Yankee 12-25 (1920–1922)
(1) $7,000   (2) $9,750   (3) $15,750   (4) $19,000   (5) $21,000

Andrews Tractor Company (renamed Andrews-Kinkade Co.), Minneapolis, Minnesota

Andrews Tractor (1919–1921)
(1) $7,000   (2) $10,500   (3) $13,000   (4) $16,000 (5) $19,500

18-36 (1922)
(1) $4,250   (2) $6,500   (3) $8,000   (4) $9,500   (5) $12,000

Antigo Tractor Corporation, Antigo, Wisconsin

Antigo Quadpull 15-25 (1921–1923)
(1) $8,500   (2) $12,000   (3) $15,000   (4) $18,000 (5) $23,000

Appleton Manufacturing Company, Batavia, Illinois

Appleton 14-28 (rerated 12-20, 1917–1924)
(1) $5,000   (2) $8,000   (3) $10,250   (4) $12,000 (5) $14,500

Arthurdale Farm Equipment Corp. (see Co-Operative Mfg.)

Atlas Engineering Company, Clintonville, Wisconsin

Model 30-45 (4-wheel drive, ca. 1927)
(1) $8,500   (2) $12,500   (3) $16,000   (4) $19,000 (5) $24,000

A restored Aultman-Taylor 15-30 similar to the one shown here sold at auction for $18,000 in 1998. The Aultman-Taylor Company was one of the oldest and most respected threshing machine manufacturers in the industry. Its loyalty to quality was passed on to its tractors and the values reflect this.

Aultman-Taylor Machinery Company, Mansfield, Ohio

Cornelius Aultman began in the thresher business in the late 1850s. In 1892 the Aultman and Taylor Machinery Company was created. Threshers and steam engines were its largest products. In 1910 the company introduced its first gas tractor, which began a line of some of the most majestic tractors on the market. The company was forced by financial losses to sell out to Advance-Rumely on the first day of January in 1924. Rumely chose not to continue manufacturing any Aultman tractors. Aultman-Taylor was one of the builders of the great prairie tractors. These tractors appeal to collectors because of their awesome size, sturdy construction, and rich history. Prices have steadily climbed in the last several years much like those of the Rumely tractors.

Model 30-60 (square radiator, 1910–1913)
(1) $15,000 (2) $22,000   (3) $28,000   (4) $40,000 (5) $45,000

Model 30-60 (round radiator, 1914–1924)
(1) $15,000 (2) $22,000 (3) $28,000 (4) $40,000 (5) $45,000

Model 18-36 (renamed 22-45, 1915–1924)
(1) $9,750 (2) $15,000 (3) $17,000 (4) $20,000 (5) $25,000

Model 25-50 (1915–1918)
(1) $15,000 (2) $22,000 (3) $25,000 (4) $28,000 (5) $32,500

Model 15-30 (1918–1924)
(1) $7,000 (2) $10,000 (3) $13,000 (4) $15,500 (5) $19,000

Automotive Corporation, Toledo, Ohio (formerly Fort Wayne, Indiana)
Automotive 12-24 (rein-drive, 1918–1922)
(1) $12,000 (2) $18,000 (3) $22,000 (4) $28,000 (5) $36,000

Avery Company, Peoria, Illinois

From its beginnings as the Avery Planter Company, Cyrus and Robert Avery's company grew into a major manufacturer that sold a wide range of farm equipment. As a well-known builder of steam traction engines since 1891, Avery worked into the gas tractor business by 1911. The company offered a wide line of tractors until it went bankrupt in 1924. Reorganized as the Avery Power Machinery Company, it continued to produce tractors until the early 1940s. Avery tractors have a special collector appeal. Many early models are the large prairie giants that always bring strong collector attention and big prices. Its wide range of sizes makes the Avery a relished tractor for the collector of early models. The rich background from the famous and impressive Avery undermount steam traction engines gives the gas tractors added historic appeal.

Model 20-35 (2-cylinder, 1911–1915)
(1) $7,000 (2) $11,250 (3) $14,250 (4) $16,000 (5) $19,500

Model 12-25 (1912–1919)
(1) $7,000 (2) $11,000 (3) $14,000 (4) $15,750 (5) $19,000

Model 40-80 (1913–1920)
(1) $15,000 (2) $22,500 (3) $28,000 (4) $34,000 (5) $42,000

Model 8-16 (1914–1922)
(1) $6,750 (2) $10,000 (3) $13,000 (4) $15,250 (5) $18,000

Model 25-50 (1914–1922)
(1) $11,250 (2) $16,750 (3) $21,000 (4) $25,500 (5) $32,000

Model 18-36 (1916–1921)
(1) $6,750 (2) $10,000 (3) $13,000 (4) $15,250 (5) $18,000

Model 5-10 (1916–1919)
(1) $5,000 (2) $7,500 (3) $9,500 (4) $11,000 (5) $14,000

Avery Motor Cultivator (1-row, 1916–1920)
(1) $3,500   (2) $5,000   (3) $6,500   (4) $7,750   (5) $9,000

Avery Motor Cultivator (2-row, 6-cylinder, 1919–1924)
(1) $3,500   (2) $5,000   (3) $6,500   (4) $7,750   (5) $9,000

Road-Razer (1919–1924)
(1) $7,000   (2) $8,750   (3) $10,500   (4) $11,500   (5) $13,000

Model 14-28 (1919–1924)
(1) $5,500   (2) $8,250   (3) $11,250   (4) $12,500   (5) $14,000

Model 45-65 (1920–1924)
(1) $14,000   (2) $21,500   (3) $27,750   (4) $32,500   (5) $40,000

Model 20-35 (4-cylinder, 1923–1924)
(1) $6,000   (2) $9,250   (3) $12,250   (4) $14,500   (5) $17,000

Ro-Trac (1938–1941)
(1) $3,750   (2) $5,000   (3) $6,500   (4) $8,750   (5) $11,250

B. F. Avery and Sons Company, Louisville, Kentucky

This company began by building a motor plow in 1915. The Avery Model A became a popular tractor on small farms during the 1940s. Minneapolis-Moline took over Avery in 1951 and continued production with a similar BF model that was built until 1958.

Model A (long hood, serial nos. 1A100-7A269, 1943-1944)
(1) $250   (2) $800   (3) $1,250   (4) $2,000   (5) $2,800

Model A (short hood, hand brakes, serial nos. 7A270-9A900, 1944-1946)
(1) $250   (2) $800   (3) $1,500   (4) $2,500   (5) $3,200

Model A (short hood, foot brakes, serial nos. 9A901-20A114, 1947-1950)
(1) $250   (2) $650   (3) $1,000   (4) $1,700   (5) $2,500

Model R (serial nos. R500-R4459, 1950-1951)
(1) $250   (2) $800   (3) $1,500   (4) $2,500   (5) $3,000

Model V (cast iron grille, hand brakes, serial nos. 1V005-1V143, 1946)
(1) $600   (2) $1,250   (3) $1,900   (4) $2,600   (5) $3,500

Model V (nonadjustable front axle, serial nos. 1V144-5V500, 1946-1949)
(1) $400   (2) $900   (3) $1,400   (4) $1,900   (5) $2,500

Model V (adjustable wide-front, serial nos. 5V501-6V206, 1950)
(1) $400   (2) $900   (3) $1,400   (4) $1,900   (5) $2,500

Model V Minneapolis Moline (serial nos. 6V207-7V271, 1950-1952)
(1) $400   (2) $900   (3) $1,400   (4) $1,900   (5) $2,500

The Avery Co. of Peoria, Illinois, built this unusual Ro-Trac that could be converted from a narrow- to a wide-front axle. A nicely restored model sold for $9,500 in a 1999 auction.

Bailor Plow Manufacturing Company, Atchison, Kansas

Bailor One-Row Motor Cultivator (Cushman 2-cylinder engine, 1919–1929)

(1) $3,600 (2) $5,200 (3) $6,800 (4) $8,100 (5) $9,500

Bailor Two-Row Motor Cultivator (Le Roi 4-cylinder engine, 1919–1929)

(1) $3,600 (2) $5,200 (3) $6,800 (4) $8,100 (5) $9,500

A. D. Baker Company, Swanton, Ohio

Model 22-40 (1926–1943)

(1) $3,500 (2) $5,750 (3) $7,250 (4) $9,000 (5) $11,000

The Baker tractor was built from some of the finest components in the industry. The quality carried on from Baker's days of the steam traction engine is evident. The sturdiness of the machine and rich history add to its appeal to collectors.

Model 25-50 (Wisconsin engine, 1927–1928)

(1) $4,100 (2) $6,500 (3) $9,250 (4) $11,000 (5) $14,250

Model 25-50 (Le Roi engine, 1928–1943)

(1) $4,000 (2) $6,250 (3) $8,500 (4) $10,000 (5) $12,750

Banting Manufacturing Company, Toledo, Ohio

Banting started building farm equipment in 1915. The company offered well-built threshing machines and two models of a steam traction engine plus a full line of threshing tools. The early gasoline tractors sold by this company were Allis-Chalmers models. Allis-Chalmers lacked an agricultural sales network in the early 1920s and Banting became its biggest agent. It sold the models 6-12, 20-35, and 15-25. The later 20-35 had the Greyhound name cast in the upper radiator tank. When this model evolved into the 25-40 in 1930, "Banting Machine Company" replaced the "Greyhound" name on the radiator. This was apparently the last year Banting was in business. Craig Detwiler, an expert on Banting tractors, points out that changes on the rear fenders occurred on 1929 models. Other changes, such as a higher-mounted gas tank, occurred at the same time. Both variations are rare and few remaining Greyhound tractors exist today, making the difference in values for the variations insignificant. These threshing tractors came with an open cab and exhaust whistle, making them a very impressive addition to any tractor gathering. A complete late model Greyhound 20-35 that was unrestored sold for $12,800 at an auction in 2000.

Greyhound Special (ribbed fenders, based on Allis-Chalmers 20-35, 1927–1928)
(1) $4,750   (2) $8,500   (3) $13,000   (4) $15,500 (5) $19,000

Thresherman's Special (smooth fenders, based on Allis-Chalmers 20-35, 1929–1930)
(1) $4,750   (2) $8,500   (3) $13,000   (4) $15,250 (5) $18,750

Bates Machine and Tractor Company, Joliet, Illinois
Model H 15-25 (1921–1924)
(1) $4,500   (2) $6,000   (3) $7,500   (4) $9,250   (5) $12,500

Bates Tractor Company, Lansing, Michigan
Bates 18-30 (opposed 2-cylinder, early style with cab, 1912–1916)
(1) $15,000 (2) $22,500   (3) $28,000   (4) $34,000 (5) $40,000

Bates 10-15 (1 cylinder, 1912–1915)
(1) $7,200   (2) $11,000   (3) $13,500   (4) $17,250 (5) $20,500

Bates All Steel Oil 15-25 (1919–1921)
(1) $5,750   (2) $9,250   (3) $11,000   (4) $13,000 (5) $16,500

Robert Bell Engine and Thresher Co.
(see Illinois Tractor Co.)

Bethlehem Motor Corporation, East Allentown, Pennsylvania
Bethlehem 18-36 (1918–1919)
(1) $7,000   (2) $9,000   (3) $12,500   (4) $15,000 (5) $18,000

Brockway Tractor Company, Bedford, Ohio
Model 49 (Continental gasoline engine, 1949–1959)
(1) $3,800   (2) $5,000   (3) $7,250   (4) $9,750   (5) $12,000

Model 49D (Continental diesel engine, 1949–1959)
(1) $4,000   (2) $5,250   (3) $7,500   (4) $10,000 (5) $13,000

Buffalo-Pitts Company, Buffalo, New York
Model 40-70 (3-cylinder, 1910–1914)
(1) $35,000 (2) $45,000 (3) $60,000 (4) $70,000 (5) $90,000

Model 40-70 (4-cylinder, 1920)
(1) $19,000 (2) $28,000 (3) $37,000 (4) $44,000 (5) $55,000

Bull Tractor Company, Minneapolis, Minnesota
The Bull tractor was the biggest seller in the year 1914. Many tractor companies scrambled to copy this design, but the fast-paced tractor industry antiquated the copies as well as the Bull in a very short time. The Fordson tractor was stealing the tractor market in a big way beginning in 1918, its first full year of production. Scores of tractor companies succumbed to the competition of Henry Ford's little tractor. Bull was one that suffered severe losses; by 1919, Bull merged with Madison Motors Corporation to survive. The following year, Bull-Madison went bust. The Bull tractor has added collector attraction due to its historical value. Being a pioneer of the affordable small farm tractor, the Bull helped change tractor history.

Little Bull 5-12 (1914–1917)
(1) $8,000   (2) $10,000 (3) $12,250 (4) $13,500 (5) $15,000

Big Bull 7-20 (rerated 12-24, 1915–1917)
(1) $8,000   (2) $10,500 (3) $13,000 (4) $14,000 (5) $16,000

J. I. Case Plow Works, Racine, Wisconsin
Not to be confused with the great tractor producer, J. I. Case Threshing Machine Company, the Plow Works became a competitor. Jerome Case funded Case, Whiting and Company in 1876 to market a new plow developed by Ebenezer Whiting. By 1878, Case bought out the Whiting interest and renamed the company the J. I. Case Plow Works. With no legal connections to the J. I. Case Threshing Machine Company, Jackson Case, son of the great Jerome Increase Case, became president of the Plow Works in 1890. Two years later, Henry Wallis, J. I. Case's son in-law took over the presidency. The Wallis tractor line began in 1912 and was consolidated with the Plow Works in 1919. Friction between the two Case companies grew after the death of J. I. Case, and by 1915 a lawsuit developed between the two companies. Battles over the Case name endured until 1927, when the Threshing Machine Company bought the Case name from Massey-Harris who had acquired the Plow Works in the same year. Wallis tractors built after this time will be found under the Massey-Harris heading.

Wallis Bear (1902)
(1) $55,000   (2) $90,000   (3) $135,000   (4) $175,000   (5) $210,000

Wallis Cub (1913–1915)
(1) $3,500   (2) $5,000   (3) $8,200   (4) $9,800   (5) $12,000

Wallis Model J Cub Jr. 13-25 (ca. 1915)
(1) $3,500   (2) $5,000   (3) $8,200   (4) $9,800   (5) $12,000

Wallis Model K (1919–1922)
(1) $3,000   (2) $4,500   (3) $7,200   (4) $8,700   (5) $11,000

Wallis Model OK 18-28 (rerated 20-30, 1922–1927)
(1) $2,400   (2) $4,300   (3) $6,000   (4) $7,300   (5) $9,000

This is perhaps one of the most valuable tractors in America. Only nine Wallis Bear tractors were ever built and this is believed to be the only one remaining. This 10-1/2-ton tractor is frequently pictured in books and calendars. Publicity usually affects the value of a tractor in a very positive way.

J. I. Case Threshing Machine Company, Racine, Wisconsin

Jerome Increase Case founded his company in 1842 as a builder of threshing machines. By 1869, Case was the largest threshing machine manufacturer in the world. This was the same year that Case built its first steam engine. Case soon became a leader in the steam traction engine business. The majestic Case steam traction engines gave way to newer gas tractors in 1911. A leader in the tractor industry for several decades, Case has a strong collector appeal. Many of its crossmotor models are genuine works of art. These models have an especially strong appeal to collectors.

Model 30-60 crossmotor (1911–1916)
(1) $50,000   (2) $78,000   (3) $100,000   (4) $125,000   (5) $160,000

Model 20-40 crossmotor (2-cylinder, 1912–1920)
(1) $27,500   (2) $47,000   (3) $52,000   (4) $74,000   (5) $80,000

Model 12-25 crossmotor (1913–1918)
(1) $8,500   (2) $12,500   (3) $15,750   (4) $18,000   (5) $23,000

Model 10-20 crossmotor (1914-approx. 1920)
(1) $9,000   (2) $13,000   (3) $16,500   (4) $19,250   (5) $24,750

Model 9-18 crossmotor (enclosed engine, 1916–1918)
(1) $5,250   (2) $9,250   (3) $12,000   (4) $14,000   (5) $18,000

Model 10-18 crossmotor (1918-1922)
(1) $1,500   (2) $4,000   (3) $6,500   (4) $8,000   (5) $10,000

Model 15-27 crossmotor (1919-1924)
(1) $3,500   (2) $6,250   (3) $8,000   (4) $9,500   (5) $12,500

Model 22-40 crossmotor (1919-1925)
(1) $7,000   (2) $11,200   (3) $14,500   (4) $16,500   (5) $21,000

Model 40-72 crossmotor (1920-1923)
(1) $26,000   (2) $42,500   (3) $50,000   (4) $60,000   (5) $75,000

Model 12-20 crossmotor (1921-1928)
(1) $1,650   (2) $3,200   (3) $6,250   (4) $8,000   (5) $9,500

Model K 18-32 crossmotor (1925-1928)
(1) $3,500   (2) $6,500   (3) $8,250   (4) $9,750   (5) $12,750

Model T 25-45 crossmotor (1924-1927)
(1) $7,000   (2) $11,000   (3) $14,250   (4) $16,000   (5) $20,500

Model L (rubber tires, 1929-1940)
(1) $800   (2) $1,700   (3) $2,700   (4) $3,800   (5) $5,000

Model L (General Motors diesel conversion, Eddings aftermarket, rubber tires, 1929-1940)
(1) $1,300   (2) $2,200   (3) $3,500   (4) $4,500   (5) $6,500

The Case 9-18 was the first of the Case crossmotor series. These crossmotor tractors are very valuable as restored units, and demand is very high. This beautiful model was built in 1918. Early versions of this model had an enclosed engine and tend to be in even higher demand.

Model L (steel wheels, 1929-1940)
(1) $800   (2) $1,800   (3) $2,800   (4) $4,000   (5) $5,000

Model LI Industrial (rubber tires, 1929-1940)
(1) $1,000   (2) $2,000   (3) $3,000   (4) $4,300   (5) $5,500

Model C (rubber tires, 1929-1939)
(1) $500   (2) $1,400   (3) $2,500   (4) $3,200   (5) $4,000

Model C (steel wheels, 1929–1939)
(1) $700   (2) $1,600   (3) $2,800   (4) $3,500   (5) $4,500

Model CI Industrial (rubber tires, 1929–1940)
(1) $1,200   (2) $1,800   (3) $3,200   (4) $4,000   (5) $4,500

Model CH High-clearance (rubber tires, 1938)
(1) $1,000   (2) $2,200   (3) $3,000   (4) $4,500   (5) $5,000

Model CO Orchard (citrus fenders, rubber tires, 1929–1938)
(1) $1,200   (2) $2,800   (3) $5,000   (4) $7,000   (5) $8,000

Model CO-VS Orchard Vineyard Special (citrus fenders, 1935–1939)
(1) $1,400   (2) $3,000   (3) $5,200   (4) $7,300   (5) $8,500

Model CC-3 (rubber tires, 1929–1939)
(1) $500   (2) $1,200   (3) $2,200   (4) $3,000   (5) $3,400

The Case 25-45 is a rare tractor that saw only 980 copies built during its four-year production. This 1925 model has scarce rear wheel extensions. Options like this often add hundreds of dollars to the value.

Model CC-3 (steel wheels, 1929–1939)
(1) $700   (2) $1,400   (3) $2,500   (4) $3,400   (5) $4,000

Model CC-4 (rubber tires, 1931–1938)
(1) $800   (2) $1,500   (3) $2,600   (4) $3,500   (5) $4,200

Model CCS Case Cane Special (rubber tires, 1937–1938)
(1) $1,500   (2) $3,000   (3) $5,000   (4) $10,000   (5) $14,000

Model R (rubber tires, steel grille, 1938)
(1) $1,000   (2) $2,000   (3) $2,800   (4) $3,500   (5) $4,000

Model R (rubber tires, cast grille, 1939–1940)
(1) $1,200   (2) $2,300   (3) $3,200   (4) $3,900   (5) $4,600

Model R (steel wheels, steel grille, 1938)
(1) $1,200   (2) $2,100   (3) $3,000   (4) $3,700   (5) $4,200

The big-selling Model CC was Case's first row-crop tractor. Almost 30,000 units were built. The Model CC-3 like the one pictured was the best-selling version of the C-Series Case tractors.

Model RC (overhead steering, rubber tires, 1935–1937)
(1) $800   (2) $1,600   (3) $2,400   (4) $3,000   (5) $3,500

Model RC (exposed radiator, side-shaft steering, rubber tires, 1937–1939)
(1) $800   (2) $1,600   (3) $2,400   (4) $3,000   (5) $3,500

Model RC (sun-burst cast-iron grille, rubber tires, 1939–1940)
(1) $1,000   (2) $1,800   (3) $2,700   (4) $3,500   (5) $4,100

Model RI Industrial (1939–1940)
(1) $1,000   (2) $2,000   (3) $2,800   (4) $3,700   (5) $4,400

Model D three-speed (rubber tires, 1939–1940)
(1) $500   (2) $925   (3) $1,050   (4) $1,300   (5) $3,250

Model D 4-speed (rubber tires, 1941–1953)
(1) $500   (2) $600   (3) $950   (4) $1,250   (5) $2,750

Model DH High-clearance (rubber tires, 1939–1940)
(1) $1,000   (2) $1,250   (3) $3,000   (4) $6,000   (5) $8,000

Model DO Orchard (full citrus fenders, rubber tires, 1939–1954)
(1) $400   (2) $500   (3) $1,000   (4) $3,000   (5) $5,250

Model DV Orchard Vineyard Special (rubber tires, 1940–1951)
(1) $400   (2) $500   (3) $1,000   (4) $3,000   (5) $5,750

Model DI Industrial (rubber tires, 1940–1952)
(1) $400   (2) $650   (3) $950   (4) $1,400   (5) $3,000

Model DI Narrow Industrial (1940–1951)
(1) $550   (2) $800   (3) $1,050   (4) $2,000   (5) $4,500

Model D LPG (rubber tires, 1951–1953)
(1) $350   (2) $600   (3) $900   (4) $1,250   (5) $3,250

Model DC-3 (rubber tires, 1939–1953)
(1) $400   (2) $550   (3) $900   (4) $1,500   (5) $3,000

Model DC-4 (rubber tires, 1939–1953)
(1) $400   (2) $575   (3) $950   (4) $1,550   (5) $3,500

Model DCS (high-clearance, rubber tires, 1939–1953)
(1) $1,000   (2) $1,350   (3) $2,750   (4) $5,000   (5) $10,000

Model S (rubber tires, 1941–1952)
(1) $600   (2) $1,000   (3) $1,600   (4) $2,500   (5) $3,000

Model SC (rubber tires, hand clutch, no Eagle Hitch, 1941–1954)
(1) $500   (2) $900   (3) $1,500   (4) $2,200   (5) $2,900

Model SC (rubber tires, foot clutch, Eagle Hitch, 1953–1954)
(1) $800   (2) $1,200   (3) $1,800   (4) $2,600   (5) $3,500

Model SC (rubber tires, hand clutch, Eagle Hitch, 1952–1954)
(1) $700   (2) $1,100   (3) $1,750   (4) $2,400   (5) $3,300

Model SC-4 (rubber tires, 1953–1954)
(1) $950   (2) $1,300   (3) $2,000   (4) $2,900   (5) $3,750

Model SO Orchard (rubber tires, 1941–1952)
(1) $1,000   (2) $1,800   (3) $2,800   (4) $4,500   (5) $5,500

Model SI Industrial (1942–1954)
(1) $800   (2) $1,400   (3) $2,100   (4) $2,800   (5) $3,500

Model LA (1940–1952)
(1) $800   (2) $1,300   (3) $2,000   (4) $3,000   (5) $4,000

Model LA (General Motors diesel conversion, Eddings aftermarket, 1940–1952)
(1) $1,300   (2) $2,000   (3) $2,900   (4) $4,200   (5) $5,500

Model LAI Industrial (1941–1952)
(1) $1,000   (2) $1,600   (3) $2,200   (4) $3,200   (5) $4,200

Model LAIM Military Industrial (1943)
(1) $1,750   (2) $2,600   (3) $3,500   (4) $4,100   (5) $5,200

Model LAH (factory diesel fuel engine, 1942–1949)
(1) $2,200   (2) $3,200   (3) $4,500   (4) $5,500   (5) $7,000

Model LAIH Industrial (factory diesel fuel engine, 1942)
(1) $2,200   (2) $3,200   (3) $4,500   (4) $5,500   (5) $7,000

Model LA with LPG engine (1952)
(1) $750   (2) $1,300   (3) $2,000   (4) $2,900   (5) $3,600

Model V (rubber tires, 1940–1942)
(1) $250   (2) $550   (3) $875   (4) $2,000   (5) $2,550

Model V (steel wheels, 1940–1942)
(1) $875   (2) $1,050   (3) $1,375   (4) $2,500   (5) $3,050

Model VC (rubber tires, 1940–1942)
(1) $350   (2) $625   (3) $1,000   (4) $1,750   (5) $2,500

Model VC (steel wheels, 1940–1942)
(1) $950   (2) $1,225   (3) $1,600   (4) $2,350   (5) $3,100

Model VC (single front wheel, rubber tires, 1940–1942)
(1) $500   (2) $750   (3) $1,325   (4) $2,075   (5) $2,875

Model VC (adjustable wide-front, rubber tires, 1940–1942)
(1) $625   (2) $1,000   (3) $1,575   (4) $2,500   (5) $3,375

Liquefied petroleum gas (LPG) versions of tractors were almost always made in very limited numbers. LPG accessories are often a challenge to locate, but the results of a correct restoration make it all worthwhile.

Model VI Industrial (rubber tires, 1941–1942)
(1) $325   (2) $500   (3) $725   (4) $1,375   (5) $2,375

Model VO Orchard (full citrus fenders, 1941–1942)
(1) $500   (2) $1,250   (3) $1,675   (4) $2,175   (5) $3,500

Model VA (1942–1953)
(1) $225   (2) $500   (3) $700   (4) $1,125   (5) $2,000

Model VAI Industrial (1942–1955)
(1) $200   (2) $500   (3) $800   (4) $1,250   (5) $2,500

Model VAO Orchard (full citrus fenders, 1942–1955)
(1) $400   (2) $900   (3) $1,375   (4) $2,000   (5) $3,250

Model VAO Orchard (without citrus fenders, 1942–1955)
(1) $300　　(2) $600　　(3) $900　　(4) $1,300　　(5) $2,600

Model VAO-15 Orchard (low-profile, 1953–1955)
(1) $550　　(2) $1,000　　(3) $1,350　　(4) $2,000　　(5) $2,750

Model VAS Offset High-clearance (1951–1954)
(1) $650　　(2) $1,150　　(3) $1,675　　(4) $2,300　　(5) $3,500

Model VAH High-clearance (1947–1955)
(1) $650　　(2) $1,250　　(3) $1,750　　(4) $2,375　　(5) $3,500

Model VAIW Industrial Warehouse (1944–1953)
(1) $625　　(2) $1,000　　(3) $2,000　　(4) $2,750　　(5) $3,375

Model VAC (rubber tires, 1942–1950)
(1) $200　　(2) $400　　(3) $1,125　　(4) $1,650　　(5) $2,025

Model VAC (steel wheels, 1942–1950)
(1) $800　　(2) $1,000　　(3) $1,725　　(4) $2,250　　(5) $2,625

Model VAC-11 (single front wheel, 1951–1953)
(1) $350　　(2) $550　　(3) $1,225　　(4) $1,875　　(5) $2,325

Model VAC-14 (low-profile with adj. wide-front axle, 1953–1954)
(1) $500　　(2) $950　　(3) $1,875　　(4) $2,500　　(5) $3,375

Model 211B (1958–1959)
(1) $1,200　(2) $1,500　　(3) $3,200　　(4) $4,000　　(5) $4,500

Model 511B (1958–1959)
(1) $800　　(2) $1,500　　(3) $2,200　　(4) $3,200　　(5) $4,200

Model 500 (1953–1956)
(1) $900　　(2) $1,500　　(3) $2,200　　(4) $3,000　　(5) $4,000

Model 300 (1955–1958)
(1) $800　　(2) $1,500　　(3) $2,700　　(4) $3,600　　(5) $4,500

The VAC-14 (left) and VAC-11 (right) are two wonderful examples of some of the many Case VA-Series variations. The VA tractors were sold from 1949 to 1955. The most sought-after versions are the VAH (high-clearance), the VAS (offset), and the VAO (orchard) with full citrus fenders.

Model 301 (diesel, 1955–1958)
(1) $1,200   (2) $1,900   (3) $3,200   (4) $4,200   (5) $5,300

Model 350 (1956–1958)
(1) $1,000   (2) $1,600   (3) $2,300   (4) $3,000   (5) $3,800

Model 311B (1956–1958)
(1) $800   (2) $1,400   (3) $2,500   (4) $3,400   (5) $4,200

Model 400 (gasoline, 1955–1957)
(1) $900   (2) $1,500   (3) $2,300   (4) $3,000   (5) $4,000

Model 400 (diesel, 1955–1957)
(1) $900   (2) $1,500   (3) $2,300   (4) $3,000   (5) $4,000

Model 400 Super Standard (diesel, 1955–1957)
(1) $1,200   (2) $1,800   (3) $2,600   (4) $3,300   (5) $4,200

Model 400 Special (diesel, full fenders, 1955–1957)
(1) $1,200   (2) $1,800   (3) $2,600   (4) $3,300   (5) $4,200

Model 400 Special Super (diesel, full fenders, 1955–1957)
(1) $1,300   (2) $1,900   (3) $2,700   (4) $3,500   (5) $4,300

Model 401 Tricycle (diesel, 1955–1957)
(1) $800   (2) $1,400   (3) $2,200   (4) $2,800   (5) $3,800

Model 402 Orchard (diesel, 1955–1957)
(1) $2,000   (2) $3,200   (3) $5,000   (4) $7,000   (5) $9,000

Model 403 High-clearance (diesel, 1955–1957)
(1) $ 2,200   (2) $3,300   (3) $5,100   (4) $7,200   (5) $9,500

Model 405 Orchard (diesel, power steering and Eagle Hitch, 1955–1957)
(1) $2,000   (2) $3,300   (3) $5,100   (4) $7,200   (5) $9,500

Model 410 Standard (gasoline, 1955–1957)
(1) $1,000   (2) $1,500   (3) $2,500   (4) $3,500   (5) $4,500

Model 410 Special (gasoline, full fenders, 1955–1957)
(1) $1,100   (2) $1,600   (3) $2,700   (4) $3,700   (5) $4,800

Model 411 and 411 Super Tricycle (gasoline, 1955–1957)
(1) $800   (2) $1,400   (3) $2,200   (4) $2,800   (5) $3,800

Model 412 Orchard (gasoline, 1955–1957)
(1) $2,000   (2) $3,200   (3) $5,000   (4) $7,000   (5) $9,000

Model 413 High-clearance (gasoline, 1955–1957)
(1) $2,200   (2) $3,300   (3) $5,100   (4) $7,200   (5) $9,500

Model 414 Orchard (LPG only, 1955–1957)
(1) $1,800   (2) $3,100   (3) $4,800   (4) $6,800   (5) $8,600

Model 415 Orchard (gasoline, 1955–1957)
(1) $2,200   (2) $3,300   (3) $5,100   (4) $7,200   (5) $9,500

Model 600 (LPG, 1957–1958)
(1) $900   (2) $1,800   (3) $2,400   (4) $3,400   (5) $4,200

Model 600 (diesel, 1957–1958)
(1) $1,000   (2) $1,900   (3) $2,500   (4) $3,500   (5) $4,300

Model 611B (1957–1958)
(1) $900   (2) $1,200   (3) $2,500   (4) $3,000   (5) $3,500

Model 700B Standard (diesel, 1958–1959)
(1) $1,200   (2) $1,700   (3) $2,600   (4) $3,600   (5) $4,600

Model 701B Tricycle (diesel, 1958–1959)
(1) $1,100   (2) $1,500   (3) $2,200   (4) $3,000   (5) $4,000

Model 702B Special (diesel, full fenders, 1958–1959)
(1) $1,500   (2) $2,000   (3) $2,800   (4) $4,000   (5) $4,800

Model 703B High-clearance (diesel, 1958–1959)
(1) $2,500   (2) $4,000   (3) $4,500   (4) $6,500   (5) $7,500

Model 705B Orchard (diesel, 1958–1959)
(1) $1,600   (2) $2,400   (3) $3,000   (4) $4,200   (5) $4,900

Model 710B Standard (gasoline, 1958–1959)
(1) $1,000   (2) $1,500   (3) $2,500   (4) $3,500   (5) $4,200

Model 711B Tricycle (gasoline, 1958–1959)
(1) $900   (2) $1,400   (3) $2,300   (4) $3,200   (5) $4,000

Model 712 (gasoline, full fenders, 1958–1959)
(1) $1,500   (2) $2,000   (3) $2,800   (4) $4,000   (5) $4,800

Model 713 High-clearance (gasoline, 1958–1959)
(1) $2,500   (2) $4,000   (3) $4,800   (4) $6,600   (5) $8,000

Model 800 Standard (diesel, 1958–1959)
(1) $800   (2) $1,200   (3) $1,900   (4) $2,600   (5) $3,200

Model 801 Tricycle (diesel, 1958–1959)
(1) $700   (2) $1,100   (3) $1,800   (4) $2,500   (5) $3,100

Model 802 Special (diesel, full fenders, 1958–1959)
(1) $1,000   (2) $1,500   (3) $2,300   (4) $2,800   (5) $3,200

Model 810 Standard (gasoline, 1958–1959)
(1) $900   (2) $1,300   (3) $2,000   (4) $2,700   (5) $3,400

Model 811 Tricycle (gasoline, 1958–1959)
(1) $800   (2) $1,200   (3) $1,800   (4) $2,500   (5) $3,200

Model 812 Special (gasoline, full fenders, 1958–1959)
(1) $1,000   (2) $1,500   (3) $2,300   (4) $2,800   (5) $3,200

Model 900 (diesel, 1958–1959)
(1) $1,000   (2) $1,600   (3) $2,600   (4) $3,600   (5) $4,600

Model 910 (LPG, 1958–1959)
(1) $900   (2) $1,500   (3) $2,500   (4) $3,400   (5) $4,300

Model 430 (gasoline, 1962–1969)
(1) $1,500   (2) $2,200   (3) $3,200   (4) $4,300   (5) $6,000

Model 430 (diesel, 1962–1969)
(1) $1,500   (2) $2,200   (3) $3,200   (4) $4,300   (5) $6,000

Model 530 (gasoline, 1962–1969)
(1) $1,800   (2) $2,500   (3) $3,500   (4) $4,500   (5) $6,500

Model 530 (diesel, 1962–1969)
(1) $1,800   (2) $2,500   (3) $3,500   (4) $4,500   (5) $6,500

Model 641 Row-crop (gasoline, 1962–1963)
(1) $1,800   (2) $2,500   (3) $3,500   (4) $4,500   (5) $6,000

Model 631 Row-crop (diesel, 1962–1963)
(1) $1,800   (2) $2,500   (3) $3,500   (4) $4,500   (5) $6,000

Model 630 Orchard (1962–1963)
(1) $1,500   (2) $2,100   (3) $3,500   (4) $4,500   (5) $6,500

Model 640 Standard Tread (gasoline, 1962–1963)
(1) $1,500   (2) $2,100   (3) $3,500   (4) $4,500   (5) $6,500

Model 741 Row-crop (gasoline, 1961–1969)
(1) $1,000   (2) $1,500   (3) $2,000   (4) $3,000   (5) $3,500

Model 730 (diesel, 1961–1969)
(1) $1,000   (2) $1,500   (3) $2,000   (4) $3,000   (5) $3,500

Model 730 Orchard (1961–1969)
(1) $1,400   (2) $2,000   (3) $3,500   (4) $4,500   (5) $7,000

Model 840 (gasoline, 1961–1969)
(1) $1,000   (2) $1,600   (3) $2,200   (4) $3,200   (5) $3,900

Model 830 (diesel, 1961–1969)
(1) $1,000   (2) $1,600   (3) $2,200   (4) $3,200   (5) $3,900

Model 843 High-crop (gasoline, 1961–1969)
(1) $1,700   (2) $2,400   (3) $3,500   (4) $4,800   (5) $8,000

Model 833 High-crop (diesel, 1961–1969)
(1) $1,700   (2) $2,400   (3) $3,500   (4) $4,800   (5) $8,000

Model 930 (6-speed standard, 1961–1969)
(1) $1,400   (2) $2,300   (3) $3,200   (4) $4,100   (5) $5,000

Model 930 Comfort King (6-speed, 1961–1969)
(1) $1,500   (2) $2,300   (3) $3,200   (4) $4,100   (5) $5,000

Model 930 Draft-O-Matic (8-speed, 1961–1969)
(1) $1,600   (2) $2,400   (3) $3,300   (4) $4,200   (5) $5,200

Model 1030 (1966–1969)
(1) $1,800   (2) $2,500   (3) $3,400   (4) $5,300   (5) $6,400

Model 1200 Traction King (4-wheel drive, 1964–1969)
(1) $3,000   (2) $5,000   (3) $8,000   (4) $10,000 (5) $12,000

Centaur Tractor Corporation, Greenwich, Ohio

The Central Tractor Company began with the little 2 1/2-5 horse-power garden-sized Centaur in 1921 and continued to produce tractors until 1948. The Centaur model name on its early tractors was adopted as the company's new name in 1928. Centaur built its Klear-View tractors for farm use, but the industrial line expanded more quickly. The Tractair was a nifty industrial tractor that used the last two of the six cylinders of the engine to compress air into a mounted tank. Contractors could drive the tractor to the work area and operate jackhammers and other high-volume air-operated equipment without having to move around a bulky trailer-type compressor. The Le Roi Company built the Tractair after it took over the financially wounded Centaur Company in 1948.

The Centaur Model G was heavily advertised in the 1920s. This low-cost tractor could make use of many of the same implements that the farmers already owned for their horses. The novelty of these early designs tends to create fairly high collector values.

Model F (5 horsepower, 1921–1925)
(1) $400   (2) $950   (3) $1,500   (4) $2,000   (5) $2,600

Model G 6-10 (1924–1929)
(1) $1,400   (2) $5,400   (3) $7,400   (4) $8,500   (5) $10,250

Model 2G 6-12 (1929–1940)
(1) $1,400   (2) $5,400   (3) $7,400   (4) $8,500   (5) $10,250

Model KV Klear-View (nonstreamlined, 1935–1939)
(1) $900   (2) $1,600   (3) $2,250   (4) $3,000   (5) $4,500

Model KV Klear-View, M, KM, KVM, KV-22, KV-30, KV-48 (stream-lined, 1939–1952)
(1) $600   (2) $1,200   (3) $2,000   (4) $2,750   (5) $3,700

Model CI (industrial, streamlined, 1939–1948)
(1) $600   (2) $1,200   (3) $2,000   (4) $2,750   (5) $3,700

Tractair 105 (industrial, 6-cylinder with built-in air compressor, ca. 1948)
(1) $1,100   (2) $1,400   (3) $1,800   (4) $2,200   (5) $3,100

Chase Motor Truck Company, Syracuse, New York
Model 8-16 (1915–1918)
(1) $4,500   (2) $7,000   (3) $9,000   (4) $10,250 (5) $12,000

Model 9-18 (1918–1919)
(1) $4,500   (2) $7,000   (3) $9,000   (4) $10,250 (5) $12,000

Model 12-25 (1919–1921)
(1) $5,000   (2) $8,000   (3) $10,500   (4) $12,000 (5) $14,000

Cleveland Tractor Company, Cleveland, Ohio
Roland White, the president of the White Motor Company, started the Cleveland Motor Plow Company in 1917. Within a few years the name changed to the Cleveland Tractor Company. As one of the most well-known crawler builders in its day, the company built the General as a feeble attempt to enter the wheeled-tractor market. B. F. Avery continued with a similar model after the General production ended in 1941. Oliver Corporation purchased the Cleveland Tractor Company in 1944. Collectors seem to be attracted to the small size of the General and the limited number available. A very earnest collector, Cork Lemmon, pointed out the added attraction of the early model with the small caps on the transmission. Prices have gone up modestly in the last few years as interest in lesser-known tractors seems to be growing.

Model GG General (serial nos. 1FA000–3FA935, small caps on transmission, 1939)
(1) $450   (2) $900   (3) $1,650   (4) $2,200   (5) $3,500

Model GG General (serial nos. 3FA936 and up, 1939–1941)
(1) $450   (2) $700   (3) $1,250   (4) $1,750   (5) $2,500

Cockshutt Plow Company, Brantford, Ontario
In 1877, James Cockshutt saw the strong demand for farm equipment and opened his blacksmith shop in Brantford, Ontario. The plows James made in the first years displeased his father Ignatius, who was the major dry goods supplier in the area. By 1882, Ignatius became vice president of his son's Cockshutt Plow Company. The business prospered and grew into a major manufacturer in Canada. Cockshutt marketed tractors in the 1920s. These tractors were built

by Goold, Shapley, and Muir, later Allis-Chalmers, and by the 1930s, Oliver Corporation. Most of the Oliver tractors were painted red and sported the Cockshutt logo on the hood or radiator. These tractors had the same serial number sequences as their Oliver counterparts. In 1946, Cockshutt built its first tractor, the Model 30. This tractor had the first true live PTO assembly. Several models followed. White Motor Company took over Cockshutt in 1962 and the Brantford-built tractors ended. The last Cockshutt tractors from the Oliver line were painted red and carried the Cockshutt name as they had before World War II. The Canadian-built Cockshutt tractors have a loyal following of collectors. These tractors are becoming more in demand as the company's rich history has begun to unfold. (Note: For Models 18-28, 28-44, 60, 70, 80, and 90, see Oliver listings with the same model numbers.)

Model 20 (dual, narrow front, 1952–1956)
(1) $675   (2) $1,200   (3) $1,850   (4) $2,875   (5) $4,000

Model 20 (wide-front, 1952–1956)
(1) $875   (2) $1,450   (3) $2,150   (4) $3,275   (5) $4,500

Model 20 Deluxe (dual, narrow front, 1956–1958)
(1) $925   (2) $1,575   (3) $2,300   (4) $3,425   (5) $4,625

The Model 50 was the biggest tractor in the Cockshutt lineup during the early 1950s. The wide-front axle is usually a more valuable option than the narrow-front models.

Model 20 Deluxe (wide-front, 1956–1958)
(1) $1,125   (2) $1,825   (3) $2,600   (4) $3,825   (5) $5,100

Model 30 Row crop (gasoline, dual narrow front, no 3-point hitch, 1946–1956)
(1) $500   (2) $1,150   (3) $1,400   (4) $2,025   (5) $2,850

Model 30 Row crop (gasoline, dual narrow front, 3-point hitch, 1946–1956)
(1) $750   (2) $1,450   (3) $1,750   (4) $2,425   (5) $3,350

Model 30 Row crop (gasoline, adjustable wide-front, no 3-point hitch, 1946–1956)
(1) $600   (2) $1,350   (3) $1,625   (4) $2,275   (5) $3,150

Model 30 Standard tread (gasoline, no 3-point hitch, 1946–1956)
(1) $525 (2) $1,225 (3) $1,475 (4) $2,125 (5) $2,975

Model 30 Row crop (diesel, dual narrow front, no 3-point hitch, 1949–1956)
(1) $950 (2) $1,500 (3) $1,975 (4) $3,200 (5) $4,000

Model 30 Row crop (diesel, adjustable wide-front, no 3-point hitch, 1949–1956)
(1) $1,125 (2) $1,900 (3) $2,475 (4) $3,700 (5) $4,500

Model 30 Standard tread (diesel, 3-point hitch, 1949–1956)
(1) $1,225 (2) $1,700 (3) $2,175 (4) $3,400 (5) $4,150

Model 30 Row crop (LPG, narrow front, no 3-point hitch, 1949–1956)
(1) $1,500 (2) $1,750 (3) $2,000 (4) $5,000 (5) $6,000

Model 35 Deluxe or Black Hawk 35 (dual, narrow front, 3-point hitch, 1956–1958)
(1) $975 (2) $1,450 (3) $1,900 (4) $3,300 (5) $4,300

Model 35 Deluxe (adjustable wide-front, 3-point hitch, 1956–1958)
(1) $1,125 (2) $1,750 (3) $2,250 (4) $3,650 (5) $4,650

Model 35 Deluxe Standard tread (3-point hitch, 1956–1958)
(1) $975 (2) $1,600 (3) $2,100 (4) $3,500 (5) $4,400

Model 35L (no 3-point hitch, 1956–1958)
(1) $1,325 (2) $1,700 (3) $2,600 (4) $3,750 (5) $4,400

Model 35L (3-point hitch, 1956–1958)
(1) $1,725 (2) $2,200 (3) $3,200 (4) $4,450 (5) $5,300

Model 40 Row crop (gasoline, dual narrow front, no 3-point hitch, 1949–1956)
(1) $750 (2) $1,200 (3) $1,500 (4) $3,000 (5) $4,000

Model 40 Row crop (gasoline, dual narrow front, 3-point hitch, 1949–1956)
(1) $1,250 (2) $1,700 (3) $2,000 (4) $3,500 (5) $4,500

Model 40 Row crop (gasoline, adjustable wide-front, no 3-point hitch, 1949–1956)
(1) $1,000 (2) $1,550 (3) $2,000 (4) $3,600 (5) $4,750

Model 40 Standard tread (gasoline, no 3-point hitch, 1949–1956)
(1) $875 (2) $1,350 (3) $1,700 (4) $3,400 (5) $4,300

Model 40 Row crop (LPG, dual narrow front, no 3-point hitch, 1949–1956)
(1) $2,000 (2) $2,500 (3) $3,000 (4) $5,000 (5) $6,000

Model 40 Row crop (diesel, dual narrow front, no 3-point hitch, 1949-1956)

(1) $750 (2) $1,100 (3) $1,350 (4) $2,900 (5) $3,725

Model 40 Row crop (diesel, adjustable wide-front, no 3-point hitch, 1949-1956)

(1) $1,050 (2) $1,450 (3) $1,750 (4) $3,350 (5) $4,225

Model 40 Standard tread (diesel, no 3-point hitch, 1949-1956)

(1) $800 (2) $1,200 (3) $1,475 (4) $3,100 (5) $4,000

Model 40 Deluxe Row crop (dual narrow front, 3-point hitch, 1956-1958)

(1) $1,000 (2) $1,425 (3) $1,800 (4) $3,425 (5) $4,375

Model 40 Deluxe Row crop (adjustable wide-front, 3-point hitch, 1956-1958)

(1) $1,250 (2) $1,800 (3) $2,300 (4) $4,050 (5) $5,125

Model 40 Deluxe Standard tread (3-point hitch, 1956-1958)

(1) $1,100 (2) $1,575 (3) $1,975 (4) $3,625 (5) $4,625

Model 50 Row crop (gasoline, dual narrow front, 1953-1958)

(1) $1,125 (2) $1,700 (3) $2,200 (4) $4,325 (5) $5,025

Model 50 (adjustable wide-front, gasoline, 1953-1956)

(1) $1,525 (2) $2,100 (3) $2,600 (4) $4,725 (5) $5,425

Model 50 Standard tread (gasoline, 1953-1956)

(1) $1,075 (2) $1,800 (3) $2,325 (4) $4,575 (5) $5,075

Model 50 Row crop (diesel, dual narrow front, 1953-1956)

(1) $900 (2) $1,600 (3) $2,225 (4) $4,050 (5) $4,725

Model 50 (adjustable wide-front, diesel, 1953-1956)

(1) $1,400 (2) $2,150 (3) $2,825 (4) $4,700 (5) $5,475

Model 50 Standard tread (diesel, 1953-1956)

(1) $1,075 (2) $1,800 (3) $2,375 (4) $4,400 (5) $5,125

Model 50 Deluxe Row crop (gasoline, dual narrow front, 1953-1958)

(1) $1,325 (2) $1,900 (3) $2,425 (4) $4,575 (5) $5,275

Model 50 Deluxe (adjustable wide-front, gasoline, 1953-1956)

(1) $1,725 (2) $2,325 (3) $4,850 (4) $4,975 (5) $6,025

Model 50 Deluxe Standard tread (gasoline, 1953-1956)

(1) $1,375 (2) $2,100 (3) $2,625 (4) $4,900 (5) $5,425

Model 50 Deluxe Row crop (diesel, dual narrow front, 1953-1956)

(1) $1,150 (2) $2,000 (3) $2,650 (4) $4,500 (5) $5,200

Model 50 Deluxe (adjustable wide-front, diesel, 1953–1956)
(1) $1,700   (2) $2,200   (3) $3,300   (4) $5,225   (5) $6,225

Model 50 Deluxe Standard tread (diesel, 1953–1956)
(1) $1,450   (2) $2,200   (3) $2,850   (4) $4,900   (5) $5,625

Model 540 (1958–1961)
(1) $925   (2) $1,550   (3) $2,500   (4) $3,850   (5) $4,750

Model 540 High Utility (1958–1961)
(1) $1,750   (2) $3,100   (3) $4,000   (4) $6,000   (5) $7,400

Model 550 Row-crop (gasoline, 1958–1961)
(1) $900   (2) $1,600   (3) $2,050   (4) $3,450   (5) $4,375

Model 550 (adjustable wide-front, gasoline, 1958–1961)
(1) $1,100   (2) $1,900   (3) $2,450   (4) $3,850   (5) $4,875

Model 550 Wheatland (gasoline, 1958–1961)
(1) $1,175   (2) $1,900   (3) $2,375   (4) $3,750   (5) $4,700

Model 550 Row-crop (diesel, 1958–1961)
(1) $1,250   (2) $2,000   (3) $2,600   (4) $3,825   (5) $4,750

Model 550 (adjustable wide-front, diesel, 1958–1961)
(1) $1,500   (2) $2,350   (3) $3,150   (4) $4,175   (5) $5,450

Model 550 Wheatland (diesel, 1958–1961)
(1) $1,350   (2) $2,200   (3) $2,800   (4) $4,075   (5) $5,000

Model 560 Row-crop (no 3-point hitch, 1958–1962)
(1) $950   (2) $1,300   (3) $1,635   (4) $3,150   (5) $4,000

Model 560 Row-crop (3-point hitch, 1958–1962)
(1) $1,200   (2) $1,550   (3) $1,885   (4) $3,400   (5) $4,250

Model 560 (adjustable wide-front, no 3-point hitch, 1958–1962)
(1) $1,200   (2) $1,525   (3) $2,100   (4) $3,650   (5) $4,450

Model 560 Wheatland (no 3-point hitch, 1958–1962)
(1) $1,050   (2) $1,300   (3) $1,750   (4) $3,300   (5) $4,150

Model 570 Row-crop (gasoline, 1958–1960)
(1) $950   (2) $2,100   (3) $2,800   (4) $3,600   (5) $4,600

Model 570 (adjustable wide-front, gasoline, 1958–1960)
(1) $1,250   (2) $2,500   (3) $3,300   (4) $4,150   (5) $5,350

Model 570 Wheatland (gasoline, 1958–1960)
(1) $1,200   (2) $2,400   (3) $3,200   (4) $4,000   (5) $4,900

Model 570 Row-crop (diesel, 1961–1962)
(1) $950   (2) $2,050   (3) $2,750   (4) $3,550   (5) $4,550

Model 570 (adjustable wide-front, diesel, 1961–1962)
(1) $1,250   (2) $2,500   (3) $3,300   (4) $4,150   (5) $5,350

Model 570 Wheatland (diesel, 1961–1962)
(1) $1,200   (2) $2,400   (3) $3,200   (4) $4,000   (5) $4,900

Model 570 Super Row-crop (diesel, 1961–1962)
(1) $1,550   (2) $2,450   (3) $3,250   (4) $4,550   (5) $6,250

Model 570 Super (adjustable wide-front, diesel, 1961–1962)
(1) $1,950   (2) $2,900   (3) $3,500   (4) $5,050   (5) $6,950

Model 570 Super Wheatland (diesel, 1961–1962)
(1) $1,750   (2) $2,700   (3) $3,300   (4) $4,850   (5) $6,750

Golden Eagle (1955–1958)
(1) $1,000   (2) $1,500   (3) $2,000   (4) $2,500   (5) $3,500

Golden Arrow (1957)
(1) $3,000   (2) $4,100   (3) $5,750   (4) $8,750   (5) $10,000

C.O.D. Tractor Company, Minneapolis, Minnesota
Model 13-24 (1916–1919)
(1) $6,000   (2) $9,000   (3) $11,750   (4) $15,000   (5) $17,000

Model B (1919)
(1) $4,500   (2) $7,000   (3) $9,000   (4) $11,000   (5) $13,500

This 1919 Model B was the last of two models made by C.O.D. Albert O. Espe was one of the finest tractor designers in the early tractor years. The C.O.D. was one of his designs as well as the Avery tractor. Rumely also used Espe patents for its GasPull tractor.

Coleman Tractor Company, Kansas City, Missouri
Model 10-20 (rerated 16-30, 1918–1920)
(1) $5,500   (2) $8,250   (3) $10,250   (4) $12,000   (5) $15,000

Comet Automobile Company, Decatur, Illinois
Model 15-30 (1919–1920)
(1) $6,750   (2) $10,250   (3) $13,000   (4) $15,500   (5) $19,000

Common Sense Gas Tractor Company, Minneapolis, Minnesota
Common Sense 20-40 (4-cylinder engine, 1916–1918)
(1) $7,000   (2) $12,000   (3) $16,000   (4) $26,000   (5) $32,000

Common Sense 20-50 (V-8 engine, 1917–1920)
(1) $7,000   (2) $12,000   (3) $16,000   (4) $26,000 (5) $32,000

Co-Op (National Farm Machinery Cooperative), Battle Creek, Michigan
Co-Op No. 1 (1936–1938)
(1) $3,000   (2) $4,000   (3) $5,000   (4) $6,250   (5) $7,500

Co-Op No. 2 (1936–1938)
(1) $2,000   (2) $2,400   (3) $3,000   (4) $3,750   (5) $4,500

Co-Op No. 3 (1936–1938)
(1) $2,400   (2) $3,000   (3) $3,750   (4) $4,250   (5) $5,200

Co-Op G (made by Cletrac, 1939–1941)
(1) $450   (2) $700   (3) $1,250   (4) $1,900   (5) $2,700

Co-Op B-1 (made by Cletrac, 1941–1944)
(1) $500   (2) $750   (3) $1,400   (4) $2,100   (5) $3,000

Co-Op B-2 (1940–1942)
(1) $1,500   (2) $2,500   (3) $5,000   (4) $7,000   (5) $9,000

Co-Op B-2 Jr. (1940–1942)
(1) $4,000   (2) $5,750   (3) $7,000   (4) $9,000   (5) $10,000

Co-Op B-3 (1940–1942)
(1) $4,000   (2) $6,250   (3) $8,600   (4) $9,200   (5) $10,100

Co-Op C (1944)
(1) $3,800   (2) $5,750   (3) $7,600   (4) $9,000   (5) $10,000

Co-Op D-3 (1945)
(1) $1,200   (2) $2,100   (3) $2,750   (4) $3,200   (5) $4,000

Co-Op 3-S (1948–1951)
(1) $2,000   (2) $3,500   (3) $4,000   (4) $4,500   (5) $7,500

The Coleman tractor weighs about 5,000 pounds and was rated 16-30 horsepower by 1919. Early tractors from little-known companies are still in highdemand by certain collectors. With the very limited numbers of surviving models, restoration is not for the average collector.

Co-Op E2 (1952–1958)
(1) $1,500　(2) $2,500　(3) $3,500　(4) $4,000　(5) $5,000

Co-Op E3 (gasoline, 1946–1956)
(1) $1,200　(2) $2,100　(3) $2,750　(4) $3,200　(5) $4,000

Co-Op E3 (diesel, 1949–1956)
(1) $1,800　(2) $2,500　(3) $3,250　(4) $4,000　(5) $5,000

Co-Op E4 (gasoline, 1950–1958)
(1) $1,250　(2) $1,800　(3) $2,600　(4) $3,200　(5) $4,100

Co-Op E4 (diesel, 1950–1958)
(1) $1,400　(2) $2,000　(3) $2,750　(4) $3,300　(5) $4,200

Co-Op E5 (gasoline, 1953–1958)
(1) $1,200　(2) $1,800　(3) $2,600　(4) $3,200　(5) $4,000

Corbitt Company, Henderson, North Carolina
Model G-50 (gasoline, ca. 1956)
(1) $4,200　(2) $6,500　(3) $8,200　(4) $9,500　(5) $12,500

Model K-50 (kerosene, ca. 1956)
(1) $4,200　(2) $6,500　(3) $8,200　(4) $9,500　(5) $12,500

Model D-50 (diesel, ca. 1956)
(1) $4,500　(2) $6,700　(3) $8,450　(4) $9,750　(5) $13,000

Craig Tractor Company, Cleveland, Ohio
Model 15-25 (1919–1921)
(1) $6,000　(2) $8,000　(3) $10,000　(4) $11,500　(5) $14,000

Crosley Corp., Marion, Indiana
This popular automobile company from the 1940s and 1950s decided to make a small jeep-like vehicle called the Farm-O-Road. All kinds of farm implements could be bought to work the fields. When a trip to town was needed, two people could travel at highway speeds with comfort. The Farm-O-Roads are an interesting attraction at farm shows and also appeal to many automobile collectors. One may expect the prices to rise on these scarce little jeeps in the next few years, as interest appears to be growing.

Farm-O-Road Model FOR (1950–1952)
(1) $2,200　(2) $4,000　(3) $5,600　(4) $6,800　(5) $8,600

Cushman Motor Works, Lincoln, Nebraska
Macdonald 12-24 (1917–1920)
(1) $3,500　(2) $7,000　(3) $10,000　(4) $12,500　(5) $16,000

Custom Tractor Manufacturing Company, Shelbyville, Indiana
Model B (1947–1953)
(1) $500　(2) $900　(3) $1,500　(4) $3,800　(5) $8,000

Model C (1947–1953)
(1) $500   (2) $900   (3) $1,500   (4) $3,800   (5) $8,000

Model HR Row-crop (1947–1953)
(1) $800   (2) $1,500   (3) $2,000   (4) $3,000   (5) $8,000

Model HW Wide-front (1947–1953)
(1) $1,000   (2) $1,700   (3) $2,250   (4) $3,500   (5) $8,000

Model E Row-crop (1947–1953)
(1) $1,000   (2) $1,700   (3) $2,200   (4) $3,200   (5) $8,000

Model E Wide-front (1947–1953)
(1) $1,300   (2) $2,000   (3) $2,800   (4) $4,000   (5) $9,000

Model 96R Row-crop (1952–1954)
(1) $1,000   (2) $1,500   (3) $2,000   (4) $3,000   (5) $8,000

Model 96W Wide-front (1952–1954)
(1) $1,300   (2) $1,700   (3) $2,250   (4) $3,500   (5) $8,000

Model 97R Row-crop (1952–1954)
(1) $1,000   (2) $1,600   (3) $2,100   (4) $3,100   (5) $8,000

Model 97W Wide-front (1952–1954)
(1) $1,200   (2) $1,800   (3) $2,300   (4) $3,800   (5) $8,300

Model 98R Row-crop (1952–1954)
(1) $1,200   (2) $1,800   (3) $2,400   (4) $4,000   (5) $8,200

Model 98W Wide-front (1952–1954)
(1) $1,500   (2) $2,100   (3) $2,700   (4) $4,400   (5) $9,500

Dart Truck and Tractor Company, Waterloo, Iowa
Model 12-25 Blue J (1920)
(1) $8,000   (2) $11,500   (3) $14,500   (4) $17,500 (5) $21,000

Model 15-30 Blue J (1920)
(1) $8,250   (2) $12,000   (3) $15,000   (4) $18,000 (5) $22,000

Dauch Manufacturing Company, Sandusky, Ohio
Model E 15-35 (1912–1920)
(1) $20,000 (2) $24,000   (3) $27,000   (4) $30,000 (5) $34,000

Model J 10-20 (1917–1920)
(1) $14,000 (2) $17,000   (3) $19,000   (4) $21,000 (5) $24,000

Dayton-Dick Company
(Renamed Dayton-Dowd Co.), Quincy, Illinois
Leader 9-15 (1916)
(1) $8,000   (2) $11,750   (3) $14,000   (4) $16,500 (5) $20,000

Leader 12-28 (ca. 1917)
(1) $12,500 (2) $15,750   (3) $20,000   (4) $23,500 (5) $28,000

55

The Sandusky tractors had little success even though the company spent a fortune in advertising. Any remaining examples of Sandusky tractors are notably scarce. Seldom does a collector find such a machine in running condition, and the restoration process can be a gigantic and expensive process.

Leader B 12-18 (two known to exist, 1917–1921)
(1) $11,000 (2) $14,000 (3) $17,000 (4) $20,000 (5) $24,000

Leader 15-25 (ca. 1917)
(1) $14,000 (2) $18,000 (3) $22,000 (4) $25,000 (5) $30,000

Leader N 16-32 (1920–1925)
(1) $6,500 (2) $8,750 (3) $11,000 (4) $13,000 (5) $16,000

Deere and Company, Moline, Illinois

John Deere was a prominent blacksmith from Rutland, Vermont. In 1836 he moved to Grand Detour, Illinois, where he built his first famous steel plow from the remains of a large discarded band-saw blade. By 1847, Deere was selling 1,000 plows a year, and in 1852 he moved his facilities to Moline, Illinois, where he was producing 4,000 plows a year. The company expanded into different types of tillage equipment to become an agricultural giant and began experimenting with tractors in 1912. Several tractor attempts proved to be financial losers in the highly competitive tractor industry. Deere finally bought the Waterloo Gasoline Engine Company on March 14, 1918, and was thrust into the tractor business. The already successful Waterloo tractors had a good reputation in the United States as well as England where they were sold under the name Overtime. In 1923, Deere built the model D standard tread tractor using the basic engine design of the later Waterloo Boy tractors; this two-cylinder design was Deere's hallmark for decades to come. One of our advisors, Larry Moit, stressed that the original serial number tag on a John Deere is crucial for its value. A missing tag, especially on the rare models, damages the value significantly. Values listed are for tractors with original tags. I learned from advisors Bill Black and Bernard Scott that the factory can track the engine numbers of the Dubuque models and will issue replacement tags. The company has extensive records on these vertical two-cylinder tractors and can cross-reference the engine numbers to find the original serial number. The John Deere two-cylinder tractors have the strongest following of all collectable tractors and are ahead of most other major brands by several years. Expect the "New Generation" early four- to six-cylinder models to surge in price within the next few years.

Waterloo Boy Model R (1915–1919)
(1) $14,000 (2) $21,000 (3) $23,000 (4) $32,500 (5) $45,000

Waterloo Boy Model N (1917–1924)
(1) $12,750 (2) $18,750 (3) $20,500 (4) $30,000 (5) $37,500

Model D (unstyled, fabricated front axle, serial nos. 30401–30450, 1923–1924)
(1) $15,000 (2) $20,000 (3) $25,000 (4) $30,500 (5) $35,000

Model D (unstyled, spoke flywheel, serial nos. 30451–31279, 1924)
(1) $9,500 (2) $13,000 (3) $17,500 (4) $21,250 (5) $27,500

Model D (unstyled, spoke flywheel, serial nos. 31280–36248, 1924–1926)
(1) $6,500 (2) $9,250 (3) $11,500 (4) $15,000 (5) $19,000

Model D (unstyled, solid flywheel, keyed crankshaft, serial nos. 36249–53387, 1926–1927)
(1) $1,500 (2) $2,125 (3) $2,850 (4) $3,750 (5) $5,375

Model D (unstyled, solid flywheel, serial nos. 53388–143799, 1927–1938)
(1) $2,000 (2) $3,125 (3) $3,850 (4) $4,750 (5) $6,375

Model D (styled, serial nos. 143800–183705, 1939–1949)
(1) $1,500 (2) $2,000 (3) $3,500 (4) $5,000 (5) $6,000

Model D (styled, turning brakes, serial nos. 183706–191578, 1949–1953)
(1) $2,500 (2) $3,000 (3) $4,000 (4) $6,000 (5) $8,000

Model D "Streeter" (serial nos. 191579–191670, 1953)
(1) $2,750 (2) $3,500 (3) $4,250 (4) $5,500 (5) $7,500

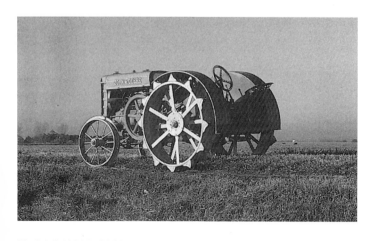

This 1923 John Deere D is an extremely desirable tractor. ny Model D with a spoked flywheel will bring a hefty price. This one, equipped with a ladder-side radiator and fabricated front axle, is one of the first fifty Model Ds made.

Model C (1927–1928)
(1) $8,000 (2) $12,500 (3) $16,675 (4) $23,000 (5) $29,325

Model GP (steel wheels, 1930–1935)
(1) $1,250 (2) $2,250 (3) $3,000 (4) $3,500 (5) $5,050

Model GPWT Wide tread (serial nos. 400000–404809, 1929–1932)
(1) $4,400 (2) $8,000 (3) $12,250 (4) $16,750 (5) $22,500

Model GPWT Wide tread (overhead steering, proper wheels, 1932-33)
(1) $8,000   (2) $11,400   (3) $15,000   (4) $21,500   (5) $28,500

Model GP-Tricycle (1928-1929)
(1) $7,000   (2) $10,000   (3) $15,000   (4) $20,000   (5) $27,000

Model GPO (orchard, 1931-1933)
(1) $4,250   (2) $5,750   (3) $10,500   (4) $11,500   (5) $12,500

Model GP-P (potato, 1930)
(1) $9,000   (2) $12,000   (3) $15,000   (4) $19,750   (5) $26,500

**Model A (open fan shaft, dual narrow front, serial nos.
410008-414808, 1934-1935)**
(1) $3,000   (2) $3,975   (3) $7,000   (4) $9,000   (5) $14,000

Model A (unstyled, steel wheels, dual narrow front, 1935-1938)
(1) $750   (2) $1,800   (3) $2,400   (4) $3,000   (5) $4,650

Model A (unstyled, rubber tires, dual narrow front, 1935-1938)
(1) $875   (2) $1,825   (3) $2,400   (4) $3,000   (5) $5,275

**Model A (unstyled, rubber tires, round spoke wheels, dual narrow
front, 1935-1938)**
(1) $1,575   (2) $2,350   (3) $2,825   (4) $3,550   (5) $6,275

Model AN (unstyled, rubber tires, single front wheel, 1935-1938)
(1) $1,900   (2) $2,350   (3) $3,750   (4) $5,300   (5) $7,000

Model AW (unstyled, rubber tires, wide-front axle, 1935-1938)
(1) $4,750   (2) $6,200   (3) $6,500   (4) $7,900   (5) $10,850

Model ANH (unstyled, rubber tires, narrow, 1935-1938)
(1) $9,000   (2) $10,500   (3) $11,500   (4) $18,000   (5) $21,500

Model AWH (unstyled, rubber tires, wide-front, 1935-1938)
(1) $9,500   (2) $12,000   (3) $14,750   (4) $18,000   (5) $24,000

Model A (styled, steel wheels, dual narrow front, 1938-1947)
(1) $750   (2) $1,475   (3) $2,200   (4) $3,050   (5) $4,400

Model A (styled, rubber tires, dual narrow front, 1938-1947)
(1) $650   (2) $1,250   (3) $1,725   (4) $2,450   (5) $3,300

Model AN (styled, rubber tires, single front wheel, 1938-1947)
(1) $1,100   (2) $1,700   (3) $2,300   (4) $3,150   (5) $4,250

Model AW (styled, rubber tires, wide-front axle, 1938-1947)
(1) $1,450   (2) $2,050   (3) $2,725   (4) $4,250   (5) $5,550

Model ANH (styled, rubber tires, narrow, 1938-1947)
(1) $1,100   (2) $2,000   (3) $3,000   (4) $3,875   (5) $4,900

Model AWH (styled, rubber tires, wide-front, 1938–1947)
(1) $2,300   (2) $4,800   (3) $5,700   (4) $6,900   (5) $7,950

Model A (styled, pressed-steel frame, rubber tires, dual narrow front, 1947–1952)
(1) $700   (2) $1,400   (3) $2,125   (4) $2,850   (5) $3,600

Model A (styled, pressed-steel frame, rubber tires, single front wheel, 1947–1952)
(1) $800   (2) $1,600   (3) $2,400   (4) $3,200   (5) $4,000

Model A (styled, pressed-steel frame, rubber tires, wide-front, 1947–1952)
(1) $900   (2) $1,800   (3) $2,700   (4) $3,600   (5) $4,500

Model AH (styled, pressed-steel frame, rubber tires, Hi-Crop, 1947–1952)
(1) $7,000   (2) $8,500   (3) $12,000   (4) $17,000   (5) $27,000

Model AR (unstyled, steel wheels, standard tread, offset radiator cap, 1935–1940)
(1) $1,750   (2) $3,000   (3) $3,750   (4) $4,750   (5) $6,500

Model AR (unstyled, steel wheels, standard tread, center radiator cap, 1941–1949)
(1) $1,150   (2) $1,950   (3) $2,375   (4) $3,500   (5) $4,750

Model AR (unstyled, rubber tires, standard tread, center radiator cap, 1941–1949)
(1) $925   (2) $1,600   (3) $2,275   (4) $3,200   (5) $4,250

Model AI (unstyled, rubber tires, industrial, 1936–1941)
(1) $6,500   (2) $9,750   (3) $12,000   (4) $13,750   (5) $17,000

Model AO (unstyled, steel wheels, orchard, 1935–1949)
(1) $3,000   (2) $4,000   (3) $6,000   (4) $8,000   (5) $13,000

Model AO (unstyled, rubber tires, orchard, 1935–1949)
(1) $2,500   (2) $3,500   (3) $5,000   (4) $7,000   (5) $12,000

Model AOS (rubber tires, streamlined orchard, 1936–1940)
(1) $4,000   (2) $5,000   (3) $7,500   (4) $10,000   (5) $15,000

Model AO (styled, rubber tires, orchard, 1949–1953)
(1) $1,625   (2) $2,875   (3) $3,625   (4) $5,250   (5) $8,000

Model AR (styled, steel wheels, standard tread, 1949–1953)
(1) $1,625   (2) $2,875   (3) $3,625   (4) $5,250   (5) $8,000

Model AR (styled, rubber tires, standard tread, 1949–1953)
(1) $1,400   (2) $2,600   (3) $3,200   (4) $4,800   (5) $7,600

Model B (unstyled, short frame, dual narrow front, 4-bolt front, steel wheels, 1935)
(1) $1,200   (2) $2,400   (3) $3,600   (4) $4,800   (5) $6,200

Model B (unstyled, short frame, dual narrow front, 8-bolt front, steel wheels, 1935–1937)
(1) $800   (2) $1,600   (3) $2,400   (4) $3,200   (5) $4,250

Model B (unstyled, long frame, dual narrow front, steel wheels, serial nos. 4220–58246, 1937–1938)
(1) $900   (2) $1,800   (3) $2,700   (4) $3,600   (5) $4,500

Model B (unstyled, long frame, dual narrow front, rubber tires, 1937–1938)
(1) $900   (2) $1,800   (3) $2,700   (4) $3,600   (5) $4,500

Model BN (unstyled, long frame, single front wheel, rubber tires, 1937–1938)
(1) $1,200   (2) $2,200   (3) $3,200   (4) $4,200   (5) $5,200

Model BW (unstyled, long frame, wide-front axle, rubber tires, 1937–1938)
(1) $5,250   (2) $8,000   (3) $10,500   (4) $12,500 (5) $15,250

Model BNH (unstyled, narrow, high 1937–1938)
(1) $4,900   (2) $6,250   (3) $8,000   (4) $9,750   (5) $12,500

The John Deere B tractors were among the most popular built in their day. For today's collectors, the unstyled versions have all the charm of the early John Deeres without the big price tag that this brand often generates.

Model BWH (unstyled, wide, high, 1937–1938)
(1) $6,250   (2) $8,500   (3) $10,500   (4) $14,750 (5) $18,750

Model BR Standard Tread (1935–1938)
(1) $1,875   (2) $3,500   (3) $4,750   (4) $5,825   (5) $7,000

Model BO Orchard (1935–1938)
(1) $2,000   (2) $3,600   (3) $4,900   (4) $6,000   (5) $7,250

Model BI Industrial (1936–1938)
(1) $6,750   (2) $9,500   (3) $12,250   (4) $16,000 (5) $19,000

Model B (styled, dual narrow front, 4-speed, 1938–1940)
(1) $500   (2) $1,000   (3) $1,500   (4) $2,000   (5) $2,500

Model BN (styled, single front wheel, 4-speed, 1938–1940)
(1) $700   (2) $1,400   (3) $2,150   (4) $2,800   (5) $3,500

Model BW (styled, wide-front axle, 4-speed, 1938–1940)
(1) $800   (2) $1,600   (3) $2,400   (4) $3,200   (5) $4,000

Model BNH (styled, narrow, high, 4-speed, 1938–1940)
(1) $2,250   (2) $2,600   (3) $3,500   (4) $4,500   (5) $5,750

Model BWH (styled, wide, high, 4-speed, 1938–1940)
(1) $2,750   (2) $3,500   (3) $4,250   (4) $5,250   (5) $7,000

Model B (styled, dual narrow front, 6-speed, 1941–1947)
(1) $500   (2) $1,000   (3) $1,500   (4) $2,000   (5) $2,500

Model BN (styled, single front wheel, 6-speed, 1941–1947)
(1) $700   (2) $1,400   (3) $2,100   (4) $2,800   (5) $3,500

Model BW (styled, wide-front axle, 6-speed, 1941–1947)
(1) $1,100   (2) $1,700   (3) $2,400   (4) $3,200   (5) $3,900

Model BNH (styled, narrow, 6-speed, 1941–1947)
(1) $1,450   (2) $1,750   (3) $2,125   (4) $2,900   (5) $3,625

Model BWH (styled, wide, 6-speed, 1941–1947)
(1) $2,000   (2) $2,125   (3) $3,000   (4) $3,375   (5) $3,875

Model B (styled, dual narrow front, pressed-steel frame, 1947–1952)
(1) $700   (2) $1,400   (3) $2,100   (4) $2,800   (5) $3,500

Model BN (styled, single front wheel, pressed-steel frame, 1947–1952)
(1) $900   (2) $1,800   (3) $2,700   (4) $3,600   (5) $4,500

Model BW (styled, wide-front axle, pressed-steel frame, 1947–1952)
(1) $1,000   (2) $2,000   (3) $3,000   (4) $4,000   (5) $5,000

Model BN (styled, narrow high-clearance, pressed-steel frame, 1947–1952)
(1) $1,100   (2) $2,200   (3) $3,300   (4) $4,400   (5) $5,500

Model BW (styled, wide high-clearance, pressed-steel frame, 1947–1952)
(1) $1,200   (2) $2,400   (3) $3,600   (4) $4,800   (5) $6,000

Model G (unstyled, steel wheels, low-radiator, dual narrow front, prior to serial no. 4251, 1938)
(1) $7,000   (2) $8,000   (3) $9,000   (4) $10,000 (5) $12,500

Model G (unstyled, rubber tires, low-radiator, dual narrow front, prior to serial no. 4251, 1938)
(1) $7,500   (2) $8,500   (3) $9,500   (4) $10,500 (5) $13,000

Model G (unstyled, steel wheels, large-radiator, dual narrow front, 1939-1941)
(1) $2,500   (2) $4,000   (3) $5,000   (4) $6,000   (5) $7,500

Model G (unstyled, rubber tires, large-radiator, dual narrow front, 1939-1941)
(1) $2,500   (2) $4,000   (3) $5,000   (4) $6,000   (5) $7,500

Model G (unstyled, rubber, round spoke wheels, large-radiator, dual narrow front, 1939-1941)
(1) $3,300   (2) $5,000   (3) $6,000   (4) $7,000   (5) $8,500

Model GM Modified (rubber tires, 1941-1946)
(1) $1,600   (2) $2,200   (3) $2,800   (4) $3,900   (5) $5,000

Model G (styled, steel wheels, dual, narrow front, 1947-1953)
(1) $2,250   (2) $2,750   (3) $3,550   (4) $4,750   (5) $6,400

Model G (styled, rubber tires, dual, narrow front, 1947-1953)
(1) $1,500   (2) $2,000   (3) $2,750   (4) $3,750   (5) $5,250

Model GN (styled, rubber tires, single front wheel, 1947-1953)
(1) $1,600   (2) $2,300   (3) $3,050   (4) $4,150   (5) $5,750

Model GW (styled, rubber tires, wide-front axle, 1947-1953)
(1) $2,250   (2) $2,625   (3) $3,250   (4) $4,250   (5) $6,000

Model GH (styled, rubber tires, high-clearance, 1947-1953)
(1) $8,000   (2) $12,000   (3) $16,000   (4) $19,750 (5) $28,000

Model H (rubber tires, dual narrow front, 1939-1947)
(1) $700   (2) $1,100   (3) $1,900   (4) $2,750   (5) $3,500

Model HN (rubber tires, single front wheel, 1939-1947)
(1) $900   (2) $1,800   (3) $2,700   (4) $3,600   (5) $4,500

Model HNH (rubber tires, single front wheel, high-clearance, 1941-1942)
(1) $5,000   (2) $10,000   (3) $15,000   (4) $20,000 (5) $25,000

Model HWH (rubber tires, wide-front axle, high-clearance, 1941-1942)
(1) $4,000   (2) $8,000   (3) $12,000   (4) $16,000 (5) $21,000

Model Y (1936)
(1) $10,000 (2) $15,000   (3) $22,500   (4) $30,000 (5) $35,000

Model 62 (1937)
(1) $10,000 (2) $15,000   (3) $22,500   (4) $30,000 (5) $35,000

Model L (unstyled, 1936-1938)
(1) $5,000   (2) $7,500   (3) $11,000   (4) $15,000 (5) $20,000

Model L (styled, 1938–1946)
(1) $800   (2) $1,500   (3) $2,500   (4) $4,500   (5) $8,000

Model LI Industrial (1942–1946)
(1) $1,500   (2) $2,500   (3) $3,500   (4) $6,000   (5) $10,000

Model LA (1940–1946)
(1) $750   (2) $1,500   (3) $2,500   (4) $4,500   (5) $8,000

Model M (1947–1952)
(1) $600   (2) $1,500   (3) $2,500   (4) $4,500   (5) $6,000

Model MI Industrial (1949–1955)
(1) $1,500   (2) $2,500   (3) $3,500   (4) $6,000   (5) $10,000

Model MT (dual narrow front axle, 1949–1952)
(1) $600   (2) $1,500   (3) $2,500   (4) $4,500   (5) $6,000

Model MT-W (wide-front axle, 1949–1952)
(1) $1,000   (2) $2,000   (3) $3,000   (4) $5,000   (5) $6,500

Model MT-N (single front wheel, 1949–1952)
(1) $1,000   (2) $2,000   (3) $3,000   (4) $5,000   (5) $6,500

Model R (1949–1954)
(1) $1,000   (2) $2,000   (3) $3,000   (4) $4,000   (5) $5,500

Model 40U Utility (gasoline, 1953–1955)
(1) $600   (2) $1,500   (3) $2,500   (4) $5,000   (5) $6,500

Model 40U Utility (all-fuel, 1953–1955)
(1) $1,100   (2) $2,000   (3) $3,000   (4) $5,500   (5) $7,000

Model 40S Standard (gasoline, 1953–1955)
(1) $600   (2) $1,500   (3) $2,500 `   (4) $5,000   (5) $6,500

Model 40S Standard (all-fuel, 1953–1955)
(1) $1,100   (2) $2,000   (3) $3,000   (4) $5,500   (5) $7,000

Model 40T-W Tricycle (wide-front axle, gasoline, 1953–1955)
(1) $600   (2) $1,500   (3) $2,500   (4) $5,000   (5) $6,500

Model 40T-W Tricycle (wide-front axle, all-fuel, 1953–1955)
(1) $1,100   (2) $2,000   (3) $3,000   (4) $5,500   (5) $7,000

Model 40T-RC Row-crop (narrow, dual-front axle, gasoline, 1953–1955)
(1) $600   (2) $1,500   (3) $2,500   (4) $4,000   (5) $6,000

Model 40T-RC Row-crop (narrow, dual-front axle, all-fuel, 1953–1955)
(1) $1,100   (2) $2,000   (3) $3,000   (4) $4,500   (5) $6,500

Model 40T-N (single front wheel, gasoline, 1953–1955)
(1) $1,000   (2) $2,000   (3) $3,000   (4) $4,500   (5) $6,500

Model 40T-N (single front wheel, all-fuel, 1953–1955)
(1) $1,500   (2) $2,500   (3) $3,500   (4) $5,000   (5) $7,000

Model 40H Hi-Crop (gasoline, 1954–1955
(1) $1,500   (2) $2,500   (3) $3,500   (4) $6,000   (5) $8,000

Model 40H Hi-Crop (all-fuel, 1954–1955)
(1) $3,000   (2) $4,000   (3) $5,000   (4) $7,500   (5) $9,500

Model 40V Special Hi-Crop (gasoline, 1955)
(1) $1,300   (2) $2,500   (3) $3,500   (4) $6,000   (5) $8,000

Model 40V Special Hi-Crop (all-fuel, 1955)
(1) $2,800   (2) $4,000   (3) $5,000   (4) $7,500   (5) $9,500

Model 50 (dual narrow front axle, gasoline, 1952–1956)
(1) $900   (2) $1,200   (3) $1,700   (4) $2,500   (5) $3,500

Model 50 (dual narrow front axle, all-fuel, 1952–1956)
(1) $1,000   (2) $1,300   (3) $1,800   (4) $2,750   (5) $4,000

Model 50 (dual narrow front axle, LPG, 1952–1956)
(1) $1,250   (2) $1,500   (3) $1,900   (4) $3,000   (5) $4,500

Model 50 (wide-front axle, gasoline, 1952–1956)
(1) $1,500   (2) $1,750   (3) $2,000   (4) $3,000   (5) $4,000

Model 50 (wide-front axle, all-fuel, 1952–1956)
(1) $1,700   (2) $2,000   (3) $2,200   (4) $3,200   (5) $4,500

Model 50 (wide-front axle, LPG, 1952–1956)
(1) $2,000   (2) $2,500   (3) $3,000   (4) $3,500   (5) $5,000

Model 50 (single front wheel, gasoline, 1952–1956)
(1) $900   (2) $1,200   (3) $1,700   (4) $2,500   (5) $3,500

Model 50 (single front wheel, all-fuel, 1952–1956)
(1) $1,000   (2) $1,300   (3) $1,800   (4) $2,600   (5) $3,750

Model 50 (single front wheel, LPG, 1952–1956)
(1) $1,500   (2) $1,700   (3) $2,000   (4) $3,000   (5) $4,200

Model 60 Tricycle (dual front wheels 1952–1956)
(1) $1,000   (2) $1,500   (3) $2,000   (4) $2,700   (5) $3,500

Model 60 Tricycle (single front wheel 1952–1956)
(1) $1,100   (2) $1,600   (3) $2,100   (4) $2,800   (5) $3,600

Model 60 Row-crop (wide-front axle , 1952–1956)
(1) $1,500   (2) $1,750   (3) $2,500   (4) $3,000   (5) $4,000

Model 60S Standard High-Seat (1954–1956)
(1) $2,000   (2) $2,500   (3) $3,000   (4) $3,500   (5) $4,500

Model 60S Standard Low-Seat (1952–1954)
(1) $1,500   (2) $2,000   (3) $2,500   (4) $3,000   (5) $4,000

Model 60-O Orchard (1952–1957)
(1) $3,000   (2) $3,500   (3) $4,000   (4) $5,000   (5) $6,000

Model 60H Hi-Crop (gasoline, 1952–1956)
(1) $12,500   (2) $15,000   (3) $20,000   (4) $25,000 (5) $30,000

Model 60H Hi-Crop (LPG, 1952–1956)
(1) $12,500   (2) $15,000   (3) $21,000   (4) $27,000 (5) $35,000

Model 60H Hi-Crop (all-fuel, 1952–1956)
(1) $12,500   (2) $15,000   (3) $21,000   (4) $27,000 (5) $35,000

Model 70 Tricycle (dual front wheels, 1953–1956)
(1) $800   (2) $1,200   (3) $1,750   (4) $2,500   (5) $3,000

Model 70 Tricycle (single front wheel, 1953–1956)
(1) $1,000   (2) $1,500   (3) $1,900   (4) $2,750   (5) $3,250

Model 70 Row-crop (wide-front axle, 1953–1956)
(1) $1,500   (2) $2,000   (3) $2,500   (4) $3,250   (5) $3,500

The citrus fenders on the John Deere 60 Orchard are often in poor shape or missing before restoration. It takes endless hours of work and dedication to bring a tractor to this beautiful state, as the price of a well-restored example will reflect.

Model 70D Tricycle (diesel, dual front wheels, 1953–1956)
(1) $800   (2) $1,200   (3) $1,750   (4) $2,500   (5) $3,250

Model 70D Tricycle (diesel, single front wheel, 1954–1956)
(1) $900   (2) $1,300   (3) $1,800   (4) $2,700   (5) $3,350

Model 70D Row-crop (diesel, wide-front axle, 1954–1956)
(1) $1,500   (2) $2,000   (3) $2,500   (4) $3,200   (5) $3,500

Model 70S Standard (gasoline, 1953–1956)
(1) $2,000   (2) $2,500   (3) $3,500   (4) $4,500   (5) $6,500

Model 70S Standard (diesel, 1954–1956)
(1) $1,800   (2) $2,200   (3) $3,000   (4) $4,000   (5) $5,000

Model 70H Hi-Crop (gasoline, 1953–1956)
(1) $12,000 (2) $15,000 (3) $20,000 (4) $25,000 (5) $30,000

Model 70H Hi-Crop (LPG, 1953–1956)
(1) $12,000 (2) $15,000 (3) $21,000 (4) $27,000 (5) $35,000

Model 70H Hi-Crop (diesel, 1954–1956)
(1) $12,000 (2) $15,000 (3) $21,000 (4) $27,000 (5) $35,000

Model 80 (1955–1956)
(1) $1,800   (2) $2,200   (3) $3,000   (4) $4,000   (5) $6,000

Model 320 Standard (direct-drive axles, 1956–1958)
(1) $2,500   (2) $3,500   (3) $5,000   (4) $7,500   (5) $10,000

Model 320 Utility (final drive bull gears, 1956–1958)
(1) $2,500   (2) $3,500   (3) $6,500   (4) $8,000   (5) $12,000

Model 420 Utility (Series I, gasoline, chrome nameplate, 1956)
(1) $800   (2) $1,400   (3) $2,400   (4) $3,900   (5) $5,400

Model 420 Utility (Series I, all-fuel, 1956)
(1) $2,300   (2) $2,900   (3) $3,900   (4) $5,400   (5) $6,900

Model 420 Utility (Series II, gasoline, yellow paint on hood, straight dash, 1956–1957)
(1) $1,000   (2) $2,000   (3) $3,000   (4) $4,500   (5) $6,000

Model 420 Utility (Series II, all-fuel, 1956–1957)
(1) $2,500   (2) $3,500   (3) $4,500   (4) $6,000   (5) $7,500

Model 420 Utility (Series III, gasoline, slant-dash, 1957–1958)
(1) $1,600   (2) $2,600   (3) $3,600   (4) $5,100   (5) $6,600

Model 420 Utility (Series III, all-fuel, 1957–1958)
(1) $3,100   (2) $4,100   (3) $5,100   (4) $6,600   (5) $8,100

Model 420 Utility (LPG, 1956–1958)
(1) $7,500   (2) $10,000 (3) $12,500 (4) $20,000 (5) $25,000

Model 420 Standard (Series I, gasoline, 1956)
(1) $800   (2) $1,400   (3) $2,400   (4) $3,900   (5) $5,400

Model 420 Standard (Series I, all-fuel, 1956)
(1) $1,800   (2) $2,400   (3) $3,400   (4) $4,900   (5) $6,400

Model 420 Standard (Series II, gasoline, 1956–1957)
(1) $1,000   (2) $2,000   (3) $3,000   (4) $4,500   (5) $6,000

Model 420 Standard (Series II, all-fuel, 1956–1957)
(1) $2,000   (2) $3,000   (3) $4,000   (4) $5,500   (5) $7,000

Model 420 Standard (Series III, gasoline, 1957–1958)
(1) $1,600   (2) $2,600   (3) $3,600   (4) $5,100   (5) $6,600

Model 420 Standard (Series III, all-fuel, 1957–1958)
(1) $2,600   (2) $3,600   (3) $4,600   (4) $6,100   (5) $7,600

Model 420 Standard (LPG, 1956–1957)
(1) $7,500   (2) $10,000   (3) $12,500   (4) $20,000 (5) $25,000

Model 420W (2-row utility, wide-front, Series I, gasoline, 1956)
(1) $800   (2) $1,400   (3) $2,400   (4) $3,900   (5) $5,400

Model 420W (2-row utility, wide-front, Series I, all-fuel, 1956)
(1) $1,300   (2) $1,900   (3) $2,900   (4) $4,400   (5) $5,900

Model 420W (2-row utility, wide-front, Series II, gasoline, 1956–1957)
(1) $1,000   (2) $2,000   (3) $3,000   (4) $4,500   (5) $6,000

Model 420W (2-row utility, wide-front, Series II, all-fuel, 1956–1957)
(1) $1,500   (2) $2,500   (3) $3,500   (4) $5,000   (5) $6,500

Model 420W (2-row utility, wide-front, Series III, gasoline, 1957–1958)
(1) $1,600   (2) $2,600   (3) $3,600   (4) $5,100   (5) $6,600

Model 420W (2-row utility, wide-front, Series III, all-fuel, 1957–1958)
(1) $2,100   (2) $3,100   (3) $4,100   (4) $5,600   (5) $7,100

Model 420W (LPG, 2-row utility, 1956–1958)
(1) $3,500   (2) $5,500   (3) $9,000   (4) $12,000   (5) $15,000

Model 420H Hi-Crop (Series I, gasoline, 1956)
(1) $900   (2) $1,900   (3) $2,900   (4) $5,400   (5) $7,400

Model 420H Hi-Crop (Series I, all-fuel, 1956)
(1) $2,900   (2) $3,900   (3) $4,900   (4) $7,400   (5) $9,400

Model 420H Hi-Crop (Series II, gasoline, 1956-12957)
(1) $1,500   (2) $2,500   (3) $3,500   (4) $6,000   (5) $8,000

Model 420H Hi-Crop (Series II, all-fuel, 1956–1957)
(1) $3,500   (2) $4,500   (3) $5,500   (4) $8,000   (5) $10,000

Model 420H Hi-Crop (Series III, gasoline, 1957–1958)
(1) $2,100   (2) $3,100   (3) $4,100   (4) $6,600   (5) $8,600

Model 420H Hi-Crop (Series III, all-fuel, 1957–1958)
(1) $4,100   (2) $5,100   (3) $6,100   (4) $8,600   (5) $10,600

Model 420H Hi-Crop (LPG, 1956–1958)
(1) $7,000   (2) $10,000   (3) $14,000   (4) $25,000 (5) $30,000

Model 420V Special (Series I, gasoline, 1956)
(1) $1,900   (2) $2,900   (3) $3,900   (4) $6,400   (5) $9,400

Model 420V Special (Series I, all-fuel, 1956)
(1) $2,900   (2) $4,900   (3) $5,900   (4) $8,400   (5) $11,400

Model 420V Special (Series II, gasoline, 1956–1957)
(1) $2,500   (2) $3,500   (3) $4,500   (4) $7,000   (5) $10,000

Model 420V Special (Series II, all-fuel, 1956–1957)
(1) $4,500   (2) $5,500   (3) $6,500   (4) $9,000   (5) $12,000

Model 420V Special (Series III, gasoline, 1957–1958)
(1) $3,100   (2) $4,100   (3) $5,100   (4) $7,600   (5) $10,600

Model 420V Special (Series III, all-fuel, 1957–1958)
(1) $5,100   (2) $6,100   (3) $7,100   (4) $9,600   (5) $12,600

Model 420I (Series I, gasoline, 1956)
(1) $1,900   (2) $2,900   (3) $3,900   (4) $6,400   (5) $9,400

Model 420I (Series I, all-fuel, 1956)
(1) $3,900   (2) $4,900   (3) $5,900   (4) $8,400   (5) $11,400

Model 420I (Series II, gasoline, 1956–1957)
(1) $2,500   (2) $3,500   (3) $4,500   (4) $7,000   (5) $10,000

Model 420I (Series II, all-fuel, 1956–1957)
(1) $4,500   (2) $5,500   (3) $6,500   (4) $9,000   (5) $12,000

Model 420I (Series III, gasoline, 1957–1958)
(1) $3,100   (2) $4,100   (3) $5,100   (4) $7,600   (5) $10,600

Model 420I (Series III, all-fuel, 1957–1958)
(1) $5,100   (2) $6,100   (3) $7,100   (4) $9,600   (5) $12,600

Model 420T RC (Series I, gasoline, 1956)
(1) $800   (2) $1,400   (3) $2,400   (4) $3,900   (5) $5,400

Model 420T RC (Series I, all-fuel, 1956)
(1) $1,300   (2) $1,900   (3) $2,900   (4) $4,400   (5) $5,900

Model 420T RC (Series II, gasoline, 1956–1957)
(1) $1,000   (2) $2,000   (3) $3,000   (4) $4,500   (5) $6,000

Model 420T RC (Series II, all-fuel, 1956–1957)
(1) $1,500   (2) $2,500   (3) $3,500   (4) $5,000   (5) $6,500

Model 420T RC (Series III, gasoline, 1957–1958)
(1) $1,600   (2) $2,600   (3) $3,600   (4) $5,100   (5) $6,600

Model 420T RC (Series III, all-fuel, 1957–1958)
(1) $2,100   (2) $3,100   (3) $4,100   (4) $5,600   (5) $7,100

Model 420T W (adjustable wide-front axle, Series I, gasoline, 1956)
(1) $900   (2) $1,900   (3) $2,900   (4) $3,900   (5) $5,900

Model 420T W (adjustable wide-front axle, Series I, all-fuel, 1956)
(1) $1,400   (2) $2,400   (3) $3,400   (4) $4,400   (5) $6,400

Model 420T W (adjustable wide-front axle, Series II, gasoline, 1956–1957)
(1) $1,500   (2) $2,500   (3) $3,500   (4) $4,500   (5) $6,500

Model 420T W (adjustable wide-front axle, Series II, all-fuel, 1956–1957)
(1) $2,000   (2) $3,000   (3) $4,000   (4) $5,000   (5) $7,000

Model 420T W (adjustable wide-front axle, Series III, gasoline, 1957–1958)
(1) $2,100   (2) $3,100   (3) $4,100   (4) $5,100   (5) $7,100

Model 420T W (adjustable wide-front axle, Series III, all-fuel, 1957–1958)
(1) $2,600   (2) $3,600   (3) $4,600   (4) $5,600   (5) $7,600

Model 420T N (single front wheel, Series I, gasoline, 1956)
(1) $900   (2) $1,900   (3) $2,900   (4) $3,900   (5) $5,900

Model 420T N (single front wheel, Series I, all-fuel, 1956)
(1) $1,400   (2) $2,400   (3) $3,400   (4) $4,400   (5) $6,400

Model 420T N (single front wheel, Series II, gasoline, 1956–1957)
(1) $1,500   (2) $2,500   (3) $3,500   (4) $4,500   (5) $6,500

Model 420T N (single front wheel, Series II, all-fuel, 1956–1957)
(1) $2,000   (2) $3,000   (3) $4,000   (4) $5,000   (5) $7,000

Model 420T N (single front wheel, Series III, gasoline, 1957–1958)
(1) $2,100   (2) $3,100   (3) $4,100   (4) $5,100   (5) $7,100

Model 420T N (single front wheel, Series III, all-fuel, 1957–1958)
(1) $2,600   (2) $3,600   (3) $4,600   (4) $5,600   (5) $7,600

Model 420T (LPG, 1956–1958)
(1) $3,500   (2) $5,500   (3) $9,000   (4) $12,000 (5) $15,000

Model 420 Forklift (1956–1958)
(1) $6,000   (2) $7,000   (3) $10,000   (4) $14,000 (5) $25,000

Model 520 (dual narrow front axle, gasoline, 1956–1958)
(1) $1,375   (2) $2,125   (3) $3,125   (4) $3,875   (5) $5,000

Model 520 (dual narrow front axle, all-fuel, 1956–1958)
(1) $1,500 (2) $2,400 (3) $3,525 (4) $4,375 (5) $5,900

Model 520 (dual narrow front axle, LPG, 1956–1958)
(1) $2,100 (2) $2,800 (3) $3,950 (4) $5,750 (5) $6,250

Model 520 (wide-front axle, gasoline, 1956–1958)
(1) $1,750 (2) $2,500 (3) $3,500 (4) $4,375 (5) $5,500

Model 520 (wide-front axle, all-fuel, 1956–1958)
(1) $1,850 (2) $2,750 (3) $3,700 (4) $4,650 (5) $5,950

Model 520 (wide-front axle, LPG, 1956–1958)
(1) $2,350 (2) $3,100 (3) $4,125 (4) $5,100 (5) $6,250

Model 520 (single front wheel, gasoline, 1956–1958)
(1) $1,375 (2) $1,875 (3) $2,625 (4) $3,625 (5) $4,500

Model 520 (single front wheel, all-fuel, 1956–1958)
(1) $1,625 (2) $2,200 (3) $3,000 (4) $4,000 (5) $5,375

Model 520 (single front wheel, LPG, 1956–1958)
(1) $1,650 (2) $2,500 (3) $3,375 (4) $4,750 (5) $6,000

Model 620 (dual narrow front axle, gasoline, 1956–1958)
(1) $1,650 (2) $2,375 (3) $3,100 (4) $3,750 (5) $5,000

Model 620 (dual narrow front axle, all-fuel, 1956–1958)
(1) $2,000 (2) $2,375 (3) $2,950 (4) $4,250 (5) $5,375

Model 620 (dual narrow front axle, LPG, 1956–1958)
(1) $1,600 (2) $1,950 (3) $2,750 (4) $4,000 (5) $4,750

Model 620 (wide-front axle, gasoline, 1956–1958)
(1) $2,100 (2) $2,500 (3) $3,000 (4) $3,750 (5) $4,750

Model 620 (wide-front axle, all-fuel, 1956–1958)
(1) $2,250 (2) $2,700 (3) $3,350 (4) $4,100 (5) $5,375

Model 620 (wide-front axle, LPG, 1956–1958)
(1) $1,950 (2) $2,500 (3) $3,500 (4) $4,250 (5) $5,125

Model 620 (single front wheel, gasoline, 1956–1958)
(1) $1,500 (2) $2,125 (3) $3,100 (4) $3,750 (5) $5,000

Model 620 (single front wheel, all-fuel, 1956–1958)
(1) $1,625 (2) $2,250 (3) $3,000 (4) $4,000 (5) $5,500

Model 620 (single front wheel, LPG, 1956–1958)
(1) $2,000 (2) $2,250 (3) $3,000 (4) $4,000 (5) $5,750

Model 620H (Hi-Crop, gasoline, 1956–1958)
(1) $10,000 (2) $12,500 (3) $15,000 (4) $20,000 (5) $25,000

Model 620H (Hi-Crop, all-fuel, 1956–1958)
(1) $10,000 (2) $13,000 (3) $16,000 (4) $22,000 (5) $27,500

Model 620H (Hi-Crop, LPG, 1956–1958)
(1) $10,000 (2) $14,000 (3) $17,000 (4) $23,000 (5) $28,000

Model 620S (standard, gasoline, 1956–1957)
(1) $1,900 (2) $2,100 (3) $2,750 (4) $3,875 (5) $5,500

Model 620S (standard, all-fuel, 1956–1957)
(1) $2,000 (2) $2,750 (3) $3,250 (4) $4,500 (5) $6,250

Model 620S (standard, LPG, 1956–1957)
(1) $2,100 (2) $2,600 (3) $3,250 (4) $4,500 (5) $6,650

Model 620-O (orchard, gasoline, 1957–1960)
(1) $1,900 (2) $2,450 (3) $3,100 (4) $4,000 (5) $5,875

Model 620-O (orchard, all-fuel, 1957–1960)
(1) $2,000 (2) $2,850 (3) $3,650 (4) $4,650 (5) $6,625

Model 620-O (orchard, LPG, 1957–1960)
(1) $2,150 (2) $2,750 (3) $3,625 (4) $5,250 (5) $6,750

Model 720 (dual narrow front axle, gasoline, 1956–1958)
(1) $1,250 (2) $2,000 (3) $2,750 (4) $3,500 (5) $4,500

Model 720 (dual narrow front axle, all-fuel, 1956–1958)
(1) $1,350 (2) $2,350 (3) $3,250 (4) $4,000 (5) $5,250

Model 720 (dual narrow front axle, LPG, 1956–1958)
(1) $1,250 (2) $1,875 (3) $2,750 (4) $3,750 (5) $5,250

Model 720D (dual narrow front axle, diesel, 1956–1958)
(1) $1,250 (2) $1,750 (3) $2,750 (4) $3,750 (5) $5,500

Model 720W (wide-front axle, gasoline, 1956–1958)
(1) $1,750 (2) $2,750 (3) $3,375 (4) $4,250 (5) $5,500

Model 720W (wide-front axle, all-fuel, 1956–1958)
(1) $1,600 (2) $2,750 (3) $4,000 (4) $5,000 (5) $6,500

Model 720W (wide-front axle, LPG, 1956–1958)
(1) $1,500 (2) $2,250 (3) $3,250 (4) $4,900 (5) $6,750

Model 720DW (wide-front axle, diesel, 1956–1958)
(1) $1,650 (2) $2,150 (3) $2,925 (4) $4,125 (5) $5,000

Model 720N (single front wheel, gasoline, 1956–1958)
(1) $1,150 (2) $1,500 (3) $2,500 (4) $3,500 (5) $5,250

Model 720N (single front wheel, all-fuel, 1956–1958)
(1) $1,625 (2) $2,750 (3) $4,000 (4) $4,750 (5) $6,500

Model 720N (single front wheel, LPG, 1956–1958)
(1) $1,250   (2) $1,875   (3) $3,250   (4) $4,500   (5) $6,250

Model 720DN (single front wheel, diesel, 1956–1958)
(1) $1,600   (2) $2,375   (3) $2,925   (4) $4,125   (5) $5,500

Model 720H (Hi-Crop, gasoline, 1956–1958)
(1) $10,000   (2) $15,000   (3) $20,000   (4) $22,000   (5) $25,000

Model 720H (Hi-Crop, all-fuel, 1956–1958)
(1) $10,000   (2) $16,000   (3) $21,000   (4) $25,000   (5) $30,000

Model 720H (Hi-Crop, LPG, 1956–1958)
(1) $10,000   (2) $17,000   (3) $25,000   (4) $30,000   (5) $35,000

Model 720DH (Hi-Crop, diesel, 1956–1958)
(1) $10,000   (2) $15,000   (3) $17,000   (4) $20,000   (5) $25,000

Model 720S (standard, gasoline, 1956–1958)
(1) $2,250   (2) $3,000   (3) $3,750   (4) $4,750   (5) $6,400

Model 720S (standard, all-fuel, 1956–1958)
(1) $2,500   (2) $3,750   (3) $4,625   (4) $5,500   (5) $7,125

Model 720S (standard, LPG, 1956–1958)
(1) $2,250   (2) $3,250   (3) $4,000   (4) $5,000   (5) $6,500

Model 720DS (standard, diesel, 1956–1958)
(1) $1,900   (2) $3,175   (3) $3,750   (4) $4,600   (5) $5,900

Model 820 (1956–1958)
(1) $2,600   (2) $3,300   (3) $4,500   (4) $5,100   (5) $6,600

Model 330S Standard (direct drive axles, 1958–1960)
(1) $5,000   (2) $7,500   (3) $10,000   (4) $14,000   (5) $18,000

Model 330U Utility (has final drive bull gears, 1958–1960)
(1) $6,000   (2) $9,000   (3) $16,000   (4) $18,000   (5) $25,000

Model 430S Standard (gasoline, 1958–1960)
(1) $1,500   (2) $3,500   (3) $5,500   (4) $8,000   (5) $10,000

Model 430S Standard (all-fuel, 1958–1960)
(1) $2,500   (2) $4,500   (3) $6,500   (4) $9,000   (5) $11,000

Model 430S Standard (LPG, 1958–1960)
(1) $7,000   (2) $10,000   (3) $13,000   (4) $22,000   (5) $25,000

Model 430U Utility (gasoline, 1958–1960)
(1) $1,500   (2) $3,500   (3) $5,500   (4) $8,000   (5) $10,000

Model 430U Utility (all-fuel, 1958–1960)
(1) $2,500   (2) $4,500   (3) $6,500   (4) $9,000   (5) $11,000

Model 430U Utility (LPG, 1958–1960)
(1) $8,000 (2) $11,000 (3) $14,000 (4) $25,000 (5) $30,000

Model 430W (gasoline, 2-row utility, wide-front axle, 1958–1960)
(1) $2,000 (2) $2,500 (3) $4,500 (4) $7,000 (5) $10,000

Model 430W (all-fuel, 2-row utility, wide-front axle, 1958–1960)
(1) $3,000 (2) $3,500 (3) $5,500 (4) $8,000 (5) $11,000

Model 430W (LPG, 2-row utility, wide-front axle, 1958–1960)
(1) $3,000 (2) $6,000 (3) $8,000 (4) $12,000 (5) $15,000

Model 430H Hi-Crop (gasoline, 1958–1960)
(1) $3,500 (2) $6,000 (3) $8,000 (4) $15,000 (5) $20,000

Model 430H Hi-Crop (all-fuel, 1958–1960)
(1) $6,500 (2) $9,000 (3) $11,000 (4) $18,000 (5) $23,000

Model 430H Hi-Crop (LPG, 1958–1960)
(1) $7,000 (2) $12,000 (3) $18,000 (4) $25,000 (5) $35,000

Model 430V Special (gasoline, 26-inch clearance, 1958–1960)
(1) $4,000 (2) $6,500 (3) $9,000 (4) $17,000 (5) $22,000

Model 430V Special (all-fuel, 26-inch clearance, 1958–1960)
(1) $7,000 (2) $9,500 (3) $12,000 (4) $20,000 (5) $25,000

Model 430T RC (gasoline, dual narrow front, 1958–1960)
(1) $1,200 (2) $2,200 (3) $3,500 (4) $6,000 (5) $8,000

Model 430T RC (all-fuel, dual narrow front, 1958–1960)
(1) $2,200 (2) $3,200 (3) $4,500 (4) $7,000 (5) $9,000

Model 430T W (gasoline, adjustable wide-front, 1958–1960)
(1) $1,800 (2) $2,800 (3) $4,000 (4) $6,500 (5) $8,500

Model 430T W (all-fuel, adjustable wide-front, 1958–1960)
(1) $2,800 (2) $3,800 (3) $5,000 (4) $7,500 (5) $9,500

Model 430T N (gasoline, single front wheel, 1958–1960)
(1) $1,800 (2) $2,800 (3) $4,000 (4) $6,500 (5) $8,500

Model 430T N (all-fuel, single front wheel, 1958–1960)
(1) $2,800 (2) $3,800 (3) $5,000 (4) $7,500 (5) $9,500

Model 430T (LPG, 1958–1960)
(1) $3,000 (2) $6,000 (3) $8,000 (4) $12,000 (5) $15,000

Model 430 Forklift (1958–1960)
(1) $6,000 (2) $8,000 (3) $12,000 (4) $16,000 (5) $27,000

Model 435 (diesel, 1958–1960)
(1) $1,200 (2) $3,000 (3) $4,500 (4) $8,500 (5) $10,000

Model 440 I (1958–1960)
(1) $1,500　(2) $3,000　(3) $5,500　(4) $8,000　(5) $10,000

Model 440 ID (1958–1960)
(1) $1,200　(2) $2,000　(3) $4,500　(4) $7,500　(5) $10,000

Model 530 (dual narrow front axle, gasoline, 1958–1960)
(1) $2,200　(2) $2,750　(3) $3,750　(4) $5,000　(5) $6,500

Model 530 (dual narrow front axle, all-fuel, 1958–1960)
(1) $3,000　(2) $3,750　(3) $4,750　(4) $6,000　(5) $7,500

Model 530 (dual narrow front axle, LPG, 1958–1960)
(1) $ 3,500　(2) $4,000　(3) $5,000　(4) $7,000　(5) $8,000

Model 530 (wide-front axle, gasoline, 1958–1960)
(1) $3,500　(2) $4,500　(3) $5,000　(4) $6,000　(5) $7,500

Model 530 (wide-front axle, all-fuel, 1958–1960)
(1) $3,500　(2) $4,000　(3) $5,000　(4) $7,000　(5) $8,000

Model 530 (wide-front axle, LPG, 1958–1960)
(1) $3,750　(2) $4,500　(3) $5,750　(4) $7,500　(5) $9,000

Model 530 (single front wheel, gasoline, 1958–1960)
(1) $2,400　(2) $3,000　(3) $4,000　(4) $5,500　(5) $6,750

Model 530 (single front wheel, all-fuel, 1958–1960)
(1) $2,700　(2) $3,200　(3) $4,000　(4) $5,000　(5) $7,500

Model 530 (single front wheel, LPG, 1958–1960)
(1) $3,500　(2) $4,250　(3) $5,500　(4) $6,500　(5) $7,500

Model 630 (dual narrow front axle, gasoline, 1958–1960)
(1) $1,750　(2) $2,250　(3) $2,750　(4) $3,900　(5) $4,900

Model 630 (dual narrow front axle, all-fuel, 1958–1960)
(1) $2,000　(2) $2,500　(3) $3,000　(4) $4,250　(5) $5,500

Model 630 (dual narrow front axle, LPG, 1958–1960)
(1) $1,200　(2) $1,750　(3) $2,500　(4) $5,000　(5) $6,500

Model 630 (wide-front axle, gasoline, 1958–1960)
(1) $2,000　(2) $2,500　(3) $3,000　(4) $4,000　(5) $6,000

Model 630 (wide-front axle, all-fuel, 1958–1960)
(1) $2,200　(2) $2,700　(3) $3,500　(4) $4,500　(5) $6,500

Model 630 (wide-front axle, LPG, 1958–1960)
(1) $1,500　(2) $2,000　(3) $2,750　(4) $4,250　(5) $5,500

Model 630 (single front wheel, gasoline, 1958–1960)
(1) $1,750　(2) $2,200　(3) $3,000　(4) $4,000　(5) $5,000

Model 630 (single front wheel, all-fuel, 1958–1960)
(1) $2,500   (2) $3,000   (3) $3,750   (4) $4,500   (5) $6,000

Model 630 (single front wheel, LPG, 1958–1960)
(1) $1,750   (2) $2,500   (3) $3,500   (4) $4,000   (5) $5,000

Model 630H (Hi-Crop, gasoline, with original tag only, 1958–1960)
(1) $10,000 (2) $12,500   (3) $20,000   (4) $25,000 (5) $30,000

Model 630H (Hi-Crop, all-fuel, 1958–1960)
(1) $12,000 (2) $14,000   (3) $22,000   (4) $27,500 (5) $35,000

Model 630H (Hi-Crop, LPG, 1958–1960)
(1) $11,000 (2) $13,000   (3) $21,000   (4) $27,000 (5) $32,500

Model 630S (standard, gasoline, 1958–1960)
(1) $2,500   (2) $3,000   (3) $3,500   (4) $4,500   (5) $5,500

Model 630S (standard, all-fuel, 1958–1960)
(1) $ 3,000   (2) $3,500   (3) $4,000   (4) $5,000   (5) $6,000

Model 630S (standard, LPG, 1958–1960)
(1) $3,500   (2) $4,000   (3) $4,500   (4) $6,000   (5) $7,000

The values of the John Deere Hi-Crops are astronomical. The fortunate collectors who purchased a Hi-Crop twenty years ago have watched the values skyrocket. This rare 1959 630H would not have been considered collectable 20 years ago; now it ranks high on the want-list of any collectors.

Model 730 (dual narrow front axle, gasoline, 1958–1961)
(1) $1,750   (2) $2,500   (3) $3,000   (4) $4,500   (5) $6,500

Model 730 (dual narrow front axle, all-fuel, 1958–1961)
(1) $2,000   (2) $3,000   (3) $3,500   (4) $5,000   (5) $7,000

Model 730 (dual narrow front axle, LPG, 1958–1961)
(1) $1,500   (2) $2,000   (3) $2,750   (4) $4,500   (5) $5,500

Model 730D (dual narrow front axle, diesel, 1958–1961)
(1) $1,500   (2) $2,000   (3) $2,750   (4) $3,750   (5) $5,000

Model 730W (wide-front axle, gasoline, 1958–1961)
(1) $2,000   (2) $2,500   (3) $3,500   (4) $5,750   (5) $7,000

Model 730W (wide-front axle, all-fuel, 1958–1961)
(1) $2,200   (2) $2,750   (3) $4,000   (4) $6,000   (5) $8,000

Model 730W (wide-front axle, LPG, 1958–1961)
(1) $1,750   (2) $2,250   (3) $3,250   (4) $5,000   (5) $6,000

Model 730DW (wide-front axle, diesel, 1958–1961)
(1) $2,500   (2) $3,000   (3) $3,500   (4) $5,000   (5) $8,000

Model 730N (single front wheel, gasoline, 1958–1961)
(1) $2,000   (2) $2,500   (3) $3,000   (4) $4,500   (5) $7,000

Model 730N (single front wheel, all-fuel, 1958–1961)
(1) $2,500   (2) $3,000   (3) $3,500   (4) $5,000   (5) $8,000

Model 730N (single front wheel, LPG, 1958–1961)
(1) $2,000   (2) $2,500   (3) $3,000   (4) $5,000   (5) $8,000

Model 730DN (single front wheel, diesel, 1958–1961)
(1) $2,000   (2) $2,500   (3) $3,000   (4) $4,500   (5) $7,000

Model 730H (Hi-Crop, gasoline, 1958–1961)
(1) $ 7,000   (2) $12,500   (3) $16,000   (4) $19,000   (5) $25,000

Model 730H (Hi-Crop, all-fuel, 1958–1961)
(1) $7,500   (2) $14,000   (3) $19,000   (4) $25,000   (5) $30,000

Model 730H (Hi-Crop, LPG, 1958–1961)
(1) $10,000   (2) $15,000   (3) $20,000   (4) $30,000   (5) $35,000

Model 730H (Hi-Crop, LPG, loaded, 1958–1961)
(1) $10,000   (2) $15,000   (3) $24,000   (4) $35,000   (5) $50,000

Model 730DH (Hi-Crop, diesel, 1958–1961)
(1) $6,000   (2) $8,000   (3) $12,500   (4) $15,000   (5) $20,000

Model 730S (standard, gasoline, 1958–1961)
(1) $4,000   (2) $5,000   (3) $8,000   (4) $9,000   (5) $12,000

Model 730S (standard, all-fuel, 1958–1961)
(1) $3,500   (2) $4,500   (3) $7,500   (4) $8,500   (5) $11,000

Model 730S (standard, LPG, 1958–1961)
(1) $3,500   (2) $4,500   (3) $7,500   (4) $8,500   (5) $10,500

Model 730DS (standard, diesel, 1958–1961)
(1) $3,000   (2) $4,000   (3) $7,000   (4) $8,000   (5) $10,000

Model 830 (1958–1960)
(1) $2,000   (2) $3,000   (3) $5,000   (4) $6,500   (5) $8,000

Denning Motor Implement Company, Cedar Rapids, Iowa

Joseph Denning was in the wire fence business and was experimenting with tractors by 1908. By 1916 the company was renamed the Denning Tractor Company. In May of 1919, Denning sold the company to General Ordnance Company. General Ordnance offered the National and G-O models until about 1922. The General Ordnance tractors are found under their own listing.

Model A 6-12 (1913)
(1) $7,000   (2) $12,000   (3) $15,000   (4) $19,000 (5) $24,000

Model B 16-24 (1913–1916)
(1) $8,000   (2) $14,000   (3) $18,000   (4) $22,000 (5) $28,000

Model Steel Clad Light Farm Tractor (1916–1919)
(1) $6,000   (2) $10,000   (3) $13,000   (4) $16,000 (5) $21,000

Model E 10-18 (1916–1919)
(1) $6,000   (2) $10,000   (3) $13,000   (4) $16,000 (5) $21,000

Depue Brothers Manufacturing Company, Clinton, Iowa
Model 20-30 (1918–1919)
(1) $10,000 (2) $15,000   (3) $20,000   (4) $24,000 (5) $30,000

Model 20-32 (1920–1924)
(1) $10,000 (2) $15,000   (3) $20,000   (4) $25,000 (5) $32,000

Detroit Tractor Corporation, Detroit, Michigan
Detroit 16 Horsepower (4-wheel drive, 1947–1949)
(1) $1,800   (2) $3,300   (3) $4,250   (4) $5,000   (5) $6,750

Detroit 35 Horsepower (4-wheel drive, 1947–1949)
(1) $2,100   (2) $3,600   (3) $4,800   (4) $5,500   (5) $7,500

Detroit 45 Horsepower (4-wheel drive, 1947–1949)
(1) $2,400   (2) $4,000   (3) $5,500   (4) $6,500   (5) $8,750

Diamond Iron Works, Minneapolis, Minnesota
Diamond 40-70 (1911–1914)
(1) $33,000 (2) $45,000   (3) $53,000   (4) $63,000 (5) $75,000

Diamond 20-36 (1913–1914)
(1) $14,000 (2) $18,000   (3) $24,000   (4) $30,000 (5) $35,000

C. H. A. Dissinger and Brothers Company, Wrightville, Pennsylvania
Capital 10-20 (1910–1920)
(1) $12,000 (2) $17,000   (3) $22,000   (4) $25,000 (5) $32,000

Capital 15-30 (1910–1920)
(1) $15,000 (2) $21,000   (3) $26,000   (4) $31,000 (5) $38,000

Capital 25-45 (1910–1920)
(1) $22,000 (2) $30,000 (3) $35,000 (4) $42,000 (5) $50,000

Capital 40-80 (1910–1920)
(1) $30,000 (2) $43,000 (3) $55,000 (4) $65,000 (5) $80,000

Dixieland Motor Truck Company, Texarkana, Texas
Dixieland 12-25 (1918–1920)
(1) $4,500 (2) $8,500 (3) $12,000 (4) $14,500 (5) $18,000

Duplex Machinery Company
(see Co-Operative Manufacturing Co.)

Eagle Manufacturing Company, Appleton, Wisconsin

Eagle was a well-known maker of agricultural implements that entered the tractor business early. In 1906 the company offered its first tractor with an opposed two-cylinder engine that was cooled with an evaporative radiator. The tractors evolved eventually into the fairly modern Model 6 series that were powered by six-cylinder engines. The heavyweight Eagle tractors are not often found in restorable or better condition. The models in operating condition are of extreme interest to collectors of early tractors. Production numbers were never high in any of the series. The style and values are not unlike those of the early Huber tractors.

Model D 8-16 (1913–1916)
(1) $16,000 (2) $18,000 (3) $20,000 (4) $25,000 (5) $30,000

Model D 12-22 (1916–1922)
(1) $12,000 (2) $14,000 (3) $18,000 (4) $20,000 (5) $22,000

Model D 16-30 (1913–1916)
(1) $12,000 (2) $14,000 (3) $18,000 (4) $20,000 (5) $22,000

Model F 16-30 (1916–1922)
(1) $10,000 (2) $12,000 (3) $16,000 (4) $18,000 (5) $20,000

Model F 12-22 (1917–1921)
(1) $10,000 (2) $12,000 (3) $16,000 (4) $18,000 (5) $20,000

Model H 13-25 (1923–1928)
(1) $10,000 (2) $12,000 (3) $17,000 (4) $20,000 (5) $22,000

Model H 16-30 (1922–1929)
(1) $8,500 (2) $9,500 (3) $14,000 (4) $18,000 (5) $20,000

Model H 20-40 Regular (1923–1925)
(1) $8,500 (2) $9,500 (3) $14,000 (4) $18,000 (5) $20,000

Model H 20-40 Improved (1926–1928)
(1) $8,500 (2) $9,500 (3) $14,000 (4) $18,000 (5) $20,000

Model H 20-40 Special (1929)
(1) $8,500 (2) $9,500 (3) $14,000 (4) $18,000 (5) $20,000

The Eagle 6C was the last model that the company made in 1937 and 1938. This Utility version is a bit more desirable than the 6A Standard Tread and the 6B Row-crop. This 1938 example bearing serial number 2494 is near to the last Eagle manufactured, which is believed to be number 2500. A serial number close to the end will add considerably to a tractor's appeal and often to its value as well.

Special Model H 22-45 (1928–1930)
(1) $8,500   (2) $9,500   (3) $14,000   (4) $18,000 (5) $20,000

Model E 20-35 (1928–1939)
(1) $8,500   (2) $9,500   (3) $14,000   (4) $18,000 (5) $20,000

Eagle 6A (standard tread, 1930–1937)
(1) $2,000   (2) $2,400   (3) $3,500   (4) $5,000   (5) $7,400

Eagle 6B Universal (row-crop, 1936–1938)
(1) $1,600   (2) $2,200   (3) $3,000   (4) $4,700   (5) $7,000

Eagle 6C Utility (1937–1938)
(1) $2,400   (2) $3,000   (3) $5,000   (4) $6,350   (5) $8,500

Earthmaster Farm Equipment, Burbank, California

Earthmaster tractors were built in Hollydale, California, while the offices were in Burbank. They built tractors in 1948 and 1949. A Philadelphia firm bought the company around 1949 and without tractor production, sold again to Charles Latham of Statesville, North Carolina, in the 1950s. Latham built about 50 Earthmaster tractors that had yellow grills. A total of around 5,000 Earthmaster tractors were built. These tractors have generated a surge of interest in the past few years. Because of the low numbers and special character, prices have been on the increase.

Model C (normal tread width, general purpose, 1948–1960)
(1) $400   (2) $850   (3) $1,900   (4) $2,950   (5) $4,400

Model CL (1948–1960)
(1) $400   (2) $850   (3) $1,900   (4) $2,950   (5) $4,400

Model CH (high-clearance, 30-inch rear tires, 1948–1960)
(1) $450   (2) $1,600   (3) $2,375   (4) $3,350   (5) $5,300

Model CN (narrow rear tread, short axles, 1948–1960)
(1) $300   (2) $900   (3) $2,000   (4) $3,150   (5) $4,600

Model CNH (narrow rear tread, high-clearance, 1948–1960)
(1) $400   (2) $1,600   (3) $2,375   (4) $3,350   (5) $5,300

Model CXH (extra high-clearance, 36-inch rear tires, 1948–1960)
(1) $550   (2) $1,800   (3) $2,500   (4) $3,300   (5) $5,600

Model D (wide rear tread, 1948–1960)
(1) $400   (2) $900   (3) $2,000   (4) $3,050   (5) $4,500

Model DH (wide rear tread, high-clearance, 1948–1960)
(1) $500   (2) $1,650   (3) $3,525   (4) $4,475   (5) $5,400

Model DXH (extra high-clearance, 36-inch rear tires, 1948–1960)
(1) $600   (2) $2,000   (3) $2,875   (4) $3,900   (5) $6,000

Model S (walk-behind, ca. 1948)
(1) $100   (2) $300   (3) $500   (4) $800   (5) $1,000

Model R (walk-behind, ca. 1948)
(1) $100   (2) $300   (3) $500   (4) $800   (5) $1,000

The little Earthmaster tractors were built during the post–World War II boom. Collector interest is increasing at a remarkable rate for these tractors. As the history of these small tractor companies unfolds in various publications, the interest picks up, and the values tend to follow.

Eimco Corporation, Salt Lake City, Utah
Eimco Model 20A Power-Horse (4-wheel drive, 1939–1949)
(1) $2,000   (2) $4,250   (3) $7,500   (4) $9,000   (5) $12,000

Electric Wheel Company, Quincy, Illinois
Using a new electrical process, the Electric Wheel Company built metal wheels beginning in 1890. By 1912 the company was selling tractors, while George White and Sons sold the Electric Wheel tractors in Canada. The company also built the Allwork tractors in limited numbers until about 1929, when it ended tractor production. Firestone Tire took over the Electric Wheel Company in 1957. The Allwork tractors have a distinctive design that appeals to many collectors. Restored examples are uncommon and demand high prices. Expect the value of these tractors to grow steadily over the next several years.

Number 1 (30-45, 1912–1917)
(1) $18,000   (2) $26,000   (3) $35,000   (4) $42,000   (5) $50,000

Allwork 14-28 (rerated 20-35, 1917–1924)
(1) $12,000   (2) $15,000   (3) $20,000   (4) $25,000   (5) $30,000

Allwork II 12-25 (renamed Model G 14-28, 1920–1927)
(1) $10,000 (2) $14,000 (3) $18,000 (4) $21,000 (5) $25,000

Allwork CA 16-30 (1925–1926)
(1) $12,000 (2) $16,000 (3) $20,000 (4) $25,000 (5) $30,000

Allwork D (1925–1928)
(1) $12,000 (2) $16,000 (3) $20,000 (4) $25,000 (5) $30,000

Allwork DA (1928–1929)
(1) $12,000 (2) $16,000 (3) $20,000 (4) $25,000 (5) $30,000

The Electric Wheel Company built this Allwork II Model F. A larger model 20-35 was sold at auction in 1998 for $20,000. The restoration on these tractors can often be a big challenge and dig deep into the pockets.

Elgin Tractor Corporation (formerly The Waite Tractor Sales Co.), Elgin, Illinois
Model 9-18 (rerated 10-20, 1916–1919)
(1) $6,000 (2) $9,500 (3) $12,000 (4) $15,000 (5) $19,000

Model 12-25 (1919–1920)
(1) $6,000 (2) $9,500 (3) $12,000 (4) $15,000 (5) $19,000

G. W. Elliott and Son, DeSmet, South Dakota
Dakota 25 horsepower (1913)
(1) $7,500 (2) $11,250 (3) $14,250 (4) $17,000 (5) $21,000

Dakota 40 horsepower (1913)
(1) $8,000 (2) $12,000 (3) $15,250 (4) $18,500 (5) $23,000

Dakota 5-12 (1914–1915)
(1) $7,000 (2) $10,500 (3) $13,250 (4) $15,500 (5) $19,000

Dakota 10-20 (1914–1915)
(1) $7,250 (2) $10,750 (3) $14,000 (4) $16,250 (5) $20,000

Dakota No. 1 (7-10, 1916)
(1) $7,000 (2) $10,500 (3) $13,250 (4) $15,500 (5) $19,000

Dakota No. 2 (14-18, 1916)
(1) $7,250 (2) $10,750 (3) $14,000 (4) $16,250 (5) $20,000

Emerson-Brantingham Implement Company, Rockford, Illinois

Ralph Emerson, cousin to the famous poet, controlled the Manny reaper business, and began adding other lines of farm equipment to it in 1895. In 1912, Emerson acquired Reeves and Company, Rockford Engine Works, Gas Traction Company, and the Geiser Manufacturing Company. The valuable Big 4 and Reeves tractors were built by E-B after 1912. Emerson-Brantingham was sold to the J. I. Case Company in 1928. The larger E-B tractors are showstoppers and demand high prices. The Big 4 "30" is one of the most impressive antique tractors ever built. This ten-ton giant had rear wheels that were over eight feet in diameter. These early giants are seldom sold in restored condition and selling prices can be shockingly high.

Big 4 "30" (30-60, 1912–1916)
(1) $35,000 (2) $50,000 (3) $60,000 (4) $75,000 (5) $100,000

Model D Big 4 "20" (20-35, 1913–1920)
(1) $8,500 (2) $14,000 (3) $22,000 (4) $29,000 (5) $36,000

Big 4 "45" (45-90, 1913–1915)
(1) $45,000 (2) $70,000 (3) $90,000 (4) $110,000 (5) $135,000

Model 40-65 (Reeves, 1912–1920)
(1) $18,000 (2) $30,000 (3) $45,000 (4) $60,000 (5) $75,000

Model L 12-20 (1916–1917)
(1) $9,600 (2) $14,250 (3) $17,500 (4) $21,750 (5) $25,500

Model 9-16 (1917–1920)
(1) $6,100 (2) $10,400 (3) $12,400 (4) $15,000 (5) $18,500

Model Q 12-20 (1917–1928)
(1) $7,500 (2) $12,100 (3) $16,400 (4) $18,600 (5) $22,300

Model AA 12-20 (1918–1928)
(1) $7,500 (2) $11,100 (3) $13,400 (4) $15,600 (5) $18,300

Model 20-35 (1919–1920)
(1) $8,000 (2) $12,750 (3) $15,500 (4) $18,750 (5) $23,000

Model 16-32 (1921–1928)
(1) $8,200 (2) $13,000 (3) $15,750 (4) $19,000 (5) $23,500

Number 101 Motor Cultivator (1923–1928)
(1) $3,800 (2) $6,000 (3) $7,500 (4) $9,250 (5) $12,000

Empire Tractor Corporation, Philadelphia, Pennsylvania

Empire tractor builders used new surplus Willys Jeep parts for much of the Empire drivetrains. Their unusual design and short-lived production add to their collector appeal. Carl Hering of the Empire Tractor Owners Club tells that sometime in 1947 the dash tag had a "90" stamped alongside the already imprinted "88." This indicates the beginning of the Model 90 series. By late 1947 the tag was stamped with only a "90." Interest in the Empire has increased in the last few years as the demand for the lesser-known brands has grown.

Model 88 (Nov. 1946–mid–1947)
(1) $700   (2) $1,700   (3) $2,600   (4) $3,900   (5) $5,000

Model 90 (mid–1947–early 1948)
(1) $600   (2) $1,500   (3) $2,400   (4) $3,700   (5) $4,900

Essex Tractor Company, Essex, Ontario
Essex 10-20 (rerated 12-20 and 15-30, 1919–1920)
(1) $5,000   (2) $9,000   (3) $12,000   (4) $14,000   (5) $18,000

Evans Manufacturing Company, Hudson, Ohio
Model 12-20 (1917–1920)
(1) $9,250   (2) $12,000   (3) $16,750   (4) $19,000   (5) $24,000

Model L 15-30 (rerated 18-30, 1918–1921)
(1) $9,250   (2) $12,000   (3) $16,750   (4) $19,000   (5) $24,000

Fageol Motors Company, Oakland, California
Fageol 6-15 (Overland engine, 1918–1919)
(1) $2,700   (2) $5,500   (3) $8,500   (4) $10,500   (5) $14,000

Fageol 9-12 (Lycoming engine, 1920–1924)
(1) $2,700   (2) $5,500   (3) $8,500   (4) $10,500   (5) $14,000

Fageol 10-15 (Built by Great Western Motor Co., Lycoming engine, 1924–1925)
(1) $2,700   (2) $5,500   (3) $8,500   (4) $10,500   (5) $14,000

Fairbanks, Morse and Company, Chicago, Illinois
The company got its start in the 1820s as a builder of Fairbanks scales. When it invented the platform scale in 1830, the Fairbanks Company grew to an industry giant. Charles Morse, who began as a Fairbanks employee, worked his way to creating Fairbanks, Morse and Company in 1865. In 1893, Morse convinced Charles Charter of Charter Engine fame to take over the Fairbanks-Morse gas-engineering department. This developed into the Fairbanks-Morse engine line. The company introduced tractors in 1910, but ended production by 1918. The Fordson tractor was beginning to swallow up the tractor market at this time, leaving little room for the Fairbanks-Morse heavyweight models.

Model 15-25 (rerated 15-30, 1911–1914)
(1) $20,000   (2) $34,000   (3) $44,000   (4) $52,000   (5) $65,000

Model 30-60 (1912–1914)
(1) $41,000   (2) $59,000   (3) $75,000   (4) $92,000   (5) $125,000

Model 12-25 (1918)
(1) $18,000 (2) $29,000 (3) $36,000 (4) $44,000 (5) $55,000

Model 10-20 (Reliable Tractor and Engine Co., 1917–1918)
(1) $14,000 (2) $22,500 (3) $28,000 (4) $32,000 (5) $40,000

Farmaster Corporation, Clifton, New Jersey
Farmaster FG-33 (gasoline, 1948–1950)
(1) $3,750 (2) $5,000 (3) $7,500 (4) $9,800 (5) $12,250

Farmaster FD-33 (diesel, 1948–1950)
(1) $4,000 (2) $5,500 (3) $8,000 (4) $10,250 (5) $13,000

Fairbanks-Morse, the same company that is famous for its scales, made this tractor. Although few F-M tractors exist today, the company's brief venture into the tractor business produced some well-built machines that will bring big dollars today.

Farm Engineering Company, Sand Springs, Oklahoma
Little Chief (1916–1918)
(1) $9,000 (2) $14,000 (3) $17,500 (4) $20,000 (5) $24,000

Farm Horse Traction Works, Hartford, South Dakota
Farm Horse 15-26 (1916–1919)
(1) $10,500 (2) $12,000 (3) $14,000 (4) $17,000 (5) $22,000

Farm Horse 18-30 (1920–1921)
(1) $10,500 (2) $12,000 (3) $14,000 (4) $17,000 (5) $22,000

Farm Motors Company, Canada
Tilsoil 18-30 (1919–1920)
(1) $18,000 (2) $25,000 (3) $33,000 (4) $40,000 (5) $50,000

Farmers Oil Tractor Company, Watertown, South Dakota
Farmers Oil Tractor 35 horsepower (1913–1914)
(1) $14,000 (2) $23,000 (3) $28,500 (4) $32,000 (5) $40,000

Farmers Tractor Corporation, Oshkosh, Wisconsin
Model MPM 25-40 (1920–1921)
(1) $11,000 (2) $15,000 (3) $17,000 (4) $20,500 (5) $24,000

Farmers Union Central Exchange
(See Co-Operative Mfg.)

A. B. Farquhar Company, York, Pennsylvania
Model "18" 18-35 (1918–1923)
(1) $25,000 (2) $37,000 (3) $47,000 (4) $55,000 (5) $66,000

Model "25" 25-50 (1919–1923)
(1) $28,000 (2) $42,000 (3) $52,000 (4) $63,000 (5) $78,000

Model 15-25 (1919–1923)
(1) $14,000 (2) $20,000 (3) $25,000 (4) $29,000 (5) $35,000

Fate-Root-Heath Company (Silver King), Plymouth, Ohio (in 1956 and after the Silver King was built in Clarksburg, West Virginia)

Fate-Root-Heath was a well-known builder of small railroad locomotives. As the sales for yard locomotives began to slow down, the company designed and built tractors to keep the factory alive. The tractor business was never a huge success, but the market allowed Fate-Root-Heath to build tractors for over 20 years. The company introduced its first model, the Plymouth, in 1933, and the Silver King in 1935. These tractors are well known for their high-speed road gear. The Silver King tractors had the reputation of being a lot of tractor for the money. However, the lack of a strong dealer network and perhaps the odd appearance of this tractor resulted in sales that were meager at best. The company began to lose interest in its tractor division after World War II. The Mountain State Fabricating Company of Clarksburg, West Virginia, took over the Silver King tractor line for the last two years of production (1956–1957). Prices for the Silver King tractors have rocketed in the last few years. Apparently only about 8,700 tractors were built under the Plymouth and Silver King name. Demand for the lesser-known tractors has been very strong in the last few years. Silver King tractors that only a few years ago brought embarrassingly low prices at auctions are now being bought up hungrily by collectors for a premium.

Plymouth 10-20 (1933–1935)
(1) $ 5,000 (2) $8,000 (3) $14,500 (4) $20,000 (5) $23,000

Model R-38 (1935–1939)
(1) $600 (2) $1,400 (3) $2,700 (4) $4,300 (5) $5,800

Model R-44 (standard tread, 1935–1937)
(1) $600 (2) $1,400 (3) $2,700 (4) $4,300 (5) $5,800

Model R-60 (single front wheel, 1935–1939)
(1) $800 (2) $1,600 (3) $2,000 (4) $3,100 (5) $5,900

Model R-66 (single front wheel, 1935–1939)
(1) $800 (2) $1,400 (3) $2,000 (4) $3,100 (5) $4,500

Model R-72 (single front wheel, 1938–1939)
(1) $800 (2) $1,400 (3) $2,000 (4) $3,100 (5) $4,500

Model S-44 (standard tread, steel wheels, 1935–1940)
(1) $800　　(2) $1,600　　(3) $2,200　　(4) $3,400　　(5) $4,800

Model 600 (single front wheel, 1940–1944)
(1) $700　　(2) $1,400　　(3) $2,000　　(4) $3,100　　(5) $4,700

Model 660 (single front wheel, 1940)
(1) $700　　(2) $1,400　　(3) $2,000　　(4) $3,100　　(5) $4,700

This early Fate-Root-Heath model carries the Plymouth name, while later tractors were named Silver King. The Plymouth carmaker challenged the use of its name only to find out in the legal conflict that the tractor had the rights to the name first. The automobile concern humbly backed off.

Model 661 (single front wheel, 1941)
(1) $700　　(2) $1,400　　(3) $2,000　　(4) $3,100　　(5) $4,600

Model 720 (single front wheel, 1940)
(1) $700　　(2) $1,400　　(3) $2,000　　(4) $3,100　　(5) $4,700

Model 144 (1944)
(1) $700　　(2) $1,800　　(3) $2,700　　(4) $3,900　　(5) $5,800

Model 146 (1946)
(1) $700　　(2) $1,800　　(3) $2,700　　(4) $3,900　　(5) $5,800

Model 147 (1947)
(1) $700　　(2) $1,800　　(3) $2,700　　(4) $3,900　　(5) $5,800

Model 148 (1948)
(1) $700　　(2) $1,800　　(3) $2,700　　(4) $3,900　　(5) $5,800

Model 149 (1949)
(1) $700　　(2) $1,800　　(3) $2,700　　(4) $3,900　　(5) $5,800

Model 150 (1950)
(1) $700　　(2) $1,800　　(3) $2,700　　(4) $3,900　　(5) $5,800

Model 151 (1951)
(1) $700　　(2) $1,800　　(3) $2,700　　(4) $3,900　　(5) $5,800

Model 152 (1952)
(1) $700　　(2) $1,800　　(3) $2,700　　(4) $3,900　　(5) $5,800

About ten years ago, these Silver King tractors were sold at auctions for ridiculously low prices. The collector demand has drastically changed these values. These former ugly ducklings are now the delight of many collectors who recognize their special character and tremendous quality.

Model 242 (single front wheel, 1942)
(1) $800   (2) $1,400   (3) $2,000   (4) $3,100   (5) $4,500

Model 244 (single front wheel, 1944)
(1) $800   (2) $1,400   (3) $2,000   (4) $3,100   (5) $4,500

Model 247 (single front wheel, 1947)
(1) $800   (2) $1,400   (3) $2,000   (4) $3,100   (5) $4,500

Model 248 (single front wheel, 1948)
(1) $800   (2) $1,400   (3) $2,000   (4) $3,100   (5) $4,500

Model 249 (single front wheel, 1949)
(1) $800   (2) $1,400   (3) $2,000   (4) $3,100   (5) $4,500

Model 250 (single front wheel, 1950)
(1) $800   (2) $1,400   (3) $2,000   (4) $3,100   (5) $4,500

Model 251 (single front wheel, 1951)
(1) $800   (2) $1,400   (3) $2,000   (4) $3,100   (5) $4,500

Model 252 (single front wheel, 1952)
(1) $800   (2) $1,400   (3) $2,000   (4) $3,100   (5) $4,500

Model 253 (single front wheel, 1953)
(1) $800   (2) $1,400   (3) $2,000   (4) $3,100   (5) $4,500

Model 340 (single front wheel, 1940–1942)
(1) $750   (2) $1,900   (3) $2,800   (4) $4,000   (5) $6,000

Model 341 (single front wheel, 1941)
(1) $750   (2) $1,900   (3) $2,800   (4) $4,000   (5) $6,000

Model 342 (single front wheel, 1942)
(1) $750   (2) $1,900   (3) $2,800   (4) $4,000   (5) $6,000

Model 343 (single front wheel, 1943–1944)
(1) $750   (2) $1,900   (3) $2,800   (4) $4,000   (5) $6,000

Model 344 (single front wheel, 1944–1945)
(1) $750   (2) $1,900   (3) $2,800   (4) $4,000   (5) $6,000

Model 345 (single front wheel, 1945)
(1) $750   (2) $1,900   (3) $2,800   (4) $4,000   (5) $6,000

Model 346 (single front wheel, 1946)
(1) $750   (2) $1,900   (3) $2,800   (4) $4,000   (5) $6,000

Model 347 (single front wheel, 1947)
(1) $750   (2) $1,900   (3) $2,800   (4) $4,000   (5) $6,000

Model 348 (single front wheel, 1948)
(1) $750   (2) $1,900   (3) $2,800   (4) $4,000   (5) $6,000

Model 349 (single front wheel, 1949)
(1) $750   (2) $1,900   (3) $2,800   (4) $4,000   (5) $6,000

Model 350 (single front wheel, 1950)
(1) $750   (2) $1,900   (3) $2,800   (4) $4,000   (5) $6,000

Model 351 (single front wheel, 1951)
(1) $750   (2) $1,900   (3) $2,800   (4) $4,000   (5) $6,000

Model 352 (single front wheel, 1952)
(1) $750   (2) $1,900   (3) $2,800   (4) $4,000   (5) $6,000

Model 355 (single front wheel, 1955–1956)
(1) $750   (2) $1,900   (3) $2,800   (4) $4,000   (5) $6,000

Model 370 (Mountain State Fabricating Co., single front wheel, 1956–1957)
(1) $1,900   (2) $3,400   (3) $5,400   (4) $7,500   (5) $10,000

Model 371 (Mountain State Fabricating Co., 1956–1957)
(1) $1,900   (2) $3,400   (3) $5,400   (4) $7,500   (5) $10,000

Model 380 (1940)
(1) $700   (2) $1,900   (3) $3,000   (4) $4,100   (5) $6,500

Model 381 (single front wheel, 1941)
(1) $700   (2) $1,900   (3) $2,800   (4) $4,000   (5) $6,000

Model 440 (1940–1941)
(1) $700   (2) $2,000   (3) $3,200   (4) $4,300   (5) $6,700

Model 441C (1941)
(1) $700   (2) $2,000   (3) $3,200   (4) $4,300   (5) $6,700

Model 442 (1942)
(1) $700   (2) $2,000   (3) $3,200   (4) $4,300   (5) $6,700

Model 444 (1944–1945)
(1) $700   (2) $2,000   (3) $3,200   (4) $4,300   (5) $6,700

Model 445 (1945)
(1) $700   (2) $2,000   (3) $3,200   (4) $4,300   (5) $6,700

Model 446 (1946)
(1) $700   (2) $2,000   (3) $3,200   (4) $4,300   (5) $6,700

Model 447 (1947)
(1) $700   (2) $2,000   (3) $3,200   (4) $4,300   (5) $6,700

Model 448 (1948)
(1) $700   (2) $2,000   (3) $3,200   (4) $4,300   (5) $6,700

Model 449 (1949)
(1) $700   (2) $2,000   (3) $3,200   (4) $4,300   (5) $6,700

Model 450 (1950-1951)
(1) $700   (2) $2,000   (3) $3,200   (4) $4,300   (5) $6,700

Model 452 (1952)
(1) $700   (2) $2,000   (3) $3,200   (4) $4,300   (5) $6,700

Model 453 (1953)
(1) $700   (2) $2,000   (3) $3,200   (4) $4,300   (5) $6,700

Harry Ferguson Company, Detroit, Michigan

Harry Ferguson invented the three-point hitch that was eventually used on the Ford 9N. According to a handshake agreement that Ferguson made with Henry Ford, Ford would build the tractors and Ferguson would market them. Henry Ford II, grandson to the famous carmaker, introduced the 8N Ford and dropped Ferguson from the mix. The enraged Ferguson sued Ford and won 9.25 million while forcing Ford to drop the 8N model. He introduced the Ferguson tractor in the United States in 1948 as a sort of lookalike to the 8N Ford. Ferguson eventually sold his American concern to Massey-Harris in 1953, resulting in the Massey-Ferguson tractors.

Model TEA-20 (United Kingdom, 1947–1956)
(1) $500   (2) $1,000   (3) $1,500   (4) $2,000   (5) $3,000

Model TO-20 (US, 1948–1951)
(1) $1,500   (2) $2,000   (3) $3,000   (4) $3,500   (5) $4,000

Model TO-30 (US, 1950–1956)
(1) $1,500   (2) $2,000   (3) $3,000   (4) $4,000   (5) $4,500

The practical value of the Ferguson TO-35 is high. The usefulness of such a handy-sized tractor with three-point hitch rivals the collector value.

Model TO-35 (US, 1954–1957)
(1) $2,000   (2) $2,500   (3) $3,500   (4) $4,500   (5) $5,000

Model TO-35 Diesel (US, 1954–1957)
(1) $3,000   (2) $3,500   (3) $4,000   (4) $5,000   (5) $6,000

Model TO-40 (Standard tread, US, 1956–1957)
(1) $2,000   (2) $2,500   (3) $3,500   (4) $4,500   (5) $5,000

Model TO-40 (high-crop, dual narrow front, US, 1956–1957)
(1) $2,000   (2) $3,000   (3) $4,500   (4) $5,500   (5) $6,000

Model TO-40 (high-crop, wide-front, US, 1956–1957)
(1) $2,000   (2) $3,000   (3) $4,000   (4) $5,000   (5) $5,500

Model TO-40 (high-crop, single front wheel, US, 1956–1957)
(1) $2,000   (2) $3,500   (3) $5,000   (4) $6,000   (5) $7,000

Ford Motor Company, Dearborn, Michigan

Henry Ford was raised as a farmer and yearned to produce an inexpensive tractor that almost anyone could afford. As the most successful car builder of his time, Henry knew that he could mass-produce a tractor that would outsell most others. Without support from the other major shareholders of Ford Motor Company, Henry started building the Fordson tractor in 1917. The Fordson name was a contracted form of "Henry Ford and Son." This little tractor was an incredible success as it gobbled up the tractor market with ruthless fury. By the early 1920s, the Fordson was dominating the market with about 70 percent of all U.S. tractor sales. The historical significance of this tractor and how it

The Fordson was, by far, the biggest seller during the early 1920s, with sales approaching almost three-quarters of the whole tractor market. Today, rare versions such as this Model 9X (experimental) are worth a lot of money. The common model Fordsons will not demand high prices but are easier to restore than many other models, due to good parts availability.

changed the industry makes it particularly attractive to certain collectors. In 1939, Henry Ford began producing the 9N tractor, using Harry Ferguson's three-point hitch. In 1945, Henry Ford II took over the reign of the company from his grandfather, and in 1946, he left Harry Ferguson out of the tractor deal, motivating Ferguson to sue Ford. Ford lost the case and was forced to stop building its popular 8N tractor and shell out $9,250,000 to Ferguson. Within a few years, Ford was building an assortment of tractors. Ford tractor models built before World War II have a loyal following and have experienced a slow but steady value increase over the last several years. Because of high production numbers of many models and their value as a useful farmhand, many later models have been considered collectable in only the last few years.

Henry Ford and Son (Fordson predecessor with Hercules engine, 1917–1918)
(1) $1,300   (2) $2,800   (3) $4,250   (4) $5,500   (5) $7,200

Fordson F (ladder-side radiator, 1918)
(1) $500   (2) $700   (3) $1,200   (4) $2,500   (5) $4,500

Fordson F (solid radiator sides, steel wheels, 1919–1928)
(1) $450   (2) $600   (3) $1,000   (4) $2,200   (5) $4,000

Fordson N (Irish, steel wheels, serial nos. 747682–779153, 1929–1933)
(1) $300   (2) $750   (3) $1,200   (4) $3,000   (5) $5,500

Fordson N (United Kingdom, steel wheels, 1933–1939)
(1) $300   (2) $500   (3) $1,000   (4) $2,500   (5) $4,000

Fordson N (United Kingdom, rubber tires, 1933–1939)
(1) $300   (2) $500   (3) $1,000   (4) $2,500   (5) $4,000

Fordson All-A-Round (tricycle, rubber tires, 1936–1940)
(1) $800   (2) $1,000   (3) $1,950   (4) $4,000   (5) $4,500

Fordson E27N (1946–1953)
(1) $500   (2) $825   (3) $1,550   (4) $2,250   (5) $3,100

Fordson Major Diesel (1953–1958)
(1) $500   (2) $1,400   (3) $3,500   (4) $4,000   (5) $4,500

Fordson Power Major (1958–1960)
(1) $500   (2) $1,500   (3) $3,500   (4) $4,000   (5) $4,500

Fordson Super Major Diesel (1960–1964)
(1) $500   (2) $1,500   (3) $4,000   (4) $4,500   (5) $5,000

Fordson Dexta (1958–1961)
(1) $600   (2) $1,500   (3) $3,000   (4) $4,000   (5) $4,500

Fordson Super Dexta (1962–1964)
(1) $1,000   (2) $1,950   (3) $3,000   (4) $3,900   (5) $5,000

This Fordson tractor has a conversion kit marketed as the Trackson D. Another brand of full-track Fordson conversion sold for $13,000 in a 1998 auction. Very few Tracksons survived the scrap drives during World War II.

The British Major Series has been slow to gather interest from most collectors, but more and more of them are beginning to manifest at tractor gatherings. This tractor is the noble grandson of the popular Model F Fordson that flooded the market in the 1920s. Although much more massive and stocky, this 1961 Power Major has several design features that can be traced directly to the 1920s Fordsons.

Ford 9N (aluminum hood and grille, serial nos. 1–approx. 800, 1939)
(1) $3,500   (2) $4,500   (3) $6,000   (4) $10,000 (5) $15,000

Ford 9N (aluminum hood, steel grille, 1939)
(1) $1,200   (2) $2,000   (3) $2,500   (4) $3,500   (5) $5,000

Ford 9N (common, 1939–1942)
(1) $1,000   (2) $1,300   (3) $1,750   (4) $2,500   (5) $3,500

Ford 2N (rubber tires, 1942–1947)
(1) $800   (2) $1,200   (3) $1,600   (4) $2,000   (5) $3,000

Ford 2N (steel wheels, 1942–1947)
(1) $1,450   (2) $1,750   (3) $2,000   (4) $2,500   (5) $3,500

The Ford 9N was the first American tractor to use a 3-point hitch. Although several were built, only a handful of early 9Ns with the original aluminum hood and grille now exist. The fragile aluminum seldom survived the 60 or so years f farming. This beautiful example of a 1939 9N has the paint removed to reveal the aluminum hood.

Ford 2NAN (all-fuel, 1942–1947)
(1) $1,500   (2) $2,000   (3) $2,500   (4) $3,250   (5) $4,000

Ford B-NO-40 (Moto-Tug, ca. 1945)
(1) $2,000   (2) $2,500   (3) $3,500   (4) $4,000   (5) $4,750

Ford 8N (1947–1952)
(1) $1,500   (2) $2,000   (3) $2,500   (4) $3,000   (5) $4,000

Ford 8NAN (all-fuel, 1947–1952)
(1) $1,750   (2) $2,250   (3) $3,000   (4) $3,500   (5) $4,500

Ford 8N Funk 6-cylinder conversion (1947–1952)
(1) $2,500   (2) $3,000   (3) $3,500   (4) $4,500   (5) $6,000

The Funk Aircraft Company of Coffeeville, Kansas, produced the conversion kits that allowed either a 226-ci six-cylinder or a 239-ci V-8 Ford engine to be installed into a stock Ford 8N tractor. This V-8 tractor is the rarer of the two conversions and would command remarkably high prices from devoted collectors.

Ford 8N Funk V-8-engine conversion (1947–1952)
(1) $3,000   (2) $3,500   (3) $5,000   (4) $10,000 (5) $15,000

Ford 8N Cane/cotton conversion (1947–1952)
(1) $2,000   (2) $2,500   (3) $3,250   (4) $4,000   (5) $5,000

Ford NAA (1953–1954)
(1) $1,250   (2) $2,000   (3) $3,500   (4) $4,750   (5) $6,000

Ford 501 (offset, 1954–1957)
(1) $2,000   (2) $2,750   (3) $3,750   (4) $5,000   (5) $6,000

Ford 601 (1957–1962)
(1) $1,500   (2) $2,250   (3) $2,750   (4) $4,000   (5) $4,750

Ford 620 (less PTO and 3-point, has 4-speed, 1954–1957)
(1) $1,500   (2) $1,750   (3) $2,000   (4) $2,500   (5) $3,000

Ford 630 (less PTO, has 4-speed, 1954–1957)
(1) $1,500   (2) $1,750   (3) $2,000   (4) $2,500   (5) $3,000

The collector value for LPG tractors is usually considerably higher than the gasoline or diesel versions. This LPG fuel 1961 Ford 971 Select-O-Speed model has been restored to look like new. In the last few years, the 1960s tractors have become the most volatile in values.

Ford 640 (4-speed, 1954–1957)
(1) $1,500   (2) $1,750   (3) $2,000   (4) $2,500   (5) $3,000

Ford 641 (1957–1962)
(1) $1,500   (2) $2,000   (3) $2,500   (4) $3,000   (5) $3,750

Ford 650 (5-speed, 1954–1957)
(1) $2,000   (2) $2,250   (3) $2,500   (4) $3,000   (5) $4,000

Ford 660 (5-speed, live PTO, 1954–1957)
(1) $2,250   (2) $2,500   (3) $3,000   (4) $3,500   (5) $4,000

Ford 700 series (tricycle, 1954–1957)
(1) $2,000   (2) $2,500   (3) $2,750   (4) $3,000   (5) $3,750

Ford 800 (1954–1957)
(1) $1,500   (2) $2,000   (3) $2,250   (4) $2,500   (5) $3,500

Ford 820 (less PTO and 3-point, has 4-speed, 1954–1957)
(1) $1,750   (2) $2,000   (3) $2,250   (4) $2,500   (5) $3,000

Ford 850 (1954–1957)
(1) $2,000   (2) $2,250   (3) $2,500   (4) $2,750   (5) $3,500

Ford 860 (live PTO, 1954–1957)
(1) $2,000   (2) $2,500   (3) $3,000   (4) $3,750   (5) $4,500

Ford 861 Powermaster (1957–1962)
(1) $2,000   (2) $2,500   (3) $3,250   (4) $4,000   (5) $4,750

Ford 900 series (tricycle, 1954–1957)
(1) $2,500   (2) $2,750   (3) $3,250   (4) $4,000   (5) $5,000

The Ford Model B is unique in that the mistakes of its creators changed history. This Minneapolis-based Ford Tractor Company hired Paul Ford as a designer solely for the sake of using his name. This clever ruse fooled many people into believing that the tractor was a product of the biggest carmaker in America, Henry Ford. The unreliability of the machine so angered the Nebraska farmer and member of the State Legislature, Wilmont Crozier, that it became his personal crusade to push the famous Nebraska Tractor Testing into existence, virtually eliminating any less-than-honest tractor companies. A 1916 Ford Model B sold for $14,500 in 1998.

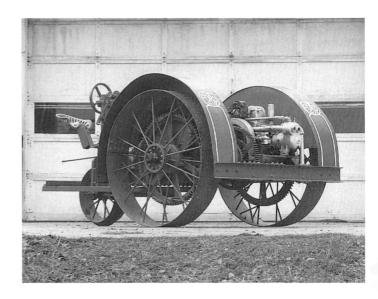

Ford Tractor Company, Minneapolis, Minnesota

The Ford Company's tractor was built by W. Baer Ewing and designed by a Mr. Kinkaid. The company hired Paul Ford simply to pose as the designer of the tractor. Because it sported the Ford name, many potential buyers falsely assumed this tractor was built by the world-famous carmaker. Henry Ford introduced his Fordson tractor in July 1917, the very same month that the Minneapolis Ford Tractor Company was brought before the U.S. Grand Jury for defrauding investors. The company folded in

December of the same year. Some believe that Henry Ford was not able to use "Ford" on his tractor because the name was already in use by this Minneapolis firm. Henry built the original Fordson (a shortened version of Henry Ford and Son) as a private venture and it was not originally connected to the Ford Motor Company. It is unlikely, however, that as one of the richest men in the world, Henry Ford would have been prevented from using his own name by such a small tractor company. Because of the ruse of the Minneapolis tractor company and the fact that its poor performance was a major factor in the formation of the Nebraska tractor tests, this tractor has much historical significance.

Ford Model B (1916–1917)
(1) $7,000 (2) $9,500   (3) $12,000 (4) $14,500 (5) $16,000

Four Drive Tractor Company, Big Rapids, Michigan
Fitch FWD 20-30 (1915–1917)
(1) $8,000 (2) $11,750 (3) $14,500 (4) $16,500 (5) $20,000

Fitch FWD 15-30 (1918–1926)
(1) $9,000 (2) $12,250 (3) $16,000 (4) $18,500 (5) $23,000

Fitch FWD 15-30 Model E "Cat" (1927–1930)
(1) $8,000 (2) $11,750 (3) $14,500 (4) $16,500 (5) $20,000

Fitch FWD 20-35 Model D (1918–1930)
(1) $8,000 (2) $12,000 (3) $15,000 (4) $17,500 (5) $22,000

Fox River Tractor Company, Appleton, Wisconsin
Fox 20-40 (1919)
(1) $6,500 (2) $9,500   (3) $12,000 (4) $14,500 (5) $18,000

Frick Company, Waynesboro, Pennsylvania
As a well-known builder of steam traction engines, Frick began building its first gas tractor in about 1918. These tractors were sold until about 1928, when the company decided to market tractors from the Minneapolis Threshing Machine Company instead. By 1930, it had dropped all tractor business to concentrate on its more successful refrigeration equipment line. Frick is still a leader in the commercial refrigeration business today.

Frick Model A 12-20 (1918–1928)
(1) $4,500 (2) $7,000   (3) $8,250   (4) $9,750   (5) $12,000

Frick Model C 15-28 (1919–1928)
(1) $5,000 (2) $8,000   (3) $9,500   (4) $11,000 (5) $14,000

Friday Tractor Company, Hartford, Michigan
With its powerful Chrysler engine, this orchard tractor has a tremendously fast road speed. Its sleek look with the rounded front end plus its low production numbers makes this tractor a standout at tractor shows. The interest in the Friday has grown tremendously in the last few years.

Friday Model O-48 (1947–1957)

(1) $3,000   (2) $4,200   (3) $5,000   (4) $6,000   (5) $7,500

Gaar, Scott and Company, Richmond, Indiana
Gaar-Scott Model 40-70 (1911)

(1) $38,000   (2) $68,000   (3) $95,000   (4) $120,000   (5) $150,000

William Galloway Company, Waterloo, Iowa
Farmobile 12-20 (1916–1919)

(1) $5,500   (2) $8,000   (3) $10,250   (4) $12,500   (5) $15,000

Galloway Bear Cat or Baby Galloway
(2 in England + 2 in US, 1916–1919)

(1) $5,250   (2) $7,500   (3) $9,500   (4) $11,000   (5) $13,000

Gamble-Skogmo, a franchise company that had several farm-supply stores in the Midwest, sold the Cockshutt Model 30 under its own logo. The Gambles Farmcrest 30 is much less common than the Cockshutt version. A nice Farmcrest sold at auction in 1999 from the late Ed Spiess' Collection for $8,000.

Gamble-Skogmo, Inc., Minneapolis, Minnesota
Farmcrest 30 (1948–1953)

(1) $1,250   (2) $2,500   (3) $4,800   (4) $6,000   (5) $7,250

Gasport Motor Company, Gasport, New York
Gasport Tractor (1911)

(1) $8,000   (2) $12,000   (3) $15,000   (4) $17,500   (5) $22,000

Gas Traction Company (see Emerson-Brantingham), Minneapolis, Minnesota
Big 4 "30" (30-60, 1910–1912)

(1) $35,000   (2) $40,000   (3) $60,000   (4) $75,000   (5) $100,000

Gehl Brothers Manufacturing Company, West Bend, Wisconsin
Gehl (drum-drive, 1916–1919)

(1) $5,500   (2) $8,000   (3) $9,250   (4) $10,000   (5) $12,750

Geiser Manufacturing Company, Waynesboro, Pennsylvania
The Geiser 25-50 (1909–1912)

(1) $18,000   (2) $25,000   (3) $31,000   (4) $35,000   (5) $45,000

General Motors Corporation, Pontiac, Michigan

The Samson Tractor Works of Stockton, California, was producing an impressive performing tractor called the Sieve-Grip. General Motors bought this company in 1918 to compete against the Fordson tractor. Henry Ford's tractor was monopolizing the market with his mass production and affordable pricing. General Motors apparently felt that they had the same capability and reputation to bring out a big seller. The Samson M was sold for only $650, but sales were not impressive. A motor cultivator followed and the new model A was in the prototype stage when General Motors ended its tractor venture in 1922.

General Motors wanted to rival the fast-selling Fordson tractor with its Samson M. This high-clearance version was another attempt to aggrandize sales. The Samson required high production to turn a profit to its mother company, but that was not to come about. In 1921, G-M stockholders voted to shut down the Samson truck and tractor division and used the facilities to build automobiles. The Samson has a special historical significance and its values are strong.

Samson Sieve-Grip 6-12
(prior to GM ownership, 1-cylinder, 1916-1917)
(1) $14,750 (2) $19,500 (3) $25,000 (4) $31,000 (5) $36,000

Samson Sieve-Grip 12-25 (1917–1918)
(1) $11,500 (2) $15,000 (3) $21,000 (4) $27,000 (5) $31,000

Very few Samson Sieve-Grip models exist today. A restored 1916 model was sold at auction for $26,000 in 1998. The demand for the Sieve-Grip models is powerful and will probably never allow the values to drop.

Samson M (1918–1922)
(1) $2,100   (2) $3,300   (3) $4,200   (4) $5,400   (5) $7,000

Samson M High-clearance (ca. 1922)
(1) $2,800   (2) $4,800   (3) $7,250   (4) $9,400   (5) $11,250

Model D Iron Horse (rein-drive motor cultivator, 1919–1922)
(1) $4,800   (2) $7,250   (3) $10,000   (4) $13,000   (5) $17,000

Samson A (one known to exist in Canandaigua, NY, 1922)
(1) $6,500   (2) $10,250   (3) $13,000   (4) $16,500 (5) $22,000

General Ordnance Company, Cedar Rapids, Iowa
G-O 14-28 (1920)
(1) $7,400   (2) $12,000   (3) $16,000   (4) $20,000 (5) $26,000

G-O 12-22 (1920)
(1) $7,000   (2) $11,250   (3) $15,000   (4) $18,500 (5) $24,000

General Tractor Company, Cleveland, Ohio
Powerbilt (4-wheel drive, ca. 1950)
(1) $1,200   (2) $2,500   (3) $3,600   (4) $4,500   (5) $6,200

Gibson Manufacturing Corporation, Longmont, Colorado, and Seattle, Washington

Wilber Gibson founded this company in 1946 and on March 2 announced production of its first 52 tractors. The early tractors were small one-cylinder Wisconsin-powered machines that weighed less than half a ton. The later six-cylinder weighed about two tons. Gibson Tractor Club founder, Dave Baas, sent me an article, written in June 1948, telling how the 150 employees at Gibson were building 2,000 tractors per month. The average assembly time was 6 minutes each and, under ideal conditions, 1-1/2 minutes. This does not take away from the high collectibility of these one-cylinder tractors today. The larger water-cooled Gibson tractors were produced in very limited numbers and demand some serious prices in nice condition. A condition five Gibson Super G (prototype) sold for $26,000 in an auction in 1999.

Gibson Model A (1-cylinder Wisconsin engine, 16-inch rear wheels, tiller steering, 1946)
(1) $250   (2) $435   (3) $720   (4) $1,050   (5) $1,300

Gibson Model A (1-cylinder Wisconsin engine, Gibson name in cast front wheels, ca. 1946)
(1) $400   (2) $750   (3) $1,000   (4) $1,400   (5) $2,400

Gibson Model D (1-cylinder Wisconsin engine, no fenders, 22- or 24-inch wheels, tiller steering, ca. 1948)
(1) $300   (2) $535   (3) $825   (4) $1,150   (5) $1,535

Gibson Model SD (1-cylinder Wisconsin engine, hood and fenders, tiller steering, 1948–1956)
(1) $490   (2) $735   (3) $1,035   (4) $1,350   (5) $1,650

Gibson Model Super D (1-cylinder Wisconsin engine, steering wheel, with optional hydraulics, 1948)
(1) $650   (2) $800   (3) $1,350   (4) $1,950   (5) $2,400

Gibson Model Super D2 (2-cylinder Wisconsin engine, ca. 1948)
(1) $950   (2) $1,200   (3) $1,700   (4) $2,450   (5) $3,100

Gibson Model E (narrow front, standard rear width, 2-cylinder, ca. 1948)
(1) $1,375   (2) $1,600   (3) $2,100   (4) $2,700   (5) $3,225

Gibson Model EF (wide-front, standard rear width, 2-cylinder, ca. 1948)
(1) $1,400   (2) $1,665   (3) $2,150   (4) $2,750   (5) $3,300

Gibson Model EW (narrow front, wide rear, 2-cylinder, ca. 1948)
(1) $1,550   (2) $1,700   (3) $2,200   (4) $2,800   (5) $3,350

Gibson Model EWF (wide-front, wide rear, 2-cylinder, ca. 1948)
(1) $1,600   (2) $1,800   (3) $2,300   (4) $2,900   (5) $3,500

Gibson Model H (narrow front, 4-cylinder, 1949–1956)
(1) $1,400   (2) $2,250   (3) $3,250   (4) $4,500   (5) $5,600

Gibson built tractors with one, two, four, and six-cylinder engines. Basically, for this brand, the more cylinders a tractor has, the higher the value. This two-cylinder Model EF was built in 1948. Gibson has a loyal following of collectors who will pay dearly for the scarcer versions.

Gibson Model HFS (fixed wide-front, 4-cylinder, 1949–1956)
(1) $1,425   (2) $2,500   (3) $3,500   (4) $5,000   (5) $6,200

Gibson Model HFA (adjustable wide-front, 4-cylinder, 1948–1956)
(1) $1,425   (2) $2,500   (3) $3,525   (4) $5,100   (5) $6,350

Gibson Model I (narrow front, 6-cylinder, 1948–1956)
(1) $1,700   (2) $2,800   (3) $4,100   (4) $6,000   (5) $8,300

Gibson Model IFS (fixed wide-front, 6-cylinder, 1948–1956)
(1) $1,725   (2) $2,900   (3) $4,275   (4) $6,200   (5) $8,550

Gibson Model IFA (adjustable wide-front, 6-cylinder, ca. 1950)
(1) $1,750   (2) $3,000   (3) $4,425   (4) $6,400   (5) $8,850

Gibson Model W Tug (ca. 1950)
(1) $1,000   (2) $1,800   (3) $3,000   (4) $4,000   (5) $5,000

Gile Tractor and Engine Company, Ludington, Michigan

Gile Model L 10-20 (single wheel, 1913–1916)
(1) $4,500   (2) $8,000   (3) $10,500   (4) $12,500 (5) $16,000

Gile Model XL 10-20 (2 front wheels, 1913–1916)
(1) $4,500   (2) $8,000   (3) $10,500   (4) $12,500 (5) $16,000

Gile Model Q 15-35 (1918–1920)
(1) $7,250   (2) $11,000   (3) $14,000   (4) $16,500 (5) $21,000

Gilson Manufacturing Company, Port Washington, Wisconsin

Gilson Model 11-20 (1917–1918)
(1) $9,000   (2) $14,000   (3) $17,000   (4) $20,000 (5) $25,000

Gilson Model 12-25 (1917)
(1) $9,000   (2) $14,000   (3) $17,000   (4) $20,000 (5) $25,000

Gilson Model 15-30 (1918–1919)
(1) $10,000 (2) $16,000   (3) $20,000   (4) $24,000 (5) $31,000

Global Trading Corporation, Washington, D. C.

Only eight Global tractors were built and only three are known to have survived. Huber Manufacturing Company made the tractor for Global. The Huber B is the same tractor, but the Global has its name down the center panel of the grille as well as in the center of the gauge cluster. Earl Scott has recorded the known Global serial numbers as 14318, 14319, and 14320. Happy hunting!

Global (made by Huber Co., 1950)
(1) $5,000   (2) $7,500   (3) $10,000   (4) $15,000 (5) $20,000

Goodfield Tractor Company, Goodfield, Illinois

Goodfield Model 9-18 (1918–1922)
(1) $8,000   (2) $12,000   (3) $15,000   (4) $17,500 (5) $21,000

Goold, Shapley and Muir Company, Brantford, Ontario

G. S. & M. Model 28-20 (1909–1912)
(1) $20,000 (2) $40,000   (3) $56,000   (4) $70,000 (5) $90,000

G. S. & M. Model 45-30 (1909–1912)
(1) $20,000 (2) $42,000   (3) $62,000   (4) $78,000(5) $100,000

G. S. & M. Model 20-35 (1909–1912)
(1) $20,000 (2) $40,000 (3) $56,000 (4) $70,000 (5) $90,000

Ideal 15-25 (ca. 1915)
(1) $20,000 (2) $40,000 (3) $56,000 (4) $70,000 (5) $90,000

Ideal 15-30 (ca. 1915)
(1) $20,000 (2) $40,000 (3) $56,000 (4) $70,000 (5) $90,000

Ideal 12-24 (ca. 1915)
(1) $20,000 (2) $35,000 (3) $48,000 (4) $62,000 (5) $80,000

Beaver 12-24 (1918–1921)
(1) $12,000 (2) $18,500 (3) $24,000 (4) $29,000 (5) $35,000

Beaver 15-30 (1918–1921)
(1) $12,000 (2) $18,500 (3) $24,000 (4) $29,000 (5) $35,000

Graham-Paige Motors Company, Detroit, Michigan

Three brothers, Joseph, Robert, and Ray Graham, bought the Paige Automobile Company in 1928. By 1937 the Graham brothers were producing a tractor that used the same six-cylinder engine as their cars used. These Graham-Bradley tractors were marketed through Sears and Roebuck catalogs in 1938 and 1939. The Grahams' focus on automobiles led to their eventual involvement with the Kaiser Frazer Corporation. The tractors were dropped as their interest in car production took priority.

Graham-Bradley Model 503-93 (1937)
(1) $4,550 (2) $5,000 (3) $6,250 (4) $7,250 (5) $8,550

Graham-Bradley Model 503-103 (narrow front, 1938–1939)
(1) $4,250 (2) $4,850 (3) $5,850 (4) $7,250 (5) $8,500

Graham-Bradley Model 503-104 (standard tread, 1938–1939)
(1) $4,800 (2) $5,500 (3) $7,500 (4) $10,000 (5) $13,500

Grain Belt Tractor Company, Fargo, North Dakota

Grain Belt Model 15-30 (rerated 18-36, 1917–1921)
(1) $3,000 (2) $5,000 (3) $7,000 (4) $10,000 (5) $16,000

Gramont Traction Plow Company, Springfield, Ohio

Gramont 50 horsepower Traction Plow (1913)
(1) $10,000 (2) $16,000 (3) $20,000 (4) $25,000 (5) $32,000

Gray Tractor Company, Minneapolis, Minnesota

Gray Tractor Model 18-36 (drum drive, 1918–1921)
(1) $5,000 (2) $7,500 (3) $9,250 (4) $13,250 (5) $15,000

Gray Tractor Model 20-36 (drum drive, 1922)
(1) $5,000   (2) $7,500   (3) $9,250   (4) $13,250 (5) $15,000

Gray Tractor Model 22-40 (drum drive, 1923–1924)
(1) $5,000   (2) $7,500   (3) $9,250   (4) $13,250(5) $15,000

Gray Canadian Special 22-40 (drum drive, 1925–1933)
(1) $5,000   (2) $7,500   (3) $9,250   (4) $13,250(5) $15,000

Great Western Tractor Company, Council Bluffs, Iowa
Great Western Senior 20-30 (1919–1921)
(1) $8,000   (2) $12,000   (3) $15,000   (4) $17,500   (5) $22,000

Haas Foundry Co. (see Metal Parts Corporation)

The Happy Farmer was a heavily advertised tractor in its day, but its reliability was far from outstanding. The publicity from its early advertising tends to create more value for this machine than for similar tractors of its day. Tractor collecting is one of the few hobbies where you can buy a known lemon and still have a valuable piece.

Happy Farmer Tractor Company, Minneapolis, Minnesota

With a style that was popular in its day, the Happy Farmer performe well in tractor demonstrations. Many of the Happy Farmer tracto were built by the La Crosse Tractor Company, which was formed par ly from the original Happy Farmer Tractor Co. and partly from th Sta-Rite Engine Co. The Oshkosh Tractor Co. bought out La Cros in 1921 and by the following year the Happy Farmer tractor w. dropped from production. There is a joke about how this tractor ma a farmer happy twice: once when he bought the tractor and aga when he sold it. Actually, the Happy Farmer was probably built bett than many other small tractors of its day. The primitive tractor sty and the low numbers of surviving examples make the demand for th tractor quite high.

Happy Farmer Tractor 8-16 (1915)
(1) $6,000   (2) $8,250   (3) $11,000   (4) $13,000   (5) $16,000

Happy Farmer Tractor 12-25 (1916)
(1) $6,000   (2) $8,250   (3) $11,000   (4) $13,000   (5) $16,000

Harris Manufacturing Company, Stockton, California
Harris PH-40 (ca. 1952)
(1) $1,400   (2) $3,000   (3) $4,500   (4) $6,250   (5) $8,000

The Harris Power Horse is an early predecessor of the now-popular skid-steer tractors. The interest in these curious-looking tractors is growing. Four-wheel-drive tractors will often have a strong collector demand, partly due to their novelty.

Harris Model F6WC (4-wheel drive, 6-cylinder Chrysler engine, 1953–1956)
(1) $1,400   (2) $3,000   (3) $4,500   (4) $6,200   (5) $8,000

Harris Model F8W (4-wheel drive, 8-cylinder Chrysler engine, 1953–1956)
(1) $1,500   (2) $3,200   (3) $4,700   (4) $6,500   (5) $8,500

Harris Model F8WC (4-wheel drive, 8-cylinder Chrysler engine, 1953–1956)
(1) $1,500   (2) $3,200   (3) $4,700   (4) $6,500   (5) $8,500

Harris Model FDWC (4-wheel drive, 2-cylinder Detroit engine, 1953–1956)
(1) $1,400   (2) $3,000   (3) $4,500   (4) $6,200   (5) $8,000

Harris Model 53 Power Horse (4-wheel drive, 6-cylinder Chrysler engine, 1953)
(1) $1,400   (2) $3,000   (3) $4,500   (4) $6,200   (5) $8,000

Hart-Parr Company, Charles City, Iowa

Two college buddies from the University of Wisconsin, Charles Hart and Charles Parr, built their first tractor in 1902 in Charles City, Iowa. Constant improvements and proper field training made this company a successful pioneer in the gas tractor business. They are falsely credited for inventing the word "tractor," but one credit they deserve is building some of the finest tractors of their day. With much money invested in improvements and customer satisfaction, Hart-Parr grew into a major tractor builder by the early 1920s. In 1929, Hart-Parr was one of four companies that merged to form the Oliver Farm Equipment Company. The Hart-Parr tractors have a strong historical attraction, and the early models are in high demand. As with many other brands of their era, the huge Hart-Parr tractors will bring huge prices. Bigger is often better when collecting early model tractors.

Hart-Parr Model 3, 18-30 (1903)
(1) $40,000   (2) $58,000   (3) $72,000   (4) $84,000   (5) $120,000

Hart-Parr Model 17-30 (1903–1906)
(1) $40,000   (2) $58,000   (3) $72,000   (4) $84,000   (5) $100,000

Hart-Parr Model 22-45 (1903–1906)
(1) $30,000   (2) $42,000   (3) $53,000   (4) $62,000   (5) $74,000

Hart-Parr is credited with coining the word "tractor." This fact is not entirely true, but Hart-Parr was the first tractor company in America to have an organized dealership and training network. The Hart-Parr Model 22-45 shown here is extremely valuable as very few examples exist today.

Old Reliable 30-60 (1907–1918)
(1) $28,000   (2) $40,000   (3) $50,000   (4) $58,000   (5) $70,000

Hart-Parr Model 40-80 (1908–1914)
(1) $50,000   (2) $70,000   (3) $80,000   (4) $100,000   (5) $110,000

Hart-Parr Model 15-30 (box radiator, 1909–1912)
(1) $40,000   (2) $58,000   (3) $72,000   (4) $84,000   (5) $100,000

Hart-Parr Model 20-40 (1912–1914)
(1) $30,000   (2) $44,000   (3) $52,000   (4) $67,000   (5) $76,000

Crop-Maker 27 (1914–1915)
(1) $40,000   (2) $58,000   (3) $70,000   (4) $84,000   (5) $100,000

Little Red Devil 15-22 (1914–1916)
(1) $20,000   (2) $29,000   (3) $40,000   (4) $45,000   (5) $60,000

Oil King Model 18-35 (1915–1918)
(1) $40,000   (2) $58,000   (3) $70,000   (4) $84,000   (5) $100,000

Hart-Parr Model "30" Type A 15-30 (1918–1922)
(1) $1,000   (2) $2,000   (3) $4,000   (4) $6,000   (5) $8,000

Road King Model 18-35 (1919)
(1) $40,000   (2) $58,000   (3) $70,000   (4) $84,000   (5) $100,000

Hart-Parr Model 12-25 (lightweight, 1918)
(1) $1,000   (2) $2,500   (3) $4,000   (4) $7,500   (5) $12,000

Hart-Parr Model B and C 10-20 (1921–1924)
(1) $2,000   (2) $4,575   (3) $8,500   (4) $12,000   (5) $18,000

Hart-Parr Model C 15-30 (1922–1924)
(1) $900   (2) $1,800   (3) $3,500   (4) $6,000   (5) $7,500

Hart-Parr Model 22-40 (4-cylinder, 1923–1927)
(1) $1,800   (2) $5,500   (3) $8,500   (4) $11,000   (5) $15,000

Hart-Parr Model E and H 12-24 (1924–1930)
(1) $900   (2) $2,500   (3) $4,000   (4) $5,500   (5) $8,500

As time goes on, more and more ultrarare tractors will end up in museums, and the values tend to reflect this trend. Private collectors must spend thousands of dollars and hundreds of hours to restore rare machines like this scarce Hart Parr 30-60.

Hart-Parr Model E 16-30 (1924–1926)
(1) $950   (2) $2,000   (3) $4,000   (4) $5,000   (5) $7,000

Hart-Parr Model G and H 18-36 (1926–1930)
(1) $1,000   (2) $2,250   (3) $4,250   (4) $5,500   (5) $7,500

Hart-Parr Model 28-50 (1927–1930)
(1) $1,000   (2) $2,500   (3) $4,500   (4) $8,000   (5) $10,000

Oliver purchased the Hart-Parr Company in 1929 and continued the use of its name until the late 1930s. Row-crop was the model name of this 1930 Hart-Parr tractor rated at 18-27. A tractor like this can fetch over $4,000 when properly restored.

Heer Engine Company, Portsmouth, Ohio
Heer Model 16-25 (FWD, 1914–1916)
(1) $30,000   (2) $45,000   (3) $65,000   (4) $80,000   (5) $100,000

Heer Model 20-28 (FWD, 1914–1916)
(1) $35,000   (2) $50,000   (3) $70,000   (4) $85,000   (5) $105,000

Heer Model 24-32 (FWD, 1914–1916)
(1) $35,000   (2) $55,000   (3) $75,000   (4) $88,000   (5) $110,000

Heider Manufacturing Company
(see Rock Island Plow Company)

Hero Manufacturing Company, Winnipeg, Manitoba
Hero 20 horsepower (1911)
(1) $9,000   (2) $12,000   (3) $15,000   (4) $22,000   (5) $28,000

Hession Tiller and Tractor Corporation, Buffalo, New York

Wheat or Hession Tractor (two known to exist, 1917–1924)

(1) $10,000 (2) $18,000 (3) $21,000 (4) $24,000 (5) $29,000

Hoke Tractor Company, South Bend, Indiana

Hoke 12-24 (1913–1917)

(1) $7,500 (2) $9,000 (3) $11,750 (4) $13,500 (5) $17,000

Hollis Tractor Company, Philadelphia, Pennsylvania

Hollis Model M 15-25 (1917–1920)

(1) $9,000 (2) $15,000 (3) $19,000 (4) $22,000 (5) $26,000

Holton Tractor Company, Indianapolis, Indiana

Holton Model 10-16 (1915–1920)

(1) $6,500 (2) $10,000 (3) $14,000 (4) $17,000 (5) $21,000

Hoosier Wheel and Tractor Company, Franklin, Indiana

Hoosier 20-35 (1920–1921)

(1) $8,000 (2) $12,000 (3) $18,000 (4) $20,000 (5) $24,000

Huber Manufacturing Company, Marion, Ohio

Edward Huber began in the farm implement business by inventing a hay rake. It was marketed in the late 1860s. He later became a recognized builder of fine steam engines and threshers. In 1898, Huber built his first tractor prototypes and began tractor production in 1911. Huber did quite well in the gas tractor business when compared to most other tractor companies of its day. With a modern design and high quality of workmanship, the Huber was perhaps one of the finest tractors built in the 1920s.

The antiquated design of Huber Super-Four tractors makes it particularly interesting to certain collectors. The transverse radiator and engine plus the oversized front wheels give this Huber its own special identity and appeal. Mainly due to its high quality, the Huber is a respected tractor among collectors and can demand some hefty prices.

Farmers Tractor 13-22 (rerated 15-30, 1910–1912)

(1) $4,000 (2) $5,000 (3) $7,000 (4) $20,000 (5) $30,000

Huber Model 30-60 (rerated 35-70, 1912–1916)

(1) $12,000 (2) $38,000 (3) $59,000 (4) $77,000 (5) $100,000

Huber Model 20-40 (1914–1917)

(1) $3,000 (2) $5,000 (3) $7,000 (4) $20,000 (5) $30,000

Huber Light Four 12-25 (1917–1928)
(1) $2,000   (2) $3,000   (3) $5,000   (4) $11,000 (5) $17,000

Huber Master Four 25-50 (rerated 40-62, 1922–1924)
(1) $3,000   (2) $5,000   (3) $7,000   (4) $10,000 (5) $16,000

Super Four 15-30 (1921–1925)
(1) $3,000   (2) $5,000   (3) $7,000   (4) $11,000 (5) $17,000

Super Four 18-36 (rerated 21-39, 1926–1929)
(1) $1,500   (2) $3,000   (3) $5,000   (4) $7,000   (5) $9,000

Super Four 20-40 (rerated 32-45, 1926–1929)
(1) $1,600   (2) $3,000   (3) $5,000   (4) $6,000   (5) $8,000

Super Four 25-50 (1926–1943)
(1) $1,600   (2) $3,000   (3) $5,000   (4) $6,000   (5) $8,000

Modern Farmer (1931–1937)
(1) $1,500   (2) $2,500   (3) $3,000   (4) $4,000   (5) $5,000

Modern Farmer L (1937–1942)
(1) $1,500   (2) $2,500   (3) $3,000   (4) $4,000   (5) $5,000

Modern Farmer LC (row-crop, 1937–1942)
(1) $1,000   (2) $1,500   (3) $2,500   (4) $3,000   (5) $4,000

Huber Light Four 20-36 (1929–1935)
(1) $1,500   (2) $2,500   (3) $3,000   (4) $4,000   (5) $6,000

Huber Model B (1936–1943)
(1) $1,200   (2) $2,000   (3) $2,500   (4) $3,000   (5) $4,000

Huber Model OB Orchard (full citrus fenders, 1937–1943)
(1) $1,200   (2) $2,000   (3) $3,000   (4) $4,500   (5) $6,000

Huber Maintainer (industrial road maintenance, ca. 1940)
(1) $900   (2) $1,100   (3) $1,800   (4) $2,500   (5) $3,300

Humber-Anderson Manufacturing Company, St. Paul, Minnesota
Little Oak (1913–1916)
(1) $6,500   (2) $10,000   (3) $16,000   (4) $18,500 (5) $22,000

Hume Manufacturing Company, Hume, Illinois
Hume 20-30 (1916)
(1) $8,000   (2) $12,000   (3) $18,000   (4) $20,000 (5) $24,000

Hunter Tractor Company, Los Angeles, California
Hunter 15-25 (1919–1920)
(1) $7,000   (2) $10,000   (3) $12,000   (4) $14,000 (5) $18,000

Huron Tractor Company, Detroit, Michigan
Boyer Four 12-25 (1917)
(1) $6,500   (2) $9,500   (3) $12,750   (4) $14,500   (5) $18,000

Illinois Tractor Company, Bloomington, Illinois
Illinois Motor Cultivator (1916–1917)
(1) $3,800   (2) $6,500   (3) $8,000   (4) $9,500   (5) $12,000

The Illinois was a refined tractor that was also marketed in Canada as the Imperial Super-Drive. This 2-1/2-ton machine was very durable and is a handsome addition to a collection.

Illinois 12-30 (1918)
(1) $3,800   (2) $6,500   (3) $8,000   (4) $9,500   (5) $12,000

Illinois 18-30 Super-Drive (1919–1921)
(1) $4,200   (2) $7,500   (3) $10,000   (4) $12,500   (5) $16,000

Illinois 22-40 Super-Drive (1920)
(1) $4,800   (2) $8,500   (3) $11,500   (4) $14,000   (5) $19,000

Imperial Manufacturing Company, Minneapolis, Minnesota
Imperial 40-70 (1910–1920)
(1) $28,000   (2) $48,000   (3) $75,000   (4) $94,000   (5) $125,000

Indiana Silo and Tractor Company, Anderson, Indiana

The Indiana was introduced in 1919 as a one-plow replacement for the horse. A popular design in its short-lived era, this front-wheel-drive tractor could use horse-drawn implements and was sold at a price that was affordable for most small-time farmers. By the early 1920s, the Fordson tractor dominated the market and pushed many companies including the Indiana out of the tractor business. Collectors are attracted to the Indiana tractor partly because it is a prime example of an early 1920s small tractor. The Moline Universal, Bull, and Allis-Chalmers Model 6-12 had a similar appearance and marketing strategies.

Indiana Tractor (front-wheel drive, 1918-ca. 1922)
(1) $3,750   (2) $5,500   (3) $7,250   (4) $9,000   (5) $10,250

Intercontinental Manufacturing Company Incorporated, Grand Prairie (Garland), Texas
Model C-26 (Continental F-162 gasoline engine, 1948–1960)
(1) $500   (2) $2,500   (3) $6,000   (4) $12,000   (5) $20,000

Model D-26 or DE (Buda 4BD-153 diesel engine, 1948–1960)
(1) $900   (2) $3,500   (3) $8,500   (4) $16,000   (5) $28,000

Model DF (Buda 4BD-182 diesel engine, 1948–1960)
(1) $900   (2) $3,500   (3) $8,500   (4) $16,000   (5) $28,000

International Harvester Company, Chicago, Illinois

Of all the American tractor companies, International Harvester has the most antique tractors available for collectors. As the largest manufacturer of farm tractors for many years, International offered numerous versions and sizes. Cyrus McCormick is credited as the inventor of the first commercially successful reaper, perhaps the most valuable of all inventions during the 1800s. His first reaper was demonstrated in 1831 and by the second half of the century, the man was a millionaire. Competition began to get fierce during the last 20 years of the century. Cyrus McCormick II took over the company after his father's death in 1884, and by 1902 he helped McCormick Harvester merge with several competitors. The merger involved William Deering, its biggest competitor, and many others. The new International Harvester Company was born. Before the turn of the century, both McCormick and Deering had experimented with self-propelled hay mowers. The first Production International Harvester tractors were being built as early as 1906. By the 1940s, International was the industry giant for farm tractors and implements. The rich history of this company and the loyalty of many enthusiasts make the International tractors popular collectibles. The pricing trend seems to be similar to that of John Deere, but perhaps lagging by ten years. Expect the prices of the high-clearance and orchard versions to increase much more over the next few years.

Titan Type D, 20 HP (1910–1914)
(1) $20,000   (2) $30,000   (3) $50,000   (4) $125,000 (5) $150,000

Titan Type D, 25 HP (1910–1914)
(1) $20,000   (2) $30,000   (3) $50,000   (4) $125,000 (5) $150,000

Titan Type D 18-35 HP (1913–1916)
(1) $14,000   (2) $24,000   (3) $40,000   (4) $58,000   (5) $80,000

Titan Type D 30-60 HP (1914–1917)
(1) $77,000   (2) $100,000   (3) $125,000   (4) $160,000 (5) $200,000

15-30 (transverse 4-cylinder, exposed flywheel, 1915–1922)
(1) $15,000 (2) $20,000   (3) $30,000   (4) $40,000 (5) $50,000

Mogul 12-25 HP (12 known to exist, 1913–1918)
(1) $12,000 (2) $15,000   (3) $25,000   (4) $40,000 (5) $50,000

Mogul 8-16 HP (single-cylinder, 1915–1917)
(1) $8,000   (2) $15,000   (3) $20,000   (4) $26,000 (5) $30,000

Mogul 10-20 HP (single-cylinder, 1916–1919)
(1) $9,500   (2) $17,000   (3) $22,500   (4) $29,000 (5) $35,000

Titan 10-20 HP (2-cylinder, 1916–1922)
(1) $2,825   (2) $4,500   (3) $6,500   (4) $9,325 (5) $13,175

8-16, chain-drive (sloping hood, 1917–1922)
(1) $2,825   (2) $4,325   (3) $6,400   (4) $7,400 (5) $10,500

Model 15-30 and 22-36 (gear drive, steel wheels, 1921–1934)
(1) $650   (2) $1,225   (3) $1,625   (4) $2,275 (5) $3,025

Model 15-30 and 22-36 (gear drive, rubber tires, 1921–1934)
(1) $600   (2) $1,025   (3) $1,425   (4) $2,175 (5) $2,825

About 33,000 International 8-16 chain-drive tractors were built during their production run from 1917 to 1922. A tractor similar to this one was used in the Robert Redford movie, *The Natural*. High publicity will sometimes boost the demand of certain models.

Model 10-20 (regular gear drive, steel wheels, 1923–1939)
(1) $450   (2) $700   (3) $1,525   (4) $1,950 (5) $2,525

Model 10-20 (regular gear drive, rubber tires, 1923–1939)
(1) $425   (2) $500   (3) $1,325   (4) $1,750 (5) $2,325

Model 10-20 NT (narrow-tread, 1926–1934)
(1) $700   (2) $1,000   (3) $1,750   (4) $2,325 (5) $3,325

Farmall "Regular" (steel wheels, 1924–1932)
(1) $425   (2) $725   (3) $1,250   (4) $2,175 (5) $2,825

Farmall "Regular" (rubber tires, 1924–1932)
(1) $325   (2) $625   (3) $1,175   (4) $1,975 (5) $2,575

Farmall "Regular Fairway" (1926–1931)
(1) $625   (2) $1,000   (3) $1,750   (4) $2,575 (5) $3,325

Farmall F-30 (steel wheels, dual narrow front, 1931–1939)
(1) $895   (2) $1,400   (3) $1,825   (4) $2,975 (5) $3,800

Farmall F-30 (rubber tires, dual narrow front, 1931–1939)
(1) $835   (2) $1,250   (3) $1,825   (4) $3,000   (5) $3,825

Farmall F-30 (steel wheels, wide-front, 1931–1939)
(1) $1,915   (2) $2,500   (3) $3,825   (4) $4,675   (5) $5,500

Farmall F-30 (rubber tires, wide-front, 1931–1939)
(1) $1,835   (2) $2,325   (3) $3,325   (4) $4,325   (5) $5,175

Farmall F-30 High-clearance (rubber tires, 1931–1939)
(1) $2,165   (2) $3,075   (3) $4,675   (4) $5,825   (5) $7,175

McCormick-Deering W-30 (steel wheels, 1932–1940)
(1) $515   (2) $1,425   (3) $2,325   (4) $3,200   (5) $4,175

McCormick-Deering W-30 (rubber tires, 1932–1940)
(1) $515   (2) $1,400   (3) $2,275   (4) $3,250   (5) $4,225

McCormick-Deering I-30 (industrial, rubber tires, 1932–1940)
(1) $800   (2) $1,825   (3) $2,925   (4) $4,000   (5) $5,175

McCormick-Deering W-30 Orchard (rubber tires, 1932–1940)
(1) $750   (2) $1,725   (3) $2,775   (4) $3,900   (5) $5,100

Farmall F-20 (steel wheels, dual narrow front, 1932–1939)
(1) $600   (2) $800   (3) $1,125   (4) $1,675   (5) $2,425

Farmall F-20 (rubber tires, dual narrow front, 1932–1939)
(1) $415   (2) $765   (3) $1,175   (4) $1,775   (5) $2,425

Farmall F-20 (steel wheels, wide-front, 1932–1939)
(1) $1,265   (2) $1,750   (3) $2,670   (4) $3,325   (5) $4,000

Farmall F-20 (rubber tires, wide-front, 1932–1939)
(1) $1,335   (2) $1,825   (3) $2,675   (4) $3,325   (5) $4,000

Farmall F-20 (dished cast wheels, wide-front, 1938)
(1) $1,300   (2) $1,775   (3) $2,650   (4) $3,350   (5) $4,975

Farmall F-20 (steel wheels, single front wheel, 1938)
(1) $900   (2) $1,275   (3) $1,725   (4) $2,275   (5) $2,900

Farmall F-12 (Waukesha engine, steel wheels, 1932–1933)
(1) $1,100   (2) $1,475   (3) $2,275   (4) $3,000   (5) $3,750

Farmall F-12 (steel wheels, single front wheel, 1933–1938)
(1) $465   (2) $985   (3) $1,275   (4) $1,575   (5) $1,925

Farmall F-12 (rubber tires, single front wheel, 1933–1938)
(1) $435   (2) $935   (3) $1,270   (4) $1,500   (5) $1,825

Farmall F-12 (steel wheels, dual narrow front, 1933–1938)
(1) $415   (2) $685   (3) $1,125   (4) $1,400   (5) $1,725

Farmall F-12 (rubber tires, dual narrow front, 1933–1938)
(1) $350　(2) $615　(3) $950　(4) $1,275　(5) $1,675

Farmall F-12 (steel wheels, wide-front, 1933–1938)
(1) $1,170　(2) $1,550　(3) $1,975　(4) $2,575　(5) $3,175

Farmall F-12 (rubber tires, wide-front, 1933–1938)
(1) $1,175　(2) $1,425　(3) $1,925　(4) $2,575　(5) $3,100

McCormick-Deering W-12 (steel wheels, 1934–1938)
(1) $1,025　(2) $1,375　(3) $2,175　(4) $3,250　(5) $3,825

McCormick-Deering W-12 (rubber tires, 1934–1938)
(1) $785　(2) $1,125　(3) $1,725　(4) $2,750　(5) $3,325

McCormick-Deering O-12 and Fairway-12 (rubber tires, 1934–1938)
(1) $1,575　(2) $2,075　(3) $3,175　(4) $4,325　(5) $5,325

McCormick-Deering I-12 (rubber tires, industrial, 1934–1938)
(1) $1,120　(2) $1,675　(3) $2,675　(4) $3,500　(5) $4,325

Farmall F-14 (steel wheels, dual narrow front, 1938–1939)
(1) $420　(2) $800　(3) $1,200　(4) $1,925　(5) $2,500

Farmall F-14 (rubber tires, dual narrow front, 1938–1939)
(1) $400　(2) $685　(3) $1,125　(4) $1,575　(5) $2,175

Farmall F-14 (steel wheels, single front wheel, 1938–1939)
(1) $550　(2) $885　(3) $1,375　(4) $1,975　(5) $2,575

Farmall F-14 (rubber tires, single front wheel, 1938–1939)
(1) $500　(2) $920　(3) $1,450　(4) $1,900　(5) $2,500

Farmall F-14 (steel wheels, wide-front, 1938–1939)
(1) $1,325　(2) $1,675　(3) $2,175　(4) $2,925　(5) $3,500

Farmall F-14 (rubber tires, wide-front, 1938–1939)
(1) $1,375　(2) $1,725　(3) $2,175　(4) $2,750　(5) $3,575

McCormick-Deering W-14 (steel wheels, 1938–1939)
(1) $1,150　(2) $1,975　(3) $3,100　(4) $4,175　(5) $5,000

McCormick-Deering W-14 (rubber tires, 1938–1939)
(1) $920　(2) $1,500　(3) $2,500　(4) $3,675　(5) $4,675

McCormick-Deering O-14 and Fairway-14 (rubber tires, 1938–1939)
(1) $1,050　(2) $1,575　(3) $2,925　(4) $4,000　(5) $5,000

McCormick-Deering W-40 (steel wheels, nondiesel, 1935–1940)
(1) $1,100　(2) $1,750　(3) $2,700　(4) $3,500　(5) $4,500

McCormick-Deering W-40 (rubber tires, nondiesel, 1935–1940)
(1) $1,000　(2) $1,600　(3) $2,500　(4) $3,250　(5) $3,900

McCormick-Deering WD-40 (steel wheels, diesel, 1935–1940)
(1) $975   (2) $2,000   (3) $2,750   (4) $4,250   (5) $6,250

McCormick-Deering WD-40 (rubber tires, diesel, 1935–1940)
(1) $800   (2) $1,250   (3) $2,375   (4) $4,125   (5) $6,000

McCormick-Deering IK-40 (rubber tires, industrial, nondiesel, 1935–1940)
(1) $1,250   (2) $2,100   (3) $3,000   (4) $3,750   (5) $5,500

McCormick-Deering ID-40 (rubber tires, industrial, diesel, 1935–1940)
(1) $1,125   (2) $1,725   (3) $2,750   (4) $3,750   (5) 5,750

Farmall A (1939–1947)
(1) $550   (2) $725   (3) $1,125   (4) $1,750   (5) $3,000

Farmall AV (high-clearance, 1939–1947)
(1) $1,350   (2) $1,750   (3) $2,250   (4) $2,900   (5) $4,000

Farmall Super A (1947–1954)
(1) $750   (2) $1,000   (3) $1,350   (4) $2,250   (5) $3,125

Farmall Super A (authentic demonstrator, painted white, 1950)
(1) $1,750   (2) $3,250   (3) $4,500   (4) $5,750   (5) $6,250

Farmall Super AV (1947–1954)
(1) $1,650   (2) $2,000   (3) $2,500   (4) $3,250   (5) $4,250

Farmall B (dual narrow front, 1939–1947)
(1) $525   (2) $825   (3) $1,000   (4) $1,400   (5) $2,250

Farmall B (single front wheel, 1939–1947)
(1) $525   (2) $750   (3) $1,125   (4) $1,500   (5) $2,425

Farmall BN (narrow tread, 1939–1947)
(1) $550   (2) $800   (3) $1,175   (4) $1,750   (5) $2,500

Farmall H (rubber tires, dual narrow front axle, 1939–1953)
(1) $535   (2) $800   (3) $1,150   (4) $1,850   (5) $2,525

Farmall H (steel wheels, dual narrow front axle, 1939–1953)
(1) $720   (2) $1,100   (3) $1,625   (4) $2,125   (5) $2,900

Farmall H (rubber tires, single front wheel, 1939–1953)
(1) $690   (2) $1,150   (3) $1,650   (4) $2,175   (5) $3,050

Farmall H (rubber tires, wide-front axle, 1939–1953)
(1) $825   (2) $1,300   (3) $1,750   (4) $2,300   (5) $3,025

Farmall HV (rubber tires, high-clearance, 1942–1953)
(1) $1,100   (2) $1,550   (3) $2,675   (4) $4,175   (5) $5,000

Farmall Super H (narrow front axle, 1953–1954)
(1) $635   (2) $800   (3) $1,225   (4) $1,900   (5) $3,500

Farmall Super H (single front wheel, 1953–1954)
(1) $650   (2) $875   (3) $1,350   (4) $2,050   (5) $3,775

Farmall Super H (wide-front axle, 1953–1954)
(1) $1,000   (2) $1,500   (3) $2,075   (4) $2,875   (5) $4,000

Farmall Super HV (high-clearance, 1953–1954)
(1) $1,500   (2) $2,325   (3) $3,325   (4) $4,325   (5) $5,325

Farmall 1939 M (rubber tires, dual narrow front, 1939)
(1) $700   (2) $1,175   (3) $2,000   (4) $2,825   (5) $4,175

Farmall M (rubber tires, dual narrow front, 1940–1952)
(1) $550   (2) $950   (3) $1,325   (4) $2,000   (5) $3,075

Farmall M (steel wheels, dual narrow front, 1940–1952)
(1) $1,100   (2) $1,450   (3) $2,075   (4) $2,775   (5) $3,825

Farmall M (rubber tires, single front wheel, 1940–1952)
(1) $970   (2) $1,350   (3) $1,825   (4) $2,600   (5) $3,775

Farmall M (rubber tires, wide-front axle, 1940–1952)
(1) $785   (2) $1,225   (3) $1,850   (4) $2,775   (5) $3,925

Farmall MV (high-clearance, rubber tires, 1942–1952)
(1) $1,385   (2) $2,000   (3) $3,325   (4) $4,675   (5) $6,000

Farmall MD diesel (rubber tires, dual narrow front, 1941–1952)
(1) $820   (2) $1,275   (3) $2,000   (4) $3,175   (5) $4,425

Farmall MD diesel (rubber tires, wide-front, 1941–1952)
(1) $1,050   (2) $1,575   (3) $2,500   (4) $3,575   (5) $4,825

Farmall MDV diesel (high-clearance, 1942–1952)
(1) $1,675   (2) $2,325   (3) $4,000   (4) $5,325   (5) $7,000

Farmall M (6M Sheppard diesel engine conversion, dual narrow front, 1939–1952)
(1) $ 2,700 (2) $4,250   (3) $5,800   (4) $7,300   (5) $8,800

Farmall Super M (narrow front axle, 1952–1954)
(1) $1,000   (2) $1,575   (3) $2,325   (4) $3,175   (5) $4,000

Farmall Super M (single front wheel, 1952–1954)
(1) $1,125   (2) $1,775   (3) $2,575   (4) $3,500   (5) $4,325

Farmall Super M (wide-front axle, 1952–1954)
(1) $1,550   (2) $2,150   (3) $3,075   (4) $3,650   (5) $4,525

Farmall Super M-TA (narrow front axle, torque amplifier, 1952–1954)
(1) $2,025   (2) $2,650   (3) $3,500   (4) $4,500   (5) $5,500

Farmall Super M-TA (wide-front axle, torque amplifier, 1952–1954)
(1) $2,250 (2) $2,925 (3) $4,000 (4) $4,900 (5) $6,000

Farmall Super MV (high-clearance, 1952–1954)
(1) $1,675 (2) $2,250 (3) $3,500 (4) $4,675 (5) $6,325

Farmall Super MV-TA (high-clearance, torque amplifier, 1952–1954)
(1) $2,325 (2) $3,175 (3) $4,500 (4) $5,675 (5) $7,500

Farmall Super MD diesel (1952–1954)
(1) $1,170 (2) $1,675 (3) $2,400 (4) $3,325 (5) $4,325

Farmall Super MD-TA diesel (torque amplifier, 1952–1954)
(1) $1,575 (2) $2,500 (3) $3,500 (4) $4,750 (5) $5,825

Farmall Super MDV diesel (high-clearance, 1952–1954)
(1) $1,750 (2) $2,575 (3) $4,275 (4) $5,750 (5) $7,075

Farmall Super MDV-TA diesel (high-clearance, torque amplifier, 1952–1954)
(1) $2,500 (2) $3,325 (3) $5,325 (4) $6,675 (5) $8,175

Farmall C (dual narrow front axle, 1948–1951)
(1) $615 (2) $965 (3) $1,400 (4) $2,025 (5) $2,800

Farmall C (authentic demonstrator, white paint, 1950)
(1) $1,500 (2) $3,000 (3) $4,250 (4) $5,500 (5) $6,000

Farmall C (single front wheel, 1948–1951)
(1) $685 (2) $1,050 (3) $1,500 (4) $2,175 (5) $3,000

Farmall C (wide-front axle, 1948–1951)
(1) $820 (2) $1,175 (3) $1,825 (4) $2,275 (5) $3,275

Farmall Super C (dual narrow front axle, 1951–1954)
(1) $835 (2) $1,250 (3) $1,875 (4) $2,475 (5) $3,125

Farmall Super C (single front wheel, 1951–1954)
(1) $870 (2) $1,275 (3) $1,900 (4) $2,550 (5) $3,225

Farmall Super C (wide-front axle, 1951–1954)
(1) $1,200 (2) $1,625 (3) $2,300 (4) $2,825 (5) $3,650

Farmall Cub (1947–1953)
(1) $735 (2) $1,175 (3) $1,425 (4) $1,925 (5) $2,675

Farmall Cub (authentic demonstrator, painted white, 1950)
(1) $2,000 (2) $3,500 (3) $4,750 (4) $6,000 (5) $6,500

Farmall Cub (1954–1958)
(1) $970 (2) $1,350 (3) $1,800 (4) $2,500 (5) $3,175

International Cub (1958–1964)
(1) $1,125 (2) $1,725 (3) $2,275 (4) $2,975 (5) $3,625

From 1921 to 1934, about 150,000 examples of the McCormick-Deering 15-30 were sold. The tractor was rerated 22-36 by 1929. This 1921 15-30 has an uncommon PTO option that adds to its value. Collectors love to have something about their tractor that makes it special. In certain cases, rare options are worth more than the unrestored tractor it equips.

International Cub Lo-Boy (1955–1964)
(1) $1,250   (2) $1,700   (3) $2,250   (4) $3,075   (5) $3,775

McCormick-Deering W-4 (steel wheels, 1940–1953)
(1) $670   (2) $1,175   (3) $1,675   (4) $2,275   (5) $2,825

McCormick-Deering W-4 (rubber tires, 1940–1953)
(1) $670   (2) $1,075   (3) $1,650   (4) $2,275   (5) $2,850

McCormick-Deering OS-4 Orchard Special (rubber tires, no citrus fenders, 1940–1953)
(1) $885   (2) $1,425   (3) $1,925   (4) $2,675   (5) $3,275

McCormick-Deering O-4 Orchard (rubber tires, full citrus fenders, 1940–1953)
(1) $1,250   (2) $1,825   (3) $2,575   (4) $3,850   (5) $4,675

International I-4 (industrial, regular-duty, 1940–1953)
(1) $650   (2) $1,175   (3) $1,675   (4) $2,300   (5) $3,000

International I-4 Heavy-duty (heavy-duty axles, hydraulic brakes, 1940–1953)
(1) $670   (2) $1,225   (3) $1,800   (4) $2,500   (5) $3,225

McCormick-Deering Super W-4 (1953–1954)
(1) $900   (2) $1,425   (3) $1,875   (4) $2,425   (5) $3,075

McCormick-Deering W-6 (1952–1954)
(1) $800   (2) $1,175   (3) $1,675   (4) $2,325   (5) $2,925

McCormick-Deering W-6 (Sheppard diesel conversion, 1940–1953)
(1) $3,200   (2) $4,750   (3) $6,800   (4) $7,800   (5) $9,800

McCormick-Deering WD-6 (diesel, 1940–1953)
(1) $800   (2) $1,175   (3) $1,675   (4) $2,225   (5) $2,950

McCormick-Deering OS-6 Orchard Special (no citrus fenders, 1940–1953)
(1) $1,150   (2) $1,650   (3) $2,275   (4) $2,825   (5) $3,500

McCormick-Deering ODS-6 Orchard Special diesel (no citrus fenders, 1940–1953)
(1) $1,100   (2) $1,750   (3) $2,300   (4) $2,875   (5) $3,575

McCormick-Deering O-6 Orchard (citrus fenders, 1940–1953)
(1) $1,675   (2) $2,475   (3) $2,575   (4) $4,000   (5) $4,825

McCormick-Deering Super W-6 (1952–1954)
(1) $1,325   (2) $1,900   (3) $2,600   (4) $3,325   (5) $4,075

McCormick-Deering Super WD-6 (diesel, 1952–1954)
(1) $1,275   (2) $1,925   (3) $2,775   (4) $3,475   (5) $4,325

McCormick-Deering Super W-6-TA (torque amplifier, 1952–1954)
(1) $2,000   (2) $2,900   (3) $4,325   (4) $5,825   (5) $7,500

McCormick-Deering Super W-6-TA (diesel, torque amplifier, 1952–1954)
(1) $2,075   (2) $3,000   (3) $4,500   (4) $6,000   (5) $7,825

International I-6 (industrial, regular-duty, 1940–1953)
(1) $885   (2) $1,250   (3) $1,900   (4) $2,575   (5) $3,250

International I-6 Heavy-duty (heavy-duty axles, hydraulic brakes, 1940–1953)
(1) $820   (2) $1,250   (3) $1,925   (4) $2,600   (5) $3,275

International ID-6 (diesel, industrial, 1940–1953)
(1) $720   (2) $1,125   (3) $1,650   (4) $2,250   (5) $3,000

International ID-6 Heavy-duty (diesel, heavy-duty axles, hydraulic brakes, 1940–1953)
(1) $600   (2) $1,025   (3) $1,525   (4) $2,250   (5) $2,825

McCormick-Deering W-9 (1940–1954)
(1) $750   (2) $1,375   (3) $1,850   (4) $2,575   (5) $3,075

McCormick-Deering WD-9 (diesel, 1940–1954)
(1) $985   (2) $1,475   (3) $2,075   (4) $2,675   (5) $3,325

McCormick-Deering WR-9 (rice tractor, 1940–1954)
(1) $1,200   (2) $1,725   (3) $2,425   (4) $2,975   (5) $3,825

McCormick-Deering WDR-9 (diesel, rice tractor, 1940–1954)
(1) $1,150   (2) $1,525   (3) $2,325   (4) $2,925   (5) $3,825

McCormick-Deering Super WD-9 (diesel, 1953–1956)
(1) $1,000   (2) $1,625   (3) $2,475   (4) $3,250   (5) $4,150

McCormick-Deering Super WDR-9 (diesel, rice tractor, 1953–1956)
(1) $1,225   (2) $1,675   (3) $2,625   (4) $3,500   (5) $4,500

International I-9 (industrial, 1940–1954)
(1) $1,100   (2) $1,475   (3) $2,175   (4) $2,750   (5) $3,750

International ID-9 diesel (industrial, 1940–1954)
(1) $1,000 (2) $1,450 (3) $2,150 (4) $2,725 (5) $3,750

International I-9 Heavy-duty (heavy-duty axles, hydraulic brakes, 1940–1954)
(1) $1,225 (2) $1,775 (3) $2,625 (4) $3,250 (5) $4,250

International ID-9 Heavy-duty (diesel, heavy-duty axles, hydraulic brakes, 1940–1954)
(1) $1,100 (2) $1,500 (3) $2,500 (4) $3,100 (5) $4,250

Farmall 100 (1954–1956)
(1) $1,200 (2) $1,625 (3) $2,425 (4) $2,625 (5) $3,325

Farmall 100 High-clearance (1954–1956)
(1) $1,825 (2) $2,550 (3) $3,000 (4) $4,000 (5) $4,825

International 100 (1954–1956)
(1) $1,325 (2) $1,850 (3) $2,225 (4) $2,775 (5) $3,525

Farmall 130 (1956–1958)
(1) $1,175 (2) $1,750 (3) $2,175 (4) $2,925 (5) $3,575

Farmall 130 High-clearance (1956–1958)
(1) $1,825 (2) $2,575 (3) $3,500 (4) $4,325 (5) $5,325

The Farmall Regular is a popular tractor with much character. Over 134,000 of these units were sold from 1924 to 1932. The Regular in this picture is the third one ever built. Any extremely low serial number makes a popular model tractor much more valuable. This 1924 tractor serial no. QC-503 is part of the Case-New Holland Historical Collection.

International 130 (1956–1958)
(1) $1,250 (2) $1,825 (3) $2,325 (4) $3,000 (5) $3,675

Farmall 140 (1958–1964)
(1) $1,250 (2) $1,850 (3) $2,300 (4) $3,200 (5) $3,975

Farmall 140 High-clearance (1958–1964)
(1) $1,900 (2) $2,750 (3) $3,750 (4) $4,550 (5) $5,475

International 140 (1958–1964)
(1) $1,350 (2) $1,950 (3) $2,475 (4) $3,400 (5) $4,000

Farmall 200 (narrow, dual front, 1954–1956)
(1) $920 (2) $1,750 (3) $2,250 (4) $2,920 (5) $3,750

Farmall 200 (single front wheel, 1954–1956)
(1) $1,100   (2) $1,950   (3) $2,550   (4) $3,200   (5) $4,000

Farmall 230 (1956–1958)
(1) $950   (2) $1,775   (3) $2,325   (4) $3,175   (5) $3,825

Farmall 300 (1954–1956)
(1) $920   (2) $1,375   (3) $1,967   (4) $2,775   (5) $3,500

Farmall 300 High-clearance (1954–1956)
(1) $1,750   (2) $2,325   (3) $3,000   (4) $4,000   (5) $4,825

International 300 Utility (1955–1956)
(1) $835   (2) $1,475   (3) $2,175   (4) $2,825   (5) $3,550

International 330 (1957–1958)
(1) $965   (2) $1,475   (3) $2,175   (4) $2,750   (5) $3,500

Farmall 350 (gasoline, 1956–1958)
(1) $1,075   (2) $1,675   (3) $2,075   (4) $2,675   (5) $3,325

Farmall 350 (diesel, 1956–1958)
(1) $1,125   (2) $1,775   (3) $2,225   (4) $3,000   (5) $3,675

Farmall 350 High-clearance (gasoline, 1956–1958)
(1) $1,675   (2) $2,250   (3) $3,225   (4) $4,900   (5) $6,000

Farmall 350 High-clearance (diesel, 1956–1958)
(1) $2,025   (2) $2,575   (3) $3,500   (4) $5,175   (5) $6,175

International 350 Utility (1956–1958)
(1) $900   (2) $1,600   (3) $2,400   (4) $3,100   (5) $3,750

International 350 Utility (diesel, 1956–1958)
(1) $850   (2) $1,350   (3) $2,250   (4) $3,000   (5) $3,750

International 350 Utility (LPG, 1956–1958)
(1) $750   (2) $1,250   (3) $2,000   (4) $2,750   (5) $3,500

International 350 Hi-Utility (1956–1958)
(1) $1,000   (2) $1,875   (3) $2,850   (4) $3,750   (5) $4,500

International 350 Wheatland (1956–1958)
(1) $1,100   (2) $2,100   (3) $2,875   (4) $3,500   (5) $4,375

Farmall 400 (gasoline, 1954–1956)
(1) $920   (2) $1,475   (3) $2,325   (4) $3,175   (5) $3,825

Farmall 400 (diesel, 1954–1956)
(1) $1,000   (2) $1,475   (3) $2,100   (4) $3,175   (5) $4,175

Farmall 400 High-clearance (gasoline, 1954–1956)
(1) $1,475   (2) $2,150   (3) $3,325   (4) $4,500   (5) $5,500

This International 400 Diesel high-clearance tractor stands 93-inches tall at the steering wheel. These tractors are rare and very desirable to collectors. The limited production combined with the stately posture make them a collector favorite.

Farmall 400 High-clearance (diesel, 1954–1956)
(1) $1,425   (2) $2,100   (3) $3,325   (4) $4,550   (5) $5,600

Farmall 450 (gasoline, 1956–1958)
(1) $1,475   (2) $2,025   (3) $2,825   (4) $3,725   (5) $4,575

Farmall 450 (diesel, 1956–1958)
(1) $1,525   (2) $2,000   (3) $2,875   (4) $3,850   (5) $4,750

Farmall 450 (LPG, 1956–1958)
(1) $1,725   (2) $2,575   (3) $2,975   (4) $3,750   (5) $4,575

Farmall 450 High-clearance (1956–1958)
(1) $2,175   (2) $2,675   (3) $4,000   (4) $5,500   (5) $6,500

Farmall 450 High-clearance (diesel, 1956–1958)
(1) $2,325   (2) $3,150   (3) $4,175   (4) $6,325   (5) $7,175

International W-400 (1954–1956)
(1) $2,000   (2) $2,500   (3) $3,500   (4) $4,500   (5) $5,000

International W-400 (diesel, 1954–1956)
(1) $2,000   (2) $3,000   (3) $4,000   (4) $4,750   (5) $5,500

International W-400 (LPG, 1954–1956)
(1) $2,000   (2) $3,500   (3) $4,500   (4) $5,500   (5) $6,000

International W-450 (gasoline, 1956–1958)
(1) $2,000   (2) $3,500   (3) $4,500   (4) $5,500   (5) $6,000

International W-450 (diesel, 1956–1958)
(1) $2,500   (2) $4,000   (3) $5,000   (4) $6,000   (5) $7,500

International W-450 (LPG, 1956–1958)
(1) $3,500   (2) $4,000   (3) $5,000   (4) $6,000   (5) $7,500

International W-600 (1956–1957)
(1) $6,250   (2) $10,000   (3) $12,000   (4) $14,250 (5) $18,000

International W-600 (diesel, 1956–1957)
(1) $2,400   (2) $3,200   (3) $4,400   (4) $6,000   (5) $8,000

International W-650 (diesel, 1956–1958)
(1) $2,200 (2) $3,350 (3) $5,000 (4) $5,750 (5) $8,000

International W-650 (LPG, 1956–1958)
(1) $2,300 (2) $3,500 (3) $5,500 (4) $7,000 (5) $9,000

Interstate Tractor and Engine Company, Waterloo, Iowa
Plow Boy 10-20 (1917)
(1) $4,500 (2) $6,200 (3) $9,000 (4) $11,000 (5) $14,000

Plow Man 13-30 (1917–1919)
(1) $4,800 (2) $6,700 (3) $9,500 (4) $11,750 (5) $15,000

Plow Man 15-30 (1918–1919)
(1) $4,800 (2) $6,700 (3) $9,500 (4) $11,750 (5) $15,000

Joliet Oil Tractor Company, Joliet, Illinois
Joliet 22-40 (ca. 1914)
(1) $14,000 (2) $17,500 (3) $20,000 (4) $26,000 (5) $34,000

Jumbo Steel Products, Azusa, California
Simpson Jumbo Model B (tricycle, Chrysler 6-cylinder, ca. 1947)
(1) $1,400 (2) $2,750 (3) $6,800 (4) $10,800 (5) $14,500

Jumbo Steel Products sold the Simpson Jumbo after World War II, when the demand for farm tractors was at a peak. An impeccable copy with a narrow-front axle was sold from the late Ed Spiess' collection in 1999 for $14,000.

Simpson Jumbo Model C
(standard tread, Chrysler 6-cylinder, ca. 1947)
(1) $1,400 (2) $2,800 (3) $7,000 (4) $11,000 (5) $15,000

Kansas City Hay Press Company, Kansas City, Missouri
Model L Prairie Dog 9-18 (rerated 10-18, 1918–1921)
(1) $9,000 (2) $14,000 (3) $17,000 (4) $21,000 (5) $26,000

Model D Prairie Dog 15-30 (1920)
(1) $10,000 (2) $16,000 (3) $21,000 (4) $25,000 (5) $30,000

Kardell Tractor and Truck Company, St. Louis, Missouri
Kardell Four-In-One 20-32 (1917–1918)
(1) $7,500 (2) $10,500 (3) $13,000 (4) $15,000 (5) $19,000

Kardell Utility 10-20 (1918–1921)
(1) $5,000   (2) $8,000   (3) $9,500   (4) $12,000 (5) $15,000

Kardell Standard (1918–1921)
(1) $7,500   (2) $8,500   (3) $11,000   (4) $17,000 (5) $22,000

Kaywood Corporation, Benton Harbor, Michigan

"Kay" was the first name and "Wood" was the last name of the wives of the two founders of this company. Built only in 1937 as a variation of the Parrett tractor, the Kaywood is a rare tractor today.

Kaywood Model D (five known to exist, 1937)
(1) $3,500   (2) $4,500   (3) $8,000   (4) $11,250 (5) $13,500

Keck-Gonnerman Company, Mt. Vernon, Indiana
Model 12-24 (rerated 15-30, 1917–1928)
(1) $9,000   (2) $12,000   (3) $14,500   (4) $16,000 (5) $19,000

Kay-Gee 18-35 (1928–1935)
(1) $3,500   (2) $5,500   (3) $7,000   (4) $8,500   (5) $11,000

Kay-Gee 25-50 (1928–1930)
(1) $4,500   (2) $8,000   (3) $10,000   (4) $11,500 (5) $14,000

Kay-Gee 27-55 (rerated 30-60, 1928–1937)
(1) $6,000   (2) $11,000   (3) $13,500   (4) $15,000 (5) $18,000

Kay-Gee ZW (1935–1946)
(1) $3,500   (2) $5,500   (3) $7,000   (4) $8,500   (5) $11,000

Kimble and Dentler Company, Vicksburg, Michigan
Kimble 40 horsepower (1913)
(1) $11,000   (2) $15,000   (3) $18,000   (4) $20,000 (5) $24,000

Kinkead Tractor Company, Minneapolis, Minnesota
K. T. 16 (12-25, 2 rear drive wheels, 1917)
(1) $6,000   (2) $8,500   (3) $10,000   (4) $12,500 (5) $15,000

K. T. 17 (12-30, single rear drive wheel, 1917)
(1) $6,000   (2) $8,500   (3) $10,000   (4) $12,500 (5) $15,000

Kinnard-Haines Company, Minneapolis, Minnesota
Flour City 30 horsepower (1908–1910)
(1) $20,000   (2) $28,000   (3) $33,000   (4) $40,000 (5) $48,000

Flour City 40-70 (1910–1927)
(1) $36,000   (2) $60,000   (3) $80,000   (4) $100,000 (5) $125,000

Flour City 20-35 (rerated 18-35, 1911–1927)
(1) $19,000   (2) $26,000   (3) $31,000   (4) $38,000 (5) $44,000

Flour City 30-50 (1911–1927)
(1) $34,000   (2) $45,000   (3) $53,000   (4) $64,000 (5) $79,000

Flour City Junior 12-20 (1918)
(1) $14,000   (2) $18,000   (3) $24,000   (4) $30,000   (5) $35,000

Kinnard Four-Plow (1915–1917)
(1) $12,000   (2) $17,000   (3) $22,000   (4) $25,000   (5) $32,000

Flour City 15-25 (1918–1919)
(1) $15,000   (2) $21,000   (3) $26,000   (4) $31,000   (5) $38,000

Flour City Junior 14-24 (1919–1927)
(1) $14,000   (2) $18,000   (3) $24,000   (4) $30,000   (5) $35,000

Knickerbocker Motors Incorporated, Poughkeepsie, New York
Kingwood 5-10 (1919–1920)
(1) $6,500   (2) $10,000   (3) $12,000   (4) $14,500   (5) $18,000

L. A. Auto Tractor Company, Los Angeles, California
Little Bear (Ford car parts, 1919–1921)
(1) $8,000   (2) $12,000   (3) $15,000   (4) $18,000   (5) $22,000

La Crosse Boiler Company, La Crosse, Wisconsin
La Crosse 12-25 (1931–1937)
(1) $10,000   (2) $16,000   (3) $21,000   (4) $25,000   (5) $30,000

La Crosse 20-40 (steam-style gasoline tractor, 1931–1937)
(1) $13,000   (2) $20,000   (3) $28,000   (4) $33,000   (5) $40,000

La Crosse 30-60 (steam-style gasoline tractor, 1931–1937)
(1) $20,000   (2) $32,000   (3) $40,000   (4) $50,000   (5) $64,000

La Crosse Tractor Company, La Crosse, Wisconsin
The Sta-Rite Engine Company and the Happy Farmer Tractor Company joined in 1916 to form the La Crosse Tractor Company. By 1922 the Oshkosh Tractor Company bought out the La Crosse interests and although they showed good intentions, the tractor production ended. The Happy Farmer and La Crosse tractors have significant interest to collectors. The primitive appearance (by today's standards) and the historical significance of these tractors make them expensive items. The reign-drive units are extremely scarce. As new museums sprout up, one may expect the availability of La Crosse tractors to become very poor. Restored models are popular attractions wherever displayed.

La Crosse Model A 8-16 (3 wheel, 1916–1918)
(1) $5,500   (2) $8,000   (3) $10,500   (4) $12,250   (5) $15,000

La Crosse Model B 12-24 (3 wheel, 1916–1918)
(1) $5,000   (2) $7,500   (3) $10,000   (4) $11,750   (5) $13,500

La Crosse Model F 12-24 (3 wheel, 1919–1920)
(1) $5,000   (2) $7,500   (3) $10,000   (4) $11,750   (5) $13,500

La Crosse Model G 12-25 (4 wheel, 1919–1920)
(1) $5,000   (2) $7,750   (3) $10,250   (4) $12,250   (5) $14,000

La Crosse Model M 7-12 Rein-Drive (1921–1922)
(1) $18,000   (2) $25,000   (3) $33,000   (4) $40,000   (5) $50,000

La Crosse Model H 12-24 Rein-Drive (1921–1922)
(1) $18,000   (2) $25,000   (3) $33,000   (4) $40,000   (5) $50,000

Lambert Gas Engine Company, Anderson, Indiana
Lambert Orchard Tractor (1913–1914)
(1) $10,000   (2) $16,000   (3) $20,000   (4) $25,000   (5) $32,000

Lambert Steel Hoof (1913–1914)
(1) $10,000   (2) $16,000   (3) $20,000   (4) $25,000   (5) $32,000

Lang Tractor Company, Minneapolis, Minnesota
Lang 15-30 (1917–1920)
(1) $4,500   (2) $7,500   (3) $10,000   (4) $14,000   (5) $19,000

Laughlin Tractor Incorporated, Marshall, Texas
Laughlin C-27 (1948)
(1) $4,450   (2) $5,950   (3) $8,550   (4) $10,750   (5) $14,000

John Lauson Manufacturing Company, New Holstein, Wisconsin
Lauson 15-25 (1916–1919)
(1) $6,000   (2) $8,500   (3) $11,750   (4) $13,750   (5) $17,000

Lauson 20-35 (1916)
(1) $6,250   (2) $10,000   (3) $13,500   (4) $16,500   (5) $20,000

Lauson 15-30 (1920–1921)
(1) $5,500   (2) $9,000   (3) $12,000   (4) $15,000   (5) $18,250

Lauson 15-30 Road Tractor (1920–1921)
(1) $6,000   (2) $9,750   (3) $13,000   (4) $16,000   (5) $19,000

Lauson 12-25 (1922–1925)
(1) $4,250   (2) $7,750   (3) $10,000   (4) $12,250   (5) $16,000

Lauson 20-35 Model S-10 (1926–1930)
(1) $6,000   (2) $9,750   (3) $13,000   (4) $16,000   (5) $19,000

Lauson 20-40 (1926–1930)
(1) $6,000   (2) $9,750   (3) $13,000   (4) $16,000   (5) $19,000

Lauson 20-40 Thresherman (1926–1930)
(1) $7,000   (2) $11,250   (3) $15,000   (4) $19,000   (5) $21,500

Lauson 25-45 (6-cylinder, 1929–1937)
(1) $6,750   (2) $11,000   (3) $14,750   (4) $18,750   (5) $21,000

Lauson 25-45 Thresherman (6-cylinder, 1929–1937)
(1) $8,250   (2) $13,000   (3) $17,250   (4) $21,000   (5) $24,000

Leader Gas Engine Company, Grand Rapids, Michigan
Leader 12-18 (1913–1914)
(1) $7,000　(2) $9,750　(3) $13,250　(4) $15,500　(5) $19,000

Leader Tractor Manufacturing Company (1920s), Des Moines, Iowa
Rex 12-25 (1918–1920)
(1) $6,500　(2) $9,500　(3) $12,500　(4) $15,000　(5) $18,250

Leader Tractor Manufacturing Company (1940s), Chagrin Falls, Ohio
Leader A (narrow front, 6-cylinder Chrysler engine, 1944–1945)
(1) $1,000　(2) $2,200　(3) $3,200　(4) $4,000　(5) $5,400

Leader B (4-cylinder Hercules engine, 1945–1947)
(1) $500　(2) $1,200　(3) $1,800　(4) $2,500　(5) $3,800

Leader D (4-cylinder Hercules engine, 1947–1949)
(1) $450　(2) $1,050　(3) $1,500　(4) $2,200　(5) $3,400

Lehr Equipment Sales, Richmond, Indiana
Lehr Big Boy B (row crop, 1947–1953)
(1) $500　(2) $900　(3) $1,500　(4) $3,800　(5) $8,000

Lehr Big Boy C (standard tread, 1947–1953)
(1) $500　(2) $900　(3) $1,500　(4) $3,800　(5) $8,000

Leonard Tractor Company, Gary, Indiana
Leonard Four-Wheel Drive (all sizes, 1918–1922)
(1) $11,000　(2) $16,500　(3) $20,000　(4) $24,000　(5) $30,000

Le Roi Company, Milwaukee, Wisconsin
Le Roi was an engine builder who started in business around 1916. The company's engines were very popular and were used in several different brands of tractors through the years. One company, Central Tractor Co. (later renamed Centaur), began using the popular Le Roi engines in its tractors in the 1930s. One of the last tractors built by Centaur was an industrial tractor called the Tractair. The Tractair was a six-cylinder tractor that used the two rear engine cylinders to compress air into a small tank found on the left side of the tractor. In 1948, Centaur ran into financial problems and the company was taken over by Le Roi. The old Centaur name continued to be used for about a year before it was replaced with the Le Roi name. The older 105-cubic feet per minute model was increased to 125 cfm at this time. Westinghouse Air Brake Company took over Le Roi sometime around 1954 and continued limited production of the Tractairs into the 1960s.

Le Roi Tractair 125 (industrial, 6-cylinder with built-in air compressor, 1948-ca. 1960)
(1) $1,100　(2) $1,400　(3) $1,800　(4) $2,200　(5) $3,100

Liberty Tractor Company, Minneapolis, Minnesota
Liberty 15-30 (ca. 1917)
(1) $8,500　(2) $13,500　(3) $18,000　(4) $21,000　(5) $26,000

Lion Tractor Company, Minneapolis, Minnesota
Lion 8-16 (1914–1918)
(1) $8,500   (2) $11,500   (3) $16,000   (4) $20,000   (5) $25,000

Little Giant Company, Mankato, Minnesota
Model A 26-35 (rerated 18-35, 1919–1927)
(1) $21,000   (2) $28,000   (3) $34,000   (4) $38,500   (5) $45,000

Model B 16-22 (rerated 12-22, 1919–1927)
(1) $18,000   (2) $24,000   (3) $29,500   (4) $35,500   (5) $42,000

London Motor Plow Company, Springfield, Ohio
London Motor Plow 12-25S (1922–1923)
(1) $6,000   (2) $9,000   (3) $12,000   (4) $14,500   (5) $17,000

Long Manufacturing Company, Tarboro, North Carolina
Long Model A (1948–1949)
(1) $1,800   (2) $3,200   (3) $5,500   (4) $7,000   (5) $9,000

Love Manufacturing Company, Eau Claire, Michigan
Tructor Row Crop (ca. 1950)
(1) $2,250   (2) $4,500   (3) $5,500   (4) $6,500   (5) $8,000

Tructor Orchard (ca. 1950)
(1) $2,500   (2) $4,750   (3) $6,000   (4) $7,000   (5) $8,500

Love LT-50 (ca. 1950)
(1) $2,000   (2) $4,200   (3) $5,000   (4) $6,000   (5) $7,500

Love C-51 (IND-5 Chrysler 6-cylinder, ca. 1950)
(1) $2,000   (2) $4,200   (3) $5,000   (4) $6,000   (5) $7,500

Love CF-51 (IND-6 Chrysler 6-cylinder, ca. 1950)
(1) $2,000   (2) $4,200   (3) $5,000   (4) $6,000   (5) $7,500

Love J-51 (4-cylinder Jeep engine, ca. 1950)
(1) $2,000   (2) $4,200   (3) $5,000   (4) $6,000   (5) $7,500

Love F-51 (6-cylinder Ford engine, ca. 1950)
(1) $2,000   (2) $4,200   (3) $5000   (4) $6,000   (5) $7,500

Harry A. Lowther Company, Joliet, Illinois
Model HR (6-cylinder 6A Chrysler engine, dual narrow front, 1950–1952)
(1) $800   (2) $1,500   (3) $2,000   (4) $3,000   (5) $8,000

Model HW (6-cylinder 6A Chrysler engine, wide-front, 1950–1952)
(1) $1,000   (2) $1,700   (3) $2,200   (4) $3,500   (5) $8,300

Model ER (6-cylinder 8A Chrysler engine, dual narrow front, 1950–1952)
(1) $1,200   (2) $1,800   (3) $2,500   (4) $3,700   (5) $8,000

Model EW (6-cylinder 8A Chrysler engine, wide-front, 1950–1952)
(1) $1,500   (2) $2,100   (3) $3,000   (4) $4,500   (5) $9,000

Magnet Tractor Company, Minneapolis, Minnesota
Magnet 14-28 (1920–1921)
(1) $9,000   (2) $13,000   (3) $17,000   (4) $20,500   (5) $24,000

Marshall, Sons and Company (import), Gainsborough, England
Marshall 25-60 (United Kingdom import, 1908–1913)
(1) $27,000   (2) $44,000   (3) $58,000   (4) $71,000   (5) $90,000

Massey-Harris, Toronto, Canada
In 1891 the Massey Manufacturing Company and the A. Harris, Son and Company merged to form the Massey-Harris Company. Massey and Harris were both Canadian competitors in the reaper and binder business, not unlike the rival U. S. firms McCormick and Deering. McCormick and Deering joined to create the famous International Harvester Company, while Massey and Harris joined to become the largest Canadian binder and reaper company. By first buying the Johnston Harvester Company of Batavia, New York, and eventually buying the J. I. Case Plow Works, Massey-Harris had a strong foothold in the United States. The J. I. Case Threshing Machine Company paid Massey-Harris over half of its 1.3 million-dollar purchase price of the J. I. Case Plow Works to get the rights to the J. I. Case name. Both Case firms had been born by the same founder, but as independent companies, and developed into competitors with identical first names. Now the J. I. Case Threshing Machine Company had exclusive rights to the name and Massey-Harris had $700,000 in the till.

Harry Ferguson invented the three-point hitch. With a handshake agreement in 1938, Harry Ferguson and Henry Ford decided to make a Ford-built tractor with the Ferguson three-point hitch. Harry Ferguson marketed these little 9N tractors until 1946, when the agreement broke down. Henry Ford II, the great carmaker's grandson, decided to leave Ferguson out of the deal when he refused to accept concessions that diminished his role. Harry Ferguson sued Ford and won 9.25 million dollars. Ferguson went on to build his own tractors. By 1953, Ferguson merged with Massey-Harris and the Massey-Ferguson Company was born. Massey-Harris tractors have a loyal following. The prices of most Massey-Harris tractors have not grown substantially in the last few years. One might expect the prices to surge somewhat in the next several years as the antique tractor availability is decreasing, while collector interest has expanded.

Massey-Harris Number 1 (1918–1922)
(1) $1,890   (2) $2,350   (3) $2,875   (4) $5,400   (5) $11,250

Massey-Harris Number 2 (1919–1923)
(1) $1,800   (2) $2,250   (3) $2,700   (4) $5,400   (5) $11,250

Massey-Harris Number 3 (1920–1923)
(1) $1,800   (2) $2,250   (3) $2,700   (4) $5,400   (5) $11,250

Wallis 12-20 (1929–1934)
(1) $2,250   (2) $2,525   (3) $2,875   (4) $5,850 (5) $12,600

Wallis 12-20 Orchard (1930)
(1) $3,150   (2) $3,775   (3) $4,225   (4) $7,025 (5) $14,400

Wallis 20-30 (1926–1932)
(1) $2,250   (2) $2,525   (3) $3,050   (4) $5,850 (5) $10,800

Massey-Harris 15-22 General Purpose (steel wheels, 4-wheel drive, 1930–1936)
(1) $ 1,800 (2) $3,600   (3) $5,400   (4) $7,200   (5) $9,000

Massey-Harris 15-22 General Purpose (rubber tires, 4-wheel drive, 1930–1936)
(1) $ 1,600 (2) $3,300   (3) $5,100   (4) $6,700   (5) $9,500

Massey-Harris General Purpose (rubber tires, 4-wheel drive, 6-cylinder engine, 1936)
(1) $2,200   (2) $4,000   (3) $6,250   (4) $8,500 (5) $11,000

Massey-Harris General Purpose (late, rubber tires, 4-wheel drive, 1936–1938)
(1) $ 1,800 (2) $3,600   (3) $5,400   (4) $7,200   (5) $9,000

Massey-Harris Model 25 (unstyled, steel wheels, 1933–1938)
(1) $900   (2) $1,250   (3) $1,625   (4) $3,600   (5) $5,400

Massey-Harris Model 25 (styled, rubber tires, 1938–1940)
(1) $800   (2) $1,200   (3) $1,650   (4) $3,700   (5) $5,600

Massey-Harris Challenger (unstyled, steel wheels, 1936–1937)
(1) $1,150   (2) $1,800   (3) $2,250   (4) $3,150   (5) $5,000

Massey-Harris Challenger (unstyled, rubber tires, 1936–1937)
(1) $1,150   (2) $1,975   (3) $2,700   (4) $3,600   (5) $5,500

Massey-Harris Twin-Power Challenger (styled, rubber tires, 1937–1939)
(1) $1,325   (2) $2,250   (3) $2,875   (4) $3,600   (5) $5,400

Massey-Harris Twin-Power Challenger (styled, steel wheels, 1937–1939)
(1) $1,450   (2) $2,375   (3) $3,000   (4) $3,750   (5) $5,600

Massey-Harris Pacemaker (unstyled, steel wheels, 1936–1937)
(1) $1,625   (2) $2,250   (3) $3,150   (4) $3,600   (5) $6,100

Massey-Harris Pacemaker (unstyled, rubber tires, 1936–1937)
(1) $1,325   (2) $1,950   (3) $2,800   (4) $3,200   (5) $5,280

Massey-Harris Pacemaker Orchard (unstyled, citrus fenders and rubber tires, 1936)
(1) $2,150   (2) $2,875   (3) $4,200   (4) $7,050   (5) $8,700

Massey-Harris Twin-Power Pacemaker (styled, 1937–1939)
(1) $1,625   (2) $2,250   (3) $3,150   (4) $3,600   (5) $5,575

Massey-Harris Twin-Power Pacemaker Orchard (1937–1939)
(1) $2,250   (2) $3,150   (3) $3,775   (4) $7,225   (5) $8,300

Massey-Harris 81 Row-crop (rubber tires, 1941–1946)
(1) $575   (2) $800   (3) $1,250   (4) $2,250   (5) $3,425

Massey-Harris 81 Standard tread (rubber tires, 1941–1946)
(1) $675   (2) $975   (3) $1,525   (4) $2,600   (5) $3,600

Massey-Harris 82 Row-crop (1941–1946)
(1) $800   (2) $1,225   (3) $1,900   (4) $3,250   (5) $4,500

Massey-Harris 82 Standard tread (1941–1946)
(1) $900   (2) $1,250   (3) $1,900   (4) $3,250   (5) $4,500

Massey-Harris 101 Junior Row-crop (1939–1946)
(1) $675   (2) $800   (3) $1,025   (4) $2,050   (5) $2,900

Massey-Harris 101 Junior Standard tread (1939–1946)
(1) $800   (2) $1,150   (3) $1,525   (4) $2,500   (5) $3,750

Massey-Harris 101 Senior Row-crop (1942–1946)
(1) $800   (2) $1,150   (3) $1,600   (4) $2,950   (5) $4,200

Massey-Harris 101 Senior Standard tread (1942–1946)
(1) $900   (2) $1,350   (3) $1,875   (4) $3,225   (5) $4,375

Massey-Harris 101 Super Row-crop (twin-power, 1939–1946)
(1) $800   (2) $1,250   (3) $1,800   (4) $3,150   (5) $4,500

The Massey-Harris 101 Super Row-crop is an impressive machine when fully restored like this 1939 model. Acquiring restorable engine covers and trim is often a tremendous challenge for the restorer, but they increase the value of the tractor substantially.

Massey-Harris 101 Super Standard tread (twin-power, 1939–1946)
(1) $900   (2) $1,450   (3) $2,075   (4) $3,425   (5) $4,675

Massey-Harris 102 Junior Row-crop (1939–1946)
(1) $900   (2) $1,425   (3) $1,975   (4) $3,150   (5) $4,500

Massey-Harris 102 Junior Standard tread (1939–1946)
(1) $900   (2) $1,625   (3) $2,250   (4) $3,425   (5) $4,680

Massey-Harris 102 Senior Row-crop (1942–1944)
(1) $900 (2) $1,425 (3) $1,975 (4) $3,150 (5) $4,500

Massey-Harris 102 Senior Standard tread (1941–1945)
(1) $900 (2) $1,625 (3) $2,250 (4) $3,425 (5) $4,680

Massey-Harris 201 (1940–1942)
(1) $1,350 (2) $1,800 (3) $2,875 (4) $4,050 (5) $5,400

Massey-Harris 202 (gasoline, 1941–1944)
(1) $1,350 (2) $1,800 (3) $2,875 (4) $4,050 (5) $5,400

Massey-Harris 202 (diesel, 1940–1942)
(1) $1,625 (2) $2,150 (3) $3,150 (4) $4,500 (5) $6,300

Massey-Harris 203 (1940–1947)
(1) $1,625 (2) $2,075 (3) $2,775 (4) $4,050 (5) $5,575

Massey-Harris 303 Work Bull (gasoline, 1956–1959)
(1) $1,800 (2) $2,100 (3) $3,150 (4) $4,500 (5) $5,850

Massey-Harris 303 Work Bull (gasoline, torque converter, 1956–1959)
(1) $2,550 (2) $3,250 (3) $4,325 (4) $6,300 (5) $9,000

Massey-Harris 303 Work Bull (gasoline, #500 loader, 1956–1959)
(1) $3,425 (2) $4,050 (3) $5,400 (4) $8,100 (5) $10,800

Massey-Harris 303 Work Bull (diesel, 1956–1959)
(1) $2,700 (2) $4,050 (3) $4,775 (4) $8,550 (5) $11,250

Massey-Harris 404 (gasoline, 1956–1957)
(1) $2,250 (2) $2,600 (3) $3,600 (4) $7,200 (5) $9,000

Massey-Harris 404 (gasoline, #500 loader, 1956–1957)
(1) $3,425 (2) $4,050 (3) $5,400 (4) $8,100 (5) $10,800

Massey-Harris 404 (diesel, 1956–1957)
(1) $3,150 (2) $3,775 (3) $4,325 (4) $8,000 (5) $10,750

Massey-Harris 404 (diesel, #500 loader, 1956–1957)
(1) $3,425 (2) $4,050 (3) $5,400 (4) $8,100 (5) $10,800

Massey-Harris 30 Row-crop (1946–1952)
(1) $475 (2) $725 (3) $1,045 (4) $1,700 (5) $2,375

Massey-Harris 30 Standard tread (1946–1952)
(1) $575 (2) $750 (3) $1,150 (4) $1,800 (5) $2,475

Massey-Harris 20 Row-crop (1946–1948)
(1) $475 (2) $625 (3) $850 (4) $1,050 (5) $2,175

Massey-Harris 20 Standard tread (1946–1948)
(1) $575 (2) $725 (3) $950 (4) $1,525 (5) $2,650

Massey-Harris 22 Row-crop (1948–1953)
(1) $650   (2) $900   (3) $1,425   (4) $2,075   (5) $3,325

Massey-Harris 22 Standard tread (1948–1953)
(1) $850   (2) $1,050   (3) $1,700   (4) $2,375   (5) $3,600

Massey-Harris 23 Mustang Row-crop (1952–1956)
(1) $950   (2) $1,425   (3) $1,900   (4) $3,050   (5) $3,900

Massey-Harris 23 Mustang Standard tread (1952–1956)
(1) $1,050   (2) $1,475   (3) $2,100   (4) $3,325   (5) $4,275

Massey-Harris built 28,746 Pony tractors. Even though it is not a rare machine, the Pony is very popular with collectors because of its small size. The value of a Pony is right up there with some of the full-sized Massey-Harris tractors that have lower production numbers. The Pony weighs only 1,365 pounds and has 11 drawbar horsepower.

Massey-Harris Pony Model 11 (1947–1957)
(1) $725   (2) $950   (3) $1,425   (4) $3,325   (5) $4,750

Massey-Harris Pony Model 14 Industrial (1951–1953)
(1) $1,025   (2) $1,300   (3) $1,900   (4) $4,100   (5) $5,500

Massey-Harris 21 Colt Row-crop (1952–1953)
(1) $900   (2) $1,175   (3) $1,800   (4) $3,325   (5) $4,750

Massey-Harris 21 Colt Standard tread (1952–1953)
(1) $1,000   (2) $1,300   (3) $2,000   (4) $3,550   (5) $5,000

Massey-Harris Pacer Model 16 (1954–1956)
(1) $750   (2) $950   (3) $1,700   (4) $3,225   (5) $4,550

Massey-Harris 33 Row-crop (gasoline, dual narrow front axle, 1952–1955)
(1) $475   (2) $725   (3) $1,325   (4) $2,650   (5) $3,700

Massey-Harris 33 Standard tread (1952–1955)
(1) $675   (2) $850   (3) $1,525   (4) $2,850   (5) $3,800

Massey-Harris 33 Row-crop (diesel, dual narrow front axle, 1952–1955)
(1) $1,425   (2) $2,075   (3) $3,325   (4) $4,000   (5) $5,900

Massey-Harris 33 Standard tread (diesel, 1952–1955)
(1) $1,700   (2) $2,375   (3) $3,600   (4) $4,275   (5) $5,975

Massey-Harris 44 Row-crop (gasoline, 1947–1955)
(1) $475   (2) $725   (3) $1,425   (4) $2,075   (5) $3,800

Massey-Harris 44 Row-crop (diesel, 1949–1955)
(1) $850   (2) $1,425   (3) $3,325   (4) $4,275   (5) $5,975

Massey-Harris 44 Row-crop (LPG, 1952)
(1) $1,500   (2) $3,025   (3) $4,500   (4) $5,775   (5) $8,100

Massey-Harris 44 High-altitude Row-crop (gasoline, 1949–1955)
(1) $1,700   (2) $2,850   (3) $4,275   (4) $6,650   (5) $9,500

Massey-Harris 44 Standard tread (gasoline, 1946–1955)
(1) $1,045   (2) $1,525   (3) $1,900   (4) $2,850   (5) $4,275

Massey-Harris 44 Standard tread (diesel, 1948–1955)
(1) $1,425   (2) $2,375   (3) $3,600   (4) $4,650   (5) $6,175

Massey-Harris 44 Standard tread (LPG, 1952)
(1) $1,900   (2) $2,975   (3) $4,125   (4) $6,200   (5) $8,750

Massey-Harris 44 Orchard (gasoline, 1950–1953)
(1) $2,375   (2) $3,325   (3) $4,275   (4) $6,650   (5) $11,400

Massey-Harris 44 Orchard (diesel, 1950–1953)
(1) $2,650   (2) $3,800   (3) $4,950   (4) $9,025   (5) $14,250

Massey-Harris 44 Vineyard (gasoline, 1950–1953)
(1) $1,700   (2) $2,850   (3) $4,275   (4) $6,650   (5) $9,500

Massey-Harris 44-6 Row-crop (6-cylinder, 1946–1951)
(1) $850   (2) $1,325   (3) $2,075   (4) $3,800   (5) $5,625

Massey-Harris 44-6 Standard tread (1947–1950)
(1) $1,045   (2) $1,700   (3) $2,650   (4) $4,375   (5) $5,950

Massey-Harris 44 Special Row-crop (gasoline, 1953–1955)
(1) $850   (2) $1,225   (3) $2,175   (4) $3,800   (5) $5,700

Massey-Harris 44 Special Row-crop (diesel, 1953–1955)
(1) $1,100   (2) $1,800   (3) $3,000   (4) $5,250   (5) $7,500

Massey-Harris 44 Special Row-crop (LPG, 1953–1955)
(1) $1,300   (2) $2,200   (3) $3,500   (4) $6,500   (5) $9,000

Massey-Harris 44 Special Standard tread (gasoline, 1953–1955)
(1) $1,050   (2) $1,700   (3) $2,475   (4) $4,000   (5) $5,900

Massey-Harris 44 Special Standard tread (diesel, 1953–1955)
(1) $1,300   (2) $2,300   (3) $3,500   (4) $5,500   (5) $7,750

Massey-Harris 44 Special Standard tread (LPG, 1953–1955)
(1) $1,600   (2) $2,500   (3) $3,800   (4) $,6,700   (5) $9,300

Massey-Harris 44 Special Cane (gasoline, 1953–1955)
(1) $1,900   (2) $2,850   (3) $4,275   (4) $7,125   (5) $10,450

Massey-Harris 50 Standard tread (gasoline, 1956–1957)
(1) $850   (2) $1,325   (3) $2,100   (4) $4,275   (5) $5,225

Massey-Harris 50 Standard tread (LPG, 1956–1957)
(1) $1,150   (2) $1,625   (3) $2,525   (4) $4,900   (5) $6,000

Massey-Harris 50 Utility (gasoline, 1956–1957)
(1) $850   (2) $1,325   (3) $2,100   (4) $4,275   (5) $5,225

Massey-Harris 50 Utility (LPG, 1956–1957)
(1) $1,150   (2) $1,625   (3) $2,525   (4) $4,900   (5) $6,000

Massey-Harris 50 High-arch (gasoline, wide-front, 1956–1957)
(1) $850   (2) $1,150   (3) $1,900   (4) $4,000   (5) $5,025

Massey-Harris 50 High-arch (LPG, wide-front, 1956–1957)
(1) $1,150   (2) $1,450   (3) $2,325   (4) $4,725   (5) $5,800

Massey-Harris 50 Tricycle (gasoline, dual narrow front, 1955–1957)
(1) $850   (2) $1,150   (3) $1,900   (4) $4,000   (5) $5,025

Massey-Harris 50 Tricycle (LPG, dual narrow front, 1955–1957)
(1) $1,150   (2) $1,450   (3) $2,325   (4) $4,725   (5) $5,800

Massey-Harris 55 Standard tread (gasoline, 1946–1955)
(1) $1,300   (2) $2,000   (3) $3,000   (4) $5,000   (5) $7,250

Massey-Harris 55 Standard tread (diesel, 1949–1955)
(1) $1,500   (2) $2,150   (3) $3,250   (4) $5,350   (5) $7,750

Massey-Harris 55 Standard (LPG, 1946–1955)
(1) $1,800   (2) $2,350   (3) $3,600   (4) $6,000   (5) $8,250

Massey-Harris 55 Rice (gasoline, 1949–1955)
(1) $1,300   (2) $2,000   (3) $3,000   (4) $5,000   (5) $7,250

Massey-Harris 55 Rice (diesel, 1950–1955)
(1) $1,500   (2) $2,150   (3) $3,000   (4) $5,000   (5) $7,250

Massey-Harris 55 Rice (LPG, 1949–1955)
(1) $1,800   (2) $2,350   (3) $3,600   (4) $6,000   (5) $8,250

Massey-Harris 55 Cane (gasoline, 1949–1955)
(1) $1,300   (2) $2,000   (3) $3,000   (4) $5,000   (5) $7,250

Massey-Harris 55 GSW Western (gasoline, 1951–1954)
(1) $1,300   (2) $2,000   (3) $3,000   (4) $5,000   (5) $7,250

Massey-Harris 333 Row-crop (gasoline, 1956–1957)
(1) $1,000   (2) $1,750   (3) $3,100   (4) $5,150   (5) $6,750

Massey-Harris 333 Row-crop (diesel, 1956–1957)
(1) $1,650   (2) $2,400   (3) $3,500   (4) $5,500   (5) $7,250

Massey-Harris 333 Row-crop (LPG, 1956–1957)
(1) $1,850 (2) $2,750 (3) $3,750 (4) $5,750 (5) $7,750

Massey-Harris 333 Standard tread (gasoline, 1956–1957)
(1) $1,500 (2) $2,250 (3) $3,500 (4) $5,400 (5) $6,750

Massey-Harris 333 Standard tread (diesel, 1956–1957)
(1) $1,750 (2) $2,750 (3) $3,650 (4) $5,750 (5) $7,250

Massey-Harris 333 Standard tread (LPG, 1956–1957)
(1) $1,750 (2) $2,750 (3) $3,650 (4) $5,9000 (5) $7,750

Massey-Harris 333 High-arch (gasoline, 1956–1957)
(1) $1,500 (2) $2,250 (3) $3,500 (4) $5,400 (5) $6,750

Massey-Harris 333 High-arch (diesel, 1956–1957)
(1) $1,750 (2) $2,750 (3) $3,650 (4) $5,750 (5) $7,250

Massey-Harris 333 High-arch (LPG, 1956–1957)
(1) $1,750 (2) $2,750 (3) $3,650 (4) $5,900 (5) $7,750

Massey-Harris 444 Row-crop (gasoline, 1956–1958)
(1) $1,250 (2) $2,000 (3) $3,000 (4) $4,750 (5) $7,000

Massey-Harris 444 Row-crop (diesel, 1956–1958)
(1) $1,500 (2) $2,250 (3) $3,250 (4) $5,250 (5) $7,000

Massey-Harris 444 Row-crop (LPG, 1956–1958)
(1) $1,750 (2) $2,550 (3) $4,000 (4) $6,000 (5) $9,000

Massey-Harris 444 Standard tread (gasoline, 1956–1958)
(1) $1,375 (2) $2,150 (3) $3,100 (4) $4,900 (5) $7,250

Massey-Harris 444 Standard tread (diesel, 1956–1958)
(1) $1,500 (2) $2,500 (3) $3,400 (4) $5,500 (5) $7,000

Massey-Harris 444 Standard tread (LPG, 1956–1958)
(1) $1,900 (2) $2,700 (3) $3,500 (4) $6,000 (5) $9,000

Massey-Harris 555 Standard tread (gasoline, 1955–1958)
(1) $1,800 (2) $2,900 (3) $3,750 (4) $5,250 (5) $7,750

Massey-Harris 555 Standard tread (diesel, 1955–1958)
(1) $2,000 (2) $3,250 (3) $4,150 (4) $5,650 (5) $8,000

Massey-Harris 555 Standard tread (LPG, 1955–1958)
(1) $2,400 (2) $3,500 (3) $4,500 (4) $6,000 (5) $8,250

Mayer Brothers Company (see Little Giant Company)

McVicker Engineering Company, Minneapolis, Minnesota

Joy-McVicker 40-horsepower tractor (1910–1911)

(1) $35,000 (2) $50,000 (3) $70,000 (4) $85,000 (5) $100,000

Joy-McVicker 70-horsepower tractor (1910–1911)
(1) $45,000 (2) $70,000 (3) $90,000 (4) $110,000 (5) $130,000

Joy-McVicker 140-horsepower tractor (1910–1911)
(1) $65,000 (2) $100,000 (3) $130,000 (4) $160,000 (5) $195,000

Mercer-Robinson Company, New York, New York
Mercer 30-BD (diesel, ca. 1952)
(1) $3,900 (2) $5,250 (3) $7,800 (4) $10,000 (5) $13,000

Mercer 30-CK (nondiesel, ca. 1952)
(1) $4,250 (2) $5,750 (3) $8,250 (4) $10,500 (5) $13,500

Metal Parts Corporation, Racine, Wisconsin
Haas Model D (ca. 1950)
(1) $5,750 (2) $7,750 (3) $10,250 (4) $13,500 (5) $17,000

Midget Tractor Company, Minneapolis, Minnesota
Midget Tractor (1918–1919)
(1) $4,000 (2) $6,500 (3) $8,000 (4) $9,500 (5) $12,000

Minneapolis-Moline Company, Minneapolis, Minnesota

Minneapolis Steel and Machinery Company had been producing the Twin City line of tractors. By merging in 1929 with the Minneapolis Threshing Machine Company and the Moline Implement Company, the new Minneapolis-Moline Company became a major agricultural equipment concern. It continued building the Twin City line of tractors into the late 1930s when the tractor line was renamed Minneapolis-Moline. The company produced many Minneapolis-Moline tractor models. Unlike other major tractor brands, these variations seldom have huge differences in values. Prices of Minneapolis-Moline tractors will begin to climb swiftly within the next few years. The high-clearance and orchard versions should see the most dramatic rise. As only a certain number of antique tractors are available and more collectors are entering the hobby each day, many variations of this brand of tractor have a long way to go to catch up to John Deere and International in prices. A rich history plus tremendous quality make the Minneapolis-Moline tractor an excellent value.

Twin City 12-20 (rerated 17-28 Model TY, 1919–1935)
(1) $2,750 (2) $4,150 (3) $5,475 (4) $6,550 (5) $8,750

Twin City 20-35 (rerated 27-44 Model AT, 1919–1935)
(1) $4,200 (2) $6,000 (3) $8,500 (4) $10,500 (5) $13,750

Minneapolis 27-42 (1929–1934)
(1) $3,400 (2) $5,500 (3) $7,250 (4) $9,250 (5) $11,500

Minneapolis 17-30 (type A and B, 1920–1934)
(1) $2,600 (2) $4,000 (3) $5,500 (4) $6,750 (5) $8,250

Twin City 21-32 (redesignated Model FT, 1926–1934)
(1) $2,100 (2) $3,500 (3) $4,500 (4) $5,500 (5) $6,500

Model V (Avery design, serial nos. 6V207–7V271, 1951–1952)
(1) $400   (2) $900   (3) $1,400   (4) $1,900   (5) $2,500

Model BF Avery (serial nos. R4460–R6537, 1952)
(1) $500   (2) $1,000   (3) $1,700   (4) $2,500   (5) $3,000

Model BF Avery (serial nos. R6538–R7571, 1953)
(1) $500   (2) $1,000   (3) $1,700   (4) $2,500   (5) $3,000

Model BF (Avery design, dual narrow front, serial nos. 57700001–57700358, 1953)
(1) $500   (2) $800   (3) $1,500   (4) $2,200   (5) $2,500

Model BF (Avery design, dual narrow front, serial nos. 57700001–57700358, 3-point hitch, 1953)
(1) $750   (2) $1,100   (3) $1,850   (4) $2,550   (5) $2,850

Model BFS (Avery design, single front wheel, serial nos. 57600001–57600047, 1953)
(1) $600   (2) $1,100   (3) $1,900   (4) $2,800   (5) $3,500

During World War II, steel wheels were used when rubber tires became next to impossible to acquire. These wheels are now treasured by their owners and are usually very difficult to find in a complete set. The Minneapolis-Moline GTA is seldom encountered with steel wheels.

Model BFH High-Clearance (Avery design, serial nos. 58000001–58000150, 1953)
(1) $1,200   (2) $1,700   (3) $2,600   (4) $3,700   (5) $4,500

Model BG (Avery design, serial nos. 57900001–57900769, 1953–1955)
(1) $1,000   (2) $1,500   (3) $2,000   (4) $3,500   (5) $5,000

Model FT Industrial (1932–1937)
(1) $450   (2) $975   (3) $1,375   (4) $1,925   (5) $2,750

Model FTA (1935–1938)
(1) $375   (2) $825   (3) $1,300   (4) $1,800   (5) $2,775

Model GT (1938–1941)
(1) $585   (2) $1,100   (3) $1,500   (4) $2,200   (5) $3,175

Model GTA (1942–1947)
(1) $575   (2) $1,000   (3) $1,350   (4) $2,000   (5) $2,975

Model GTB (1947–1954)
(1) $450   (2) $725   (3) $1,085   (4) $1,885   (5) $2,900

Model GTB (diesel, 1953–1954)
(1) $750   (2) $1,100   (3) $1,600   (4) $2,250   (5) $3,375

Model GTC (1951–1953)
(1) $625   (2) $900   (3) $1,375   (4) $1,950   (5) $3,000

Model GB (1955–1959)
(1) $435   (2) $700   (3) $1,575   (4) $1,900   (5) $3,075

Model GB (diesel, 1955–1959)
(1) $660   (2) $1,000   (3) $1,675   (4) $2,300   (5) $3,175

Model JT (1934–1937)
(1) $375   (2) $700   (3) $1,050   (4) $1,600   (5) $2,225

Model JT Standard tread (1936–1937)
(1) $485   (2) $825   (3) $1,250   (4) $1,750   (5) $2,350

Model JT Orchard (1936–1937)
(1) $1,500   (2) $2,800   (3) $4,200   (4) $6,400   (5) $7,000

Model KT (1929–1934)
(1) $285   (2) $800   (3) $1,175   (4) $1,700   (5) $2,500

Model KT Industrial (1932–1935)
(1) $425   (2) $1,000   (3) $1,375   (4) $1,925   (5) $2,750

Model KTA (1934–1938)
(1) $250   (2) $675   (3) $1,075   (4) $1,600   (5) $2,475

Model LT (1930)
(1) $2,500   (2) $3,750   (3) $8,750   (4) $11,875   (5) $15,000

Model MT (1930–1934)
(1) $450   (2) $925   (3) $1,550   (4) $2,150   (5) $3,000

Model MTA (1934–1938)
(1) $310   (2) $725   (3) $1,275   (4) $1,800   (5) $2,575

Model RTE (1948–1953)
(1) $450   (2) $875   (3) $1,300   (4) $1,950   (5) $2,700

Model RTN (1948–1951)
(1) $450   (2) $875   (3) $1,300   (4 $1,950   (5) $2,700

Model RT High-clearance (1939–1940)
(1) $630   (2) $1,175   (3) $1,975   (4) $3,075   (5) $3,975

Model RTS (1949–1953)
(1) $450   (2) $875   (3) $1,300   (4) $1,950   (5) $2,700

The queen of all the Minneapolis-Moline tractors is the rare UDLX. In 1938 about 125 to 150 tractors were built that could also serve as automobiles. The expensive selling price of $2,155 in 1938 led to poor sales. Today, most collectors can only dream of owning a UDLX.

Model R (factory original Comfort Cab, 1939-ca. 1940)
(1) $2,500 (2) $3,000 (3) $4,000 (4) $6,000 (5) $9,000

Model RTU (1939–1954)
(1) $300 (2) $750 (3) $1,200 (4) $1,675 (5) $2,425

Model RTI-M (1953)
(1) $620 (2) $1,175 (3) $1,650 (4) $2,125 (5) $3,075

Model UDLX (1938)
(1) $11,000 (2) $16,000 (3) $27,000 (4) $48,000 (5) $66,000

Model UBU (1953–1955)
(1) $365 (2) $800 (3) $1,450 (4) $2,125 (5) $3,000

Model UBE (1953–1955)
(1) $425 (2) $950 (3) $1,625 (4) $2,300 (5) $3,150

Model UBE (diesel, 1954–1955)
(1) $600 (2) $1,100 (3) $1,975 (4) $2,650 (5) $3,550

Model UBN (1953–1955)
(1) $425 (2) $950 (3) $1,625 (4) $2,300 (5) $3,150

Model UBU (diesel, 1954–1955)
(1) $450 (2) $1,000 (3) $1,625 (4) $2,300 (5) $3,150

Model UBN (diesel, 1954)
(1) $535 (2) $1,050 (3) $1,975 (4) $2,800 (5) $3,575

Model UB Special (1955)
(1) $465 (2) $950 (3) $1,825 (4) $2,475 (5) $3,350

Model UB Special (diesel, 1955–1957)
(1) $565 (2) $1,100 (3) $1,975 (4) $2,650 (5) $3,550

Model UOPN Open Roadster (1938)
(1) $5,000 (2) $10,000 (3) $24,000 (4) $42,000 (5) $60,000

Model UTC (1948–1955)
(1) $900 (2) $1,300 (3) $2,050 (4) $3,050 (5) $4,100

Model UTE (1951–1954)
(1) $425 (2) $785 (3) $1,400 (4) $2,050 (5) $3,050

Model UTN (1950–1952)
(1) $435   (2) $835   (3) $1,450   (4) $2,100   (5) $3,200

Model UTS (1938–1955)
(1) $285   (2) $720   (3) $1,300   (4) $1,900   (5) $2,800

Model UTS Special (1956–1957)
(1) $365   (2) $800   (3) $1,450   (4) $2,125   (5) $3,000

Model UTSG Grader (ca. 1950)
(1) $800   (2) $1,250   (3) $1,800   (4) $2,500   (5) $3,000

Model UTU (1938–1955)
(1) $300   (2) $725   (3) $1,325   (4) $1,900   (5) $3,800

Model UTID (1954–1955)
(1) $885   (2) $1,300   (3) $1,900   (4) $2,650   (5) $4,025

Model UTI (?–1956)
(1) $625   (2) $900   (3) $1,375   (4) $1,950   (5) $3,000

Model UTIL (?–1957)
(1) $425   (2) $785   (3) $1,400   (4) $2,050   (5) $3,050

Model UTIL-D (1953–1959)
(1) $650   (2) $1,000   (3) $1,450   (4) $2,300   (5) $3,300

Model UTIL-M (1953)
(1) $900   (2) $1,300   (3) $2,050   (4) $3,050   (5) $4,100

The Minneapolis-Moline Model YT was an experimental tractor with only two cylinders. Only 25 units were made before the engine was replaced with a four-cylinder, and other improvements led to the development of the popular Model RT. This very rare 1937 model is among the most valuable M-M tractors in existence.

Model UDU (1952–1953)
(1) $515   (2) $935   (3) $1,675   (4) $2,450   (5) $3,450

Model UDS (1952–1956)
(1) $535   (2) $1,000   (3) $1,450   (4) $2,300   (5) $3,300

Model UTSD-M (1954–1955)
(1) $600   (2) $1,050   (3) $1,775   (4) $2,600   (5) $3,550

Model UTSD-M (Turkish export model, 1956–1958)
(1) $750   (2) $1,600   (3) $2,275   (4) $3,225   (5) $4,125

Uni-Tractor (1951–1962)
(1) $220   (2) $450   (3) $825   (4) $1,125   (5) $1,725

Model YT (1937–1938)
(1) $5,000   (2) $8,000   (3) $12,000   (4) $18,000(5) $30,000

Model ZAU (1949–1952)
(1) $275   (2) $700   (3) $1,075   (4) $1,650   (5) $2,325

Model ZAS (1949–1953)
(1) $585   (2) $1,285   (3) $2,125   (4) $2,650   (5) $4,200

Model ZAN (1949–1953)
(1) $520   (2) $1,000   (3) $1,450   (4) $2,050   (5) $3,075

Model ZAE (1949–1953)
(1) $520   (2) $1,000   (3) $1,450   (4) $2,050   (5) $3,075

Model ZASI (ca. 1950)
(1) $630   (2) $1,475   (3) $2,050   (4) $3,000   (5) $3,975

Model ZBE (1953–1955)
(1) $560   (2) $1,125   (3) $1,575   (4) $2,100   (5) $3,050

Model ZBN (1954–1955)
(1) $620   (2) $1,275   (3) $1,575   (4) $2,650   (5) $3,400

Model ZBU (1953–1955)
(1) $460   (2) $970   (3) $1,375   (4) $1,825   (5) $2,775

Model ZTE (ca. 1950)
(1) $620   (2) $1,175   (3) $1,650   (4) $2,125   (5) $3,075

Model ZTN (1936–1948)
(1) $500   (2) $1,125   (3) $1,725   (4) $2,350   (5) $3,350

Model ZTU (1936–1948)
(1) $450   (2) $920   (3) $1,350   (4) $1,975   (5) $2,825

Model ZTS (1937–1947)
(1) $485   (2) $970   (3) $1,500   (4) $2,125   (5) $3,025

Model ZTI (1936–1942)
(1) $670   (2) $1,375   (3) $2,075   (4) $2,925   (5) $4,300

Model 335 Utility (1956–1961)
(1) $510   (2) $1,175   (3) $1,750   (4) $2,500   (5) $3,325

Model 335 Universal (1957–1959)
(1) $630   (2) $1,475   (3) $2,050   (4) $3,000   (5) $3,975

Model 445 Universal (1956–1959)
(1) $440   (2) $1,175   (3) $1,775   (4) $2,700   (5) $3,775

Model 445 Utility (1956–1959)
(1) $475   (2) $1,200   (3) $1,800   (4) $2,725   (5) $3,850

Model 445 Utility (diesel, 1959)
(1) $770   (2) $1,625   (3) $2,175   (4) $3,175   (5) $4,200

Model 445 Industrial (1956–1958)
(1) $720   (2) $1,575   (3) $2,025   (4) $3,075   (5) $3,875

Model 445 Industrial (diesel, 1958)
(1) $820   (2) $1,725   (3) $2,475   (4) $3,325   (5) $4,200

Model 445 Military (1958)
(1) $750   (2) $1,600   (3) $2,275   (4) $3,225   (5) $4,125

Model 445 Universal (diesel, 1958)
(1) $650   (2) $1,550   (3) $2,150   (4) $3,150   (5) $4,100

Model Big Mo 400 Industrial (1961–1964)
(1) $920   (2) $1,600   (3) $2,250   (4) $3,175   (5) $4,125

Model Big Mo 400 Military (1959–1963)
(1) $920   (2) $1,600   (3) $2,250   (4) $3,175   (5) $4,125

Model Big Mo 500 Industrial (1960–1966)
(1) $940   (2) $1,625   (3) $2,300   (4) $3,225   (5) $4,175

Model Big Mo 500 (diesel, 1960–1965)
(1) $940   (2) $1,625   (3) $2,300   (4) $3,225   (5) $4,175

Model Big Mo 600 (1960)
(1) $950   (2) $1,650   (3) $2,325   (4) $3,275   (5) $4,225

4-Star (1959–1963)
(1) $670   (2) $1,075   (3) $1,625   (4) $2,300   (5) $3,500

4-Star (diesel, 1960–1962)
(1) $610   (2) $1,200   (3) $1,675   (4) $2,800   (5) $3,750

5-Star Universal (1957–1959)
(1) $620   (2) $1,125   (3) $1,925   (4) $3,000   (5) $3,900

5-Star Universal (diesel, 1957–1959)
(1) $630   (2) $1,175   (3) $1,975   (4) $3,075   (5) $3,975

5-Star Standard (1958)
(1) $820   (2) $1,275   (3) $2,100   (4) $3,125   (5) $4,175

5-Star Standard (diesel, 1958–1959)
(1) $970   (2) $1,475   (3) $2,150   (4) $3,175   (5) $4,225

5-Star Industrial (1957–1959)
(1) $800   (2) $1,375   (3) $2,000   (4) $2,725   (5) $3,675

5-Star Industrial (diesel, 1958–1960)
(1) $820   (2) $1,375   (3) $2,000   (4) $2,725   (5) $3,675

Jet Star (1959–1962)
(1) $870   (2) $1,400   (3) $2,000   (4) $2,925   (5) $4,400

Jet Star (diesel, 1960–1962)
(1) $900   (2) $1,525   (3) $2,200   (4) $3,175   (5) $4,500

Jet Star 2 (1963)
(1) $885   (2) $1,500   (3) $2,150   (4) $3,075   (5) $3,800

Jet Star 2 (diesel, 1963)
(1) $950   (2) $1,575   (3) $2,575   (4) $3,225   (5) $4,000

Jet Star 3 (1964–1970)
(1) $1,325   (2) $1,875   (3) $2,625   (4) $3,775   (5) $5,075

Jet Star 3 (diesel, 1964–1970)
(1) $1,375   (2) $1,900   (3) $2,675   (4) $3,900   (5) $5,125

This 1962 Minneapolis-Moline G704 with front-wheel assist and the LPG fuel option is indeed a rare machine. The late-model M-M tractors have seen a big increase in collector desirability in recent years.

Jet Star Orchard (gasoline, 1965–1967)
(1) $1,550   (2) $2,175   (3) $2,900   (4) $3,825   (5) $5,200

Jet Star Orchard (diesel, 1967)
(1) $1,800   (2) $2,275   (3) $3,125   (4) $3,975   (5) $5,425

Jet Star 3 Industrial (1966–1967)
(1) $1,350   (2) $1,925   (3) $2,600   (4) $3,625   (5) $4,825

Jet Star 3 Industrial (diesel, 1966)
(1) $1,400   (2) $1,975   (3) $2,875   (4) $3,700   (5) $4,875

Model U-302 (1964–1965)
(1) $1,075   (2) $1,575   (3) $2,175   (4) $3,425   (5) $4,725

Model U-302 Super (1966–1970)
(1) $1,250   (2) $1,775   (3) $2,450   (4) $3,825   (5) $5,150

Model U-302 Super (diesel, 1967–1970)
(1) $1,350   (2) $1,825   (3) $2,625   (4) $3,950   (5) $5,275

Model U-302 Super (LPG, 1969–1970)
(1) $1,425   (2) $2,075   (3) $2,900   (4) $4,075   (5) $5,475

Model M-5 (1960–1963)
(1) $885   (2) $1,300   (3) $1,900   (4) $2,650   (5) $4,025

Model M-5 (diesel, 1960–1963)
(1) $1,100   (2) $1,675   (3) $2,275   (4) $2,925   (5) $4,275

Model M-504 Four-Wheel Drive (1962)
(1) $1,775   (2) $2,600   (3) $3,500   (4) $4,600   (5) $6,150

Model M-504 Four-Wheel Drive (diesel, 1962)
(1) $1,775   (2) $2,600   (3) $3,500   (4) $4,600   (5) $6,150

Model M-602 (1963–1964)
(1) $1,250   (2) $1,575   (3) $2,300   (4) $2,975   (5) $4,350

Model M-602 (diesel, 1963–1964)
(1) $1,225   (2) $1,700   (3) $2,350   (4) $3,175   (5) $4,425

Model M-604 Four-Wheel Drive (1963–1964)
(1) $1,625   (2) $2,675   (3) $3,325   (4) $4,425   (5) $5,400

Model M-604 Four-Wheel Drive (diesel, 1963–1964)
(1) $1,625   (2) $2,700   (3) $3,375   (4) $4,475   (5) $5,500

Model M-670 (1964–1965)
(1) $1,425   (2) $2,025   (3) $2,600   (4) $3,425   (5) $4,825

Model M-670 (diesel, 1964–1965)
(1) $1,525   (2) $2,125   (3) $2,675   (4) $3,575   (5) $5,000

Model M-670 Super (1966–1970)
(1) $1,500   (2) $2,250   (3) $3,150   (4) $3,975   (5) $5,175

Model M-670 Super (diesel, 1966–1970)
(1) $1,500   (2) $2,250   (3) $3,150   (4) $3,975   (5) $5,175

Model G-VI (1959–1962)
(1) $700   (2) $1,075   (3) $1,400   (4) $2,450   (5) $3,225

Model G-VI (diesel, 1959–1962)
(1) $820   (2) $1,175   (3) $1,675   (4) $2,500   (5) $3,625

Model G-704 (LPG, 1962)
(1) $1,725   (2) $3,075   (3) $4,175   (4) $5,625   (5) $6,575

Model G-704 (diesel, 1962)
(1) $1,675   (2) $2,925   (3) $4,075   (4) $5,500   (5) $6,400

Model G-705 (LPG, 1962–1965)
(1) $1,075   (2) $1,575   (3) $2,125   (4) $3,200   (5) $3,875

Model G-705 (diesel, 1962–1965)
(1) $1,000   (2) $1,525   (3) $2,075   (4) $3,200   (5) $3,875

Model G-706 (LPG, 1962–1965)
(1) $1,500   (2) $2,500   (3) $3,375   (4) $4,475   (5) $5,325

Model G-706 (diesel, 1962–1965)
(1) $1,500   (2) $2,450   (3) $3,300   (4) $4,450   (5) $5,300

Model G-707 (LPG, 1965)
(1) $1,275   (2) $1,725   (3) $2,450   (4) $3,600   (5) $4,225

Model G-707 (diesel, 1965)
(1) $1,200   (2) $1,675   (3) $3,125   (4) $3,650   (5) $4,225

Model G-708 (LPG, 1965)
(1) $1,900   (2) $2,925   (3) $4,275   (4) $5,750   (5) $7,175

Model G-708 (diesel, 1965)
(1) $1,850   (2) $2,775   (3) $4,100   (4) $5,575   (5) $6,925

Model G-900 (gasoline, 1967–1969)
(1) $1,500   (2) $2,175   (3) $2,925   (4) $4,425   (5) $4,975

Model G-900 (LPG, 1967–1969)
(1) $1,525   (2) $2,275   (3) $3,075   (4) $4,525   (5) $5,325

Model G-900 (diesel, 1967–1969)
(1) $1,825   (2) $2,175   (3) $3,050   (4) $4,925   (5) $5,400

Model G-950 (1969–1971)
(1) $2,075   (2) $3,125   (3) $4,475   (4) $5,600   (5) $6,225

Model G-955 (1973–1974)
(1) $2,350   (2) $3,375   (3) $5,000   (4) $6,025   (5) $6,600

Model G-1000 Row-crop (gasoline, 1965–1968)
(1) $1,475   (2) $2,175   (3) $3,375   (4) $4,625   (5) $5,400

Model G-1000 Row-crop (LPG, 1965–1968)
(1) $1,575   (2) $2,325   (3) $3,575   (4) $4,775   (5) $5,575

Model G-1000 Row-crop (diesel, 1965–1968)
(1) $1,675   (2) $2,375   (3) $3,625   (4) $4,825   (5) $5,700

Model G-1000 Wheatland (1966–1969)
(1) $1,425   (2) $2,125   (3) $3,300   (4) $4,525   (5) $5,375

Model G-1000 Vista (LPG, 1967–1969)
(1) $1,725   (2) $2,425   (3) $3,825   (4) $4,875   (5) $6,400

Model G-1000 Vista (diesel, 1967–1969)
(1) $1,725   (2) $2,375   (3) $3,625   (4) $4,625   (5) $6,100

Model G-1050 (LPG, 1969–1972)
(1) $2,175 (2) $3,725 (3) $5,300 (4) $6,600 (5) $7,875

Model G-1050 (diesel, 1969–1971)
(1) $2,125 (2) $3,675 (3) $5,250 (4) $6,575 (5) $7,775

Model G-1350 Row-crop (LPG, 1969–1972)
(1) $2,275 (2) $3,700 (3) $5,300 (4) $6,625 (5) $7,825

Model G-1350 Row-crop (diesel, 1970–1972)
(1) $2,350 (2) $3,700 (3) $4,900 (4) $6,125 (5) $7,275

Model G-1350 Wheatland (1969)
(1) $3,375 (2) $4,800 (3) $6,575 (4) $7,625 (5) $9,475

Model G-1355 (1973–1974)
(1) $2,100 (2) $3,500 (3) $4,875 (4) $6,225 (5) $7,325

Model A4T-1400 (1969–1970)
(1) $2,175 (2) $3,575 (3) $4,975 (4) $6,475 (5) $8,175

Model A4T-1600 (diesel, 1970–1972)
(1) $1,975 (2) $3,475 (3) $4,900 (4) $6,350 (5) $8,025

Model A4T-1600 (LPG, 1970–1972)
(1) $2,000 (2) $3,500 (3) $4,925 (4) $6,400 (5) $8,100

Model A4T-1600 (800 LPG engine, ca. 1972)
(1) $5,350 (2) $6,450 (3) $7,450 (4) $8,550 (5) $9,950

955 (LPG, 1973–1974)
(1) $3,200 (2) $4,000 (3) $4,400 (4) $5,400 (5) $6,000

1355 (LPG, 1973–1974)
(1) $2,500 (2) $3,500 (3) $4,500 (4) $5,500 (5) $6,500

Minneapolis Steel and Machinery Company, Minneapolis, Minnesota

Twin City 40 (1911–1924)
(1) $18,500 (2) $29,500 (3) $37,250 (4) $43,000 (5) $55,000

Twin City 60-90 (two known to exist, 1913–1920)
(1) $50,000 (2) $85,000 (3) $125,000 (4) $155,000 (5) $200,000

Twin City 25-45 (1913–1920)
(1) $14,000 (2) $23,000 (3) $29,000 (4) $37,500 (5) $45,000

Twin City 27-44 Road King (1926–1929)
(1) $4,000 (2) $6,000 (3) $7,500 (4) $8,500 (5) $11,000

Twin City 15 (1913–1917)
(1) $9,000 (2) $15,000 (3) $19,000 (4) $22,500 (5) $29,000

Twin City 16-30 (1918–1920)
(1) $8,000   (2) $13,000   (3) $14,500   (4) $16,500 (5) $22,000

Twin City 12-20 (rerated 17-28, 1919–1935)
(1) $2,750   (2) $4,150   (3) $5,475   (4) $6,550   (5) $8,750

Valuable tractor model of the Minneapolis Threshing Machine Company is the colossal Model 35-70. This tractor weighs over 11 tons and stands more than 11 feet high. A nice Minneapolis 35-70 sold for $37,500 at Oscar's Dreamland Museum Auction in September 1998.

Twin City 20-35 (rerated 27-44, 1919–1935)
(1) $4,200   (2) $6,000   (3) $8,500   (4) $10,500 (5) $13,750

Twin City 21-32 (redesignated Model FT, 1926–1934)
(1) $2,100   (2) $3,500   (3) $4,500   (4) $5,500   (5) $6,500

Minneapolis Threshing Machine Company, Hopkins, Minnesota

Universal 20 horsepower (1911–1913)
(1) $9,000   (2) $14,000   (3) $18,000   (4) $21,000 (5) $26,000

Minneapolis Farm Motor (1911)
(1) $4,000   (2) $6,000   (3) $7,250   (4) $8,500   (5) $11,000

The Minneapolis 25-50 (1912–1914)
(1) $16,000   (2) $25,000   (3) $32,000   (4) $38,500   (5) $50,000

The Minneapolis 40-80 (rerated 35-70, 1918–1928)
(1) $15,000   (2) $22,500   (3) $27,500   (4) $32,000   (5) $40,000

The Minneapolis 20-40 (1918–1919)
(1) $13,000   (2) $17,250   (3) $23,000   (4) $25,500   (5) $34,000

The Minneapolis 15 (15-30 rerated 12-25, 1915–1920)
(1) $8,000   (2) $12,500   (3) $15,250   (4) $17,000   (5) $21,000

The Minneapolis 22-44 (1921–1927)
(1) $12,000   (2) $16,000   (3) $20,000   (4) $24,000   (5) $32,000

Minneapolis 27-42 (1929–1934)
(1) $2,000   (2) $4,000   (3) $6,250   (4) $7,500   (5) $9,000

Minneapolis 17-30 (type A and B, 1920–1934)
(1) $1,800   (2) $3,600   (3) $6,000   (4) $7,250   (5) $8,250

Moline Plow Company, Moline, Illinois
Moline Universal (2-cylinder, 1915–1917)
(1) $4,500   (2) $6,500   (3) $8,250   (4) $10,000 (5) $12,000

Moline Universal Model D (4-cylinder, 1918–1923)
(1) $4,250   (2) $6,250   (3) $8,000   (4) $9,500 (5) $11,000

National Farm Equipment Corp. (See Co-Operative Mfg.)

National Tractor Company, Cedar Rapids, Iowa
National Model E 9-16 (1919–1920)
(1) $7,000   (2) $11,250   (3) $15,000   (4) $18,500 (5) $24,000

National Model F 12-22 (1919–1920)
(1) $7,400   (2) $12,000   (3) $16,000   (4) $20,000 (5) $26,000

New Age Tractor Company, Minneapolis, Minnesota
New Age 10-18 (rerated 16-28, 1916–1919)
(1) $ 10,000 (2) $17,000   (3) $23,000   (4) $28,000 (5) $35,000

Nichols and Shepard Company, Battle Creek, Michigan
Nichols-Shepard 35-70 (1919–1920)
(1) $55,000   (2) $75,000   (3) $85,000   (4) $100,000 (5) $130,000

Nichols-Shepard 20-40 Oil-Gas (1919–1927)
(1) $40,000   (2) $55,000   (3) $72,000   (4) $85,000 (5) $100,000

Nichols-Shepard 25-50 Oil-Gas (1919–1928)
(1) $22,000   (2) $33,000   (3) $40,000   (4) $47,000 (5) $55,000

Nichols-Shepard 18-36 Oil-Gas (rerated 20-42, 1918–1925)
(1) $35,000   (2) $50,000   (3) $65,000   (4) $77,000 (5) $90,000

Nichols-Shepard 16-32 (Lauson Tractor, 1927–1929)
(1) $5,500   (2) $9,000   (3) $12,000   (4) $15,000 (5) $18,250

Nichols-Shepard 20-40 (Lauson Tractor, 1927–1929)
(1) $6,000   (2) $9,750   (3) $13,000   (4) $16,000 (5) $19,000

Nichols-Shepard 20-40 Thresherman (Lauson Tractor, 1927–1929)
(1) $7,000   (2) $11,250   (3) $15,000   (4) $19,000 (5) $21,500

Nilson Tractor Company, Minneapolis, Minnesota
Nilson 20-40 (1915–1916)
(1) $12,000   (2) $18,000   (3) $24,000   (4) $28,500 (5) $34,000

Nilson Senior 24-36 (1917–1919)
(1) $12,000   (2) $18,000   (3) $24,000   (4) $28,500 (5) $34,000

Nilson Junior 15-30 (rerated 16-27, 1917–1929)
(1) $10,000   (2) $15,000   (3) $20,000   (4) $24,000 (5) $30,000

Northwest Thresher Company (see Advance Rumely, Gaspull)

Oliver Corporation, Chicago, Illinois

Oliver Hart-Parr Row-crop 18-27 (single front wheel, 1930–1931)
(1) $1,050   (2) $1,775   (3) $2,500   (4) $3,425   (5) $4,575

Oliver Row-crop 18-27 (dual-front wheels, 1931–1937)
(1) $835   (2) $1,550   (3) $2,125   (4) $2,725   (5) $3,925

Oliver 18-28 (1930–1937)
(1) $1,075   (2) $1,775   (3) $2,475   (4) $3,175   (5) $4,475

Oliver 18 Industrial (1931–1932)
(1) $1,300   (2) $1,800   (3) $2,525   (4) $3,375   (5) $4,625

Oliver 28 Industrial (1931–1937)
(1) $1,300   (2) $1,800   (3) $2,525   (4) $3,375   (5) $4,625

Oliver 28-44 (1930–1937)
(1) $1,100   (2) $1,600   (3) $2,300   (4) $3,150   (5) $4,400

Oliver 80 Industrial (1932–1947)
(1) $1,200   (2) $1,700   (3) $2,325   (4) $3,275   (5) $4,525

Oliver 80 Row-crop (nondiesel, rubber tires, 1937–1948)
(1) $1,000   (2) $1,675   (3) $2,500   (4) $3,300   (5) $4,600

Oliver 80 Row-crop (diesel, rubber tires, 1937–1948)
(1) $3,000   (2) $6,325   (3) $10,000   (4) $19,000(5) $24,325

Oliver 80 Standard tread (1937–1948)
(1) $850   (2) $1,550   (3) $2,150   (4) $2,725   (5) $3,925

Oliver 99 Industrial (1932–1947)
(1) $1,000   (2) $1,550   (3) $2,300   (4) $3,250   (5) $4,550

Oliver 90 (steel wheels, 1937–1952)
(1) $685   (2) $1,200   (3) $2,400   (4) $3,725   (5) $5,100

Oliver 90 (rubber tires, 1937–1952)
(1) $670   (2) $1,175   (3) $2,375   (4) $3,675   (5) $4,925

Oliver 99 (rubber tires, 1953–1957)
(1) $670   (2) $1,175   (3) $2,375   (4) $3,675   (5) $4,925

Oliver 50 Industrial (rubber tires, 1937–1948)
(1) $1,125   (2) $2,125   (3) $3,175   (4) $4,325   (5) $5,325

Oliver Hart-Parr 70 Row-crop (steel wheels, nonstreamlined, 1936–1937)
(1) $930   (2) $1,275   (3) $1,825   (4) $2,925   (5) $3,475

The Oliver 70 Standard Tread is more valuable than the more popular 70 Row-crop. Oliver produced 15,420 Standard Tread models compared to 67,866 Row-crop 70s. The collector interest in the Oliver tractors is healthy and flourishing.

Oliver Hart-Parr 70 Row-crop (rubber tires, nonstreamlined, 1935–1937)
(1) $880   (2) $1,200   (3) $1,725   (4) $2,725   (5) $3,250

Oliver 70 Row-crop (steel wheels, streamlined, 1937–1948)
(1) $830   (2) $1,125   (3) $1,650   (4) $2,625   (5) $3,250

Oliver 70 Row-crop (rubber tires, streamlined, 1937–1948)
(1) $750   (2) $1,025   (3) $1,575   (4) $2,550   (5) $3,150

Oliver Hart-Parr 70 Standard tread (steel wheels, nonstreamlined, 1935–1937)
(1) $1,200   (2) $1,750   (3) $2,600   (4) $3,725   (5) $5,325

Oliver Hart-Parr 70 Standard tread (rubber tires, nonstreamlined, 1935–1937)
(1) $1,000   (2) $1,575   (3) $2,375   (4) $3,525   (5) $5,100

Oliver 70 Standard tread (steel wheels, streamlined, 1937–1948)
(1) $1,225   (2) $1,925   (3) $2,725   (4) $4,225   (5) $5,075

Oliver 70 Standard tread (rubber tires, streamlined, 1937–1948)
(1) $1,200   (2) $1,900   (3) $2,700   (4) $4,200   (5) $5,000

Oliver Hart-Parr 70 High-clearance (nonstreamlined, rubber tires, wide-front axle, 1935–1937)
(1) $1,000   (2) $1,600   (3) $2,325   (4) $3,325   (5) $4,300

Oliver 70 High-clearance (streamlined, rubber tires, wide-front axle, 1937–1948)
(1) $965   (2) $1,475   (3) $2,275   (4) $3,225   (5) $3,950

Oliver 70 Orchard (rubber tires, citrus fenders, 1937–1948)
(1) $1,465   (2) $2,350   (3) $3,900   (4) $5,425   (5) $6,825

Oliver 70 Industrial (1936–1948)
(1) $635   (2) $1,200   (3) $1,850   (4) $2,925   (5) $3,850

Oliver 25 Airport (1937–1948)
(1) $1,100   (2) $1,925   (3) $2,825   (4) $4,325   (5) $5,425

Oliver built 27,966 units of the 88 Standard Tread. This Model 88 was completed in 1947, the last year that the tractor had the early style screen-type grille. This early style usually brings more money than the later bar-type grille models in the same condition. Most Oliver Standard Tread tractors will command a large sum of money in nice condition.

Oliver 35 Industrial (rubber tires, 1937–1938)
(1) $765   (2) $1,525   (3) $2,500   (4) $3,500   (5) $4,825

Oliver 60 Row-crop (rubber tires, dual narrow front, 1940–1948)
(1) $460   (2) $1,050   (3) $2,225   (4) $2,500   (5) $3,000

Oliver 60 Standard tread (rubber tires, 1940–1948)
(1) $650   (2) $1,225   (3) $2,125   (4) $3,125   (5) $4,025

Oliver 60 Industrial (1946–1948)
(1) $635   (2) $1,200   (3) $2,025   (4) $3,050   (5) $4,025

Oliver 900 Industrial (1946–1951)
(1) $1,100   (2) $1,950   (3) $3,000   (4) $4,250   (5) $4,950

Oliver 88 Row-crop (screen-type grille, 1947–1948)
(1) $850   (2) $1,725   (3) $2,800   (4) $4,200   (5) $5,325

Oliver 88 Row-crop (bar-type grille, gasoline, 1948–1954)
(1) $465   (2) $1,025   (3) $1,625   (4) $2,500   (5) $3,450

Oliver 88 Row-crop (diesel, 1951–1954)
(1) $465   (2) $1,025   (3) $1,625   (4) $2,500   (5) $3,500

Oliver 88 Standard tread (screen-type grille, 1946–1947)
(1) $1,100   (2) $1,900   (3) $2,825   (4) $3,925   (5) $4,950

Oliver 88 Standard tread (bar-type grille, 1948–1952)
(1) $600   (2) $1,200   (3) $2,025   (4) $3,000   (5) $4,025

Oliver 88 Orchard (1948–1952)
(1) $1,800   (2) $3,250   (3) $4,800   (4) $6,500   (5) $8,750

Oliver 88 Industrial (screen-type grille, 1946–1947)
(1) $2,600   (2) $3,600   (3) $4,800   (4) $7,250   (5) $9,000

Oliver 88 Industrial (bar-type grille, 1947–1952)
(1) $560   (2) $1,200   (3) $1,725   (4) $2,550   (5) $3,300

Oliver 77 Row-crop (gasoline, dual narrow front, 1948–1954)
(1) $435   (2) $900   (3) $1,575   (4) $2,300   (5) $3,025

Oliver 77 Row-crop (diesel, dual narrow front, 1951–1954)
(1) $470   (2) $950   (3) $1,625   (4) $2,350   (5) $3,325

Oliver 77 Row-crop (LPG, dual narrow front, 1951–1954)
(1) $1,100   (2) $1,725   (3) $2,525   (4) $3,450   (5) $4,825

Oliver 77 Row-crop (wide-front, gasoline, 1948–1954)
(1) $670   (2) $1,025   (3) $1,700   (4) $2,400   (5) $3,400

Oliver 77 Standard tread (gasoline, 1948–1952)
(1) $815   (2) $1,750   (3) $2,250   (4) $2,950   (5) $3,500

Oliver 77 Standard tread (diesel, 1951–1952)
(1) $900   (2) $1,850   (3) $2,425   (4) $3,200   (5) $3,900

Oliver 77 Orchard (gasoline, 1948–1952)
(1) $1,475   (2) $2,150   (3) $3,350   (4) $5,350   (5) $7,200

Oliver 77 Orchard (diesel, 1951–1952)
(1) $1,125   (2) $2,000   (3) $3,325   (4) $5,500   (5) $7,500

Oliver 77 Industrial (1948–1952)
(1) $850   (2) $1,700   (3) $2,575   (4) $3,325   (5) $4,150

Oliver 77 High-clearance (gasoline, ca. 1952)
(1) $1,600   (2) $3,100   (3) $5,250   (4) $7,250   (5) $9,500

Oliver 66 Row-crop (gasoline, 1949–1954)
(1) $1,000   (2) $1,250   (3) $1,950   (4) $2,900   (5) $3,550

Oliver 66 Row-crop (diesel, 1954–1958)
(1) $1,050   (2) $1,800   (3) $2,600   (4) $3,350   (5) $4,400

Oliver 66 Standard tread (gasoline, 1949–1952)
(1) $700   (2) $1,550   (3) $2,400   (4) $3,300   (5) $4,500

Oliver 66 Standard tread (diesel, 1949–1952)
(1) $800   (2) $1,450   (3) $2,350   (4) $3,200   (5) $4,300

Oliver 66 Orchard (gasoline, 1949–1952)
(1) $925   (2) $1,750   (3) $3,050   (4) $4,350   (5) $5,550

Oliver 66 Orchard (diesel, 1949–1952)
(1) $1,125   (2) $2,100   (3) $3,525   (4) $4,750   (5) $6,100

Oliver 66 Industrial (1949–1952)
(1) $900   (2) $1,525   (3) $2,225   (4) $3,150   (5) $4,700

Oliver Super 44 Utility (1957–1958)
(1) $1,550   (2) $2,975   (3) $4,650   (4) $6,150   (5) $8,325

Oliver Super 55 (gasoline, 1954–1958)
(1) $1,150   (2) $2,125   (3) $3,250   (4) $4,250   (5) $5,425

Oliver Super 55 (diesel, 1954–1958)
(1) $1,250   (2) $2,450   (3) $3,425   (4) $4,425   (5) $5,975

Oliver Super 55 Industrial (1954–1958)
(1) $1,150   (2) $2,150   (3) $3,100   (4) $4,000   (5) $5,325

Oliver Super 66 (gasoline, 1954–1958)
(1) $1,025   (2) $1,925   (3) $3,025   (4) $4,125   (5) $5,575

Oliver Super 66 (diesel, 1954–1958)
(1) $1,125   (2) $2,075   (3) $2,900   (4) $4,300   (5) $5,825

Oliver Super 66 Industrial (1954–1958)
(1) $925   (2) $1,850   (3) $3,000   (4) $3,550   (5) $4,725

Oliver Super 77 Row-crop (gasoline, dual narrow front, 1954–1958)
(1) $625   (2) $1,225   (3) $1,650   (4) $2,750   (5) $3,850

Oliver Super 77 LPG Row-crop (dual narrow front, 1954–1958)
(1) $1,100   (2) $1,800   (3) $2,850   (4) $3,525   (5) $5,075

Oliver Super 77 Row-crop (gasoline, wide-front, 1954–1958)
(1) $725   (2) $1,325   (3) $1,850   (4) $3,000   (5) $4,100

Oliver Super 77 LPG Row-crop (wide-front, 1954–1958)
(1) $1,200   (2) $1,900   (3) $3,050   (4) $3,775   (5) $5,325

Oliver Super 77 High-clearance (gasoline, 1954–1958)
(1) $1,750   (2) $2,875   (3) $5,450   (4) $7,250   (5) $9,750

Oliver Super 77 High-clearance (diesel, 1954–1958)
(1) $1,700   (2) $2,900   (3) $5,500   (4) $7,450   (5) $10,000

Oliver Super 77 High-clearance (LPG, 1954–1958)
(1) $1,500   (2) $3,250   (3) $5,750   (4) $9,000   (5) $12,750

Oliver Super 77 Standard tread (gasoline, 1954–1958)
(1) $925   (2) $1,575   (3) $2,325   (4) $3,350   (5) $5,750

Oliver Super 77 Standard tread (LPG, 1954–1958)
(1) $1,150   (2) $2,000   (3) $3,200   (4) $4,250   (5) $6,600

Oliver Super 77 Orchard (gasoline, 1954–1958)
(1) $1,425   (2) $2,250   (3) $3,475   (4) $4,950   (5) $7,825

Oliver Super 77 Orchard (LPG, 1954–1958)
(1) $1,550   (2) $2,925   (3) $4,500   (4) $6,850   (5) $10,075

Oliver Super 77 Industrial (1954–1958)
(1) $1,025   (2) $1,575   (3) $2,500   (4) $3,500   (5) $4,750

Oliver Super 88 (1954–1958)
(1) $925   (2) $1,750   (3) $2,800   (4) $3,725   (5) $4,850

Oliver Super 88 Standard (LPG, no 3-point hitch, 1954–1958)
(1) $3,000   (2) $4,500   (3) $6,000   (4) $8,250 (5) $10,000

Oliver Super 88 Industrial (1954–1958)
(1) $1,125   (2) $1,850   (3) $2,825   (4) $4,250   (5) $5,425

Oliver Super 88 High-clearance (gasoline, no 3-point hitch, 1954–1958)
(1) $5,150   (2) $8,500   (3) $12,250   (4) $15,875   (5) $20,000

Oliver Super 88 High-clearance (LPG, no 3-point hitch, 1954–1958)
(1) $5,550   (2) $10,000   (3) $15,200   (4) $18,000   (5) $23,000

Oliver Super 88 High-clearance (diesel, no 3-point hitch, 1954–1958)
(1) $5,050   (2) $9,400   (3) $14,725   (4) $17,000   (5) $22,000

Oliver Super 99 (gasoline, 1957–1958)
(1) $1,400   (2) $3,100   (3) $4,500   (4) $6,000   (5) $7,325

Oliver Super 99 (General Motors diesel, 1957–1958)
(1) $1,500   (2) $3,250   (3) $4,925   (4) $6,825   (5) $8,325

Oliver Super 99 (Oliver diesel, 1957–1958)
(1) $1,500   (2) $2,650   (3) $4,150   (4) $5,825   (5) $6,825

Oliver 950 (gasoline, 1958–1961)
(1) $1,250   (2) $2,750   (3) $4,000   (4) $5,000   (5) $6,000

Oliver 950 (diesel, 1958–1961)
(1) $1,150   (2) $2,375   (3) $3,625   (4) $4,750   (5) $5,750

Oliver 990 (General Motors diesel, 1958–1961)
(1) $1,350   (2) $3,000   (3) $5,250   (4) $7,250   (5) $8,750

Oliver 995 Lugmatic (torque converter, 1958–1961)
(1) $1,625   (2) $3,750   (3) $6,300   (4) $8,900 (5) $11,000

Oliver 550 (gasoline, 1953–1975)
(1) $1,000   (2) $1,950   (3) $2,875   (4) $4,500   (5) $5,875

Oliver 550 (diesel, 1953–1975)
(1) $1,100   (2) $2,050   (3) $2,975   (4) $4,600   (5) $5,950

Oliver 660 (gasoline, dual narrow front, 1959–1964)
(1) $1,725   (2) $2,800   (3) $3,675   (4) $4,825   (5) $6,175

Oliver 660 (diesel, dual narrow front, 1959–1964)
(1) $1,500   (2) $3,050   (3) $4,225   (4) $6,250   (5) $7,325

Oliver 770 (gasoline, 1958–1967)
(1) $1,175   (2) $1,925   (3) $2,975   (4) $3,775   (5) $4,750

Oliver 770 (diesel, 1958–1967)
(1) $1,125   (2) $1,975   (3) $3,325   (4) $3,800   (5) $4,900

Oliver 770 (LPG, 1958–1967)
(1) $1,325   (2) $2,250   (3) $3,075   (4) $4,000   (5) $5,175

Oliver 770 Orchard (gasoline, 1958–1967)
(1) $1,225   (2) $2,325   (3) $3,525   (4) $4,975   (5) $7,175

Oliver 770 Orchard (diesel, 1958–1967)
(1) $1,325   (2) $2,600   (3) $3,975   (4) $5,525   (5) $7,575

Oliver 770 High-clearance (gasoline, wide-front axle, 1958–1967)
(1) $1,400   (2) $2,575   (3) $3,800   (4) $5,700   (5) $8,325

Oliver 770 High-clearance (LPG, wide-front, 1958–1967)
(1) $1,650   (2) $3,025   (3) $5,000   (4) $8,700 (5) $12,000

Oliver 770 High-clearance (diesel, wide-front axle, 1958–1967)
(1) $1,575   (2) $3,175   (3) $4,000   (4) $6,250   (5) $8,575

Oliver 880 (gasoline, dual narrow front, 1958–1963)
(1) $875   (2) $1,675   (3) $2,925   (4) $3,675   (5) $4,675

Oliver 880 (diesel, dual narrow front, 1958–1963)
(1) $875   (2) $1,700   (3) $2,975   (4) $3,725   (5) $4,925

Oliver 880 High-clearance (gasoline, wide-front, 1958–1963)
(1) $1,525   (2) $3,025   (3) $4,450   (4) $5,975   (5) $8,825

Oliver 880 High-clearance (LPG, wide-front, 1958–1963)
(1) $1,850   (2) $4,550   (3) $6,500   (4) $9,000 (5) $12,800

Oliver 440 (offset, 1960)
(1) $1,725   (2) $3,100   (3) $4,675   (4) $6,825   (5) $8,575

Oliver 500 (1960–1963)
(1) $750   (2) $1,750   (3) $2,750   (4) $3,750   (5) $4,750

Olmstead Gas Traction Co., Great Falls, Montana
Olmstead (one known to exist, 4-wheel drive, 1912)
(1) $35,000   (2) $60,000   (3) $77,000   (4) $92,000 (5) $125,000

Ostenberg Manufacturing Company, Salina, Kansas
OMC Tractor and Norseman (1939–1950)
(1) $3,800   (2) $7,000   (3) $10,000   (4) $12,250   (5) $16,000

Parrett Tractor Company, Chicago, Illinois
Parrett 10-20 (1915–1917)
(1) $10,000   (2) $15,000   (3) $20,000   (4) $24,000   (5) $30,000

Parrett Model E and H 12-25 (1917–1920)
(1) $8,500   (2) $13,500   (3) $18,000   (4) $22,000   (5) $28,000

Parrett Model K 15-30 or 16-28 (1919–1922)
(1) $7,500   (2) $12,000   (3) $16,000   (4) $20,000   (5) $25,000

Parrett Tractor (built in Benton Harbor, MI, row-crop, 1935–1936)
(1) $2,500   (2) $4,500   (3) $6,000   (4) $8,000   (5) $10,000

Peoria Tractor Company, Peoria, Illinois
Peoria 8-20 (single rear drive wheel, 1914–1917)
(1) $4,500   (2) $7,500   (3) $10,500   (4) $12,500   (5) $16,000

Peoria 12-25 (single front wheel, 1918–1919)
(1) $3,750   (2) $5,500   (3) $7,000   (4) $8,750   (5) $11,000

Peoria 12-25 Model J (streamlined, 4-wheeled version, 1919–1921)
(1) $4,250   (2) $6,000   (3) $7,750   (4) $9,500   (5) $12,000

Peoria 12-25 Model L (streamlined, 4-wheeled version, 1920–1921)
(1) $4,250   (2) $6,000   (3) $7,750   (4) $9,500   (5) $12,000

Pioneer Tractor Manufacturing Company, Winona, Minnesota
Pioneer 40-75 (1916)
(1) $40,000   (2) $65,000   (3) $90,000   (4) $115,000 (5) $150,000

Pioneer 30-60 (1918–1927)
(1) $40,000   (2) $65,000   (3) $90,000   (4) $115,000 (5) $150,000

Pioneer Pony (1916)
(1) $8,000   (2) $20,000   (3) $25,000   (4) $35,000 (5) $40,000

Pioneer Special 15-30 (1917–1919)
(1) $6,500   (2) $15,000   (3) $20,000   (4) $30,000 (5) $35,000

Pioneer Special 18-36 (1919–1927)
(1) $5,000   (2) $12,000   (3) $18,000   (4) $25,000 (5) $30,000

Plow Man Tractor Company (see Interstate Tractor Company)

Port Huron Engine and Thresher Company, Port Huron, Michigan
Port Huron Model A 12-25 (1918–1922)
(1) $12,000 (2) $18,000   (3) $24,000   (4) $28,000 (5) $34,000

Reeves and Company, Columbus, Indiana
Reeves 40 (1911–1912)
(1) $18,000 (2) $30,000   (3) $45,000   (4) $60,000 (5) $75,000

Rock Island Plow Company, Rock Island, Illinois
Heider Model A (one known to exist in Carroll, Iowa, 1911)
(1) $15,000 (2) $22,000   (3) $28,000   (4) $34,000 (5) $40,000

Heider Model B (one known to exist in Canandaigua, NY, 1912)
(1) $12,000 (2) $18,000   (3) $24,000   (4) $28,500 (5) $34,000

Heider Model C 12-20 (1917–1927)
(1) $3,000   (2) $4,000   (3) $5,000   (4) $8,000 (5) $25,000

The friction drive was a nifty feature of the Heider Model C. The speed and the direction of the tractor changed without the need for a conventional clutch. Tractors that have their own special features without copying other companies in their day tend to draw added interest from collectors. Therefore, the values of the Heiders are high.

Heider Model D 9-16 (1916–1929)
(1) $3,500   (2) $4,500   (3) $5,500   (4) $8,000 (5) $15,000

Heider 15-27 (1924–1927)
(1) $3,000   (2) $4,000   (3) $5,000   (4) $8,000 (5) $15,000

Heider M Motor Cultivator (1-row, 1920–1926)
(1) $4,000   (2) $5,000   (3) $7,000   (4) $8,500 (5) $13,000

Heider M2 Motor Cultivator (2-row, 1920–1927)
(1) $4,800   (2) $6,500   (3) $9,000   (4) $11,000 (5) $14,000

Rock Island 18-35 (1927–1936)
(1) $3,500   (2) $4,250   (3) $5,000   (4) $7,000 (5) $10,000

Rock Island Model G-2 15-25 (1929–1932)
(1) $2,500   (2) $3,500   (3) $4,500   (4) $5,500 (5) $10,000

Rock Island 25-45 Canadian Special (1930)
(1) $5,000   (2) $6,000   (3) $8,000   (4) $10,000 (5) $15,000

Rock Island Model H3 15-25 (1933)
(1) $3,000   (2) $3,500   (3) $4,500   (4) $6,500 (5) $10,000

Rock Island H4 15-25 (1934)
(1) $3,000   (2) $3,500   (3) $4,500   (4) $6,500 (5) $10,000

Rock Island Model H5 15-25 (1935)
(1) $3,000   (2) $3,500   (3) $4,500   (4) $6,500 (5) $10,000

Rock Island H22 22-40 (1935)
(1) $4,000   (2) $5,000   (3) $7,500   (4) $10,000 (5) $15,000

Rock Oil Company, Edmonton, Alberta
Rockol C (6-cylinder Chrysler engine, dual-narrow front, 1945–1950)
(1) $500   (2) $900   (3) $1,500   (4) $3,800 (5) $8,000

Rockol B (6-cylinder Chrysler engine, wide-front, 1945–1950)
(1) $500   (2) $900   (3) $1,500   (4) $3,800 (5) $8,000

Russell and Company, Massillon, Ohio

Three brothers—Charles, Nahum, and Clement Russell—formed C. M. Russell and Company in 1842. They specialized in the manufacturing of threshing machines and railroad cars. In 1878 they reorganized the company and with Nahum as president they began building steam engines. Russell steam traction engines were among the finest built in their day. From 1909 to 1924 the Russell Company produced about one thousand gasoline tractors, and only a handful of models still survive. The company closed in early 1927 and was auctioned off. Because of its vivid history and the fact that the machines are magnificent examples of quality for their era, the Russell tractors are rare, extremely desirable, and demand high prices.

The American (1909–1914)
(1) $10,250   (2) $15,000   (3) $19,000   (4) $22,500   (5) $28,000

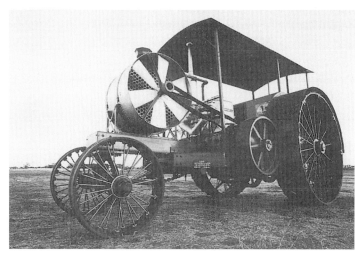

The Russell Giant is an impressive monster of a tractor. A 30-60 (older restoration) sold for $52,000 in 1998. Machines like this are out of reach for the average collector.

Russell Giant 40-80 (rerated 30-60, 3-wheel version, 1911–1913)
(1) $30,000   (2) $48,000   (3) $60,000   (4) $75,000   (5) $90,000

Russell Giant 40-80 (rerated 30-60, 4-wheel version, 1913–1914)
(1) $30,000   (2) $48,000   (3) $60,000   (4) $75,000   (5) $90,000

Russell Junior 12-24 (1915–1927)
(1) $4,500   (2) $6,500   (3) $8,750   (4) $10,750   (5) $13,000

Russell Little Boss 15-30 (one known to exist, 1917–1927)
(1) $6,750   (2) $11,750   (3) $15,000   (4) $18,000 (5) $22,000

Russell Big Boss 20-35 and 20-40 (1917–1927)
(1) $5,500   (2) $8,000   (3) $10,750   (4) $13,250   (5) $16,000

Sawyer-Massey Company, Hamilton, Ontario

Sawyer-Massey 10-20 (Waukesha 4-cylinder, 1912–1917)
(1) $10,000   (2) $12,000   (3) $18,000   (4) $22,000   (5) $26,000

Sawyer-Massey 11-22 (Erd 4-cylinder, 1918)
(1) $10,000   (2) $12,000   (3) $18,000   (4) $22,000   (5) $26,000

Sawyer-Massey 12-25 (ca. 1918)
(1) $10,000   (2) $12,000   (3) $18,000   (4) $22,000   (5) $26,000

Sawyer-Massey 16-32 (Sawyer 4-cylinder, 1912–1917)
(1) $12,000   (2) $14,000   (3) $22,000   (4) $28,000 (5) $37,000

Sawyer-Massey 17-34 (Twin City 4-cylinder, 1918–1922)
(1) $12,000   (2) $14,000   (3) $22,000   (4) $28,000 (5) $37,000

Sawyer-Massey 20-40 (Sawyer 4-cylinder, 1918)
(1) $12,000   (2) $14,000   (3) $22,000   (4) $28,000 (5) $37,000

Sawyer-Massey 22-45 (Sawyer 4-cylinder, 1911–1912)
(1) $18,000   (2) $25,000   (3) $35,000   (4) $42,000 (5) $55,000

Sawyer-Massey 25-50 (Sawyer fou4r-cylinder, 1912–1917)
(1) $18,000   (2) $25,000   (3) $35,000   (4) $42,000 (5) $55,000

Sawyer-Massey 27-50 (Sawyer 4-cylinder, 1918–1921)
(1) $18,000   (2) $25,000   (3) $35,000   (4) $42,000 (5) $55,000

Sears-Roebuck Company, Chicago, Illinois
Bradley GP (starter and lights, 1931)
(1) $4,600   (2) $5,050   (3) $6,300   (4) $7,300   (5) $8,600

Economy (used various automobile engines, ca. 1930)
(1) $900   (2) $1,300   (3) $1,950   (4) $2,800   (5) $3,800

Shaw Manufacturing Company, Galesburg, Kansas
Shaw Du-All R8 (8-horsepower Briggs & Stratton engine, ca. 1930)
(1) $250   (2) $600   (3) $1,100   (4) $1,300   (5) $1,900

Shaw Du-All R12-T (12-horsepower Wisconsin engine, ca. 1930)
(1) $350   (2) $700   (3) $1,300   (4) $1,500   (5) $2,100

Shaw-Enochs Tractor Company, Minneapolis, Minnesota
Shawnee 6-12 (1919–1921)
(1) $3,500   (2) $5,500   (3) $7,000   (4) $8,750   (5) $10,500

Shawnee 9-18 (1919–1921)
(1) $3,500   (2) $5,500   (3) $7,000   (4) $8,750   (5) $10,500

Shelby Tractor and Truck Company, Shelby, Ohio
Shelby 9-18 (1919–1921)
(1) $6,750   (2) $10,000   (3) $12,750   (4) $14,750 (5) $19,000

Shelby 15-30 (1920–1921)
(1) $7,250   (2) $11,000   (3) $14,000   (4) $16,500 (5) $21,000

Shelby 10-20 (1921)
(1) $6,750   (2) $10,000   (3) $12,750   (4) $14,750 (5) $19,000

R. H. Sheppard Company, Hanover, Pennsylvania
Sheppard SD-1 (1949–1950)
(1) $10,000   (2) $13,500   (3) $16,500   (4) $20,000 (5) $25,000

Sheppard made tractors with its own one, two, three, and four-cylinder engines. Unlike several other brands, the little one-cylinder SD-1 shown here is worth more than any of its bigger brothers. The SD-1 sold for $1,095 in 1949 without the option of electric starting—a far cry from the value of this rare tractor today!

Sheppard SD-2 Row-crop (1949–1957)
(1) $3,250   (2) $5,250   (3) $6,600   (4) $9,250 (5) $11,000

Sheppard SDG-2 Grove (1950–1956)
(1) $3,750   (2) $5,750   (3) $7,250   (4) $11,000 (5) $14,500

Sheppard made diesel engines as power units before building tractors. The SD-3 shown here used its three-cylinder engine. In 1950 the list price for a SD-3 without the optional hydraulic power unit and independent PTO was $3,195. For an additional $87, one could have bought the 4.5-inch bore engine over the standard 4.0-inch bore. Today the values of these Sheppard tractors are strong, but the restoration is often difficult and somewhat expensive as many parts are unique to this brand. One can often obtain parts for the weak Timken differentials on this machine from certain Cockshutt tractors, but most other assemblies are Sheppard-built.

Sheppard SDO-2 Orchard (1950–1956)
(1) $ 4,000   (2) $5,750   (3) $7,500   (4) $11,250 (5) $14,750

Sheppard SDI-2 Industrial (1950–1956)
(1) $ 2,250   (2) $3,500   (3) $4,750   (4) $6,750   (5) $8,750

Sheppard SDHI-2 Heavy-duty Industrial (1950–1956)
(1) $ 2,500   (2) $4,000   (3) $6,000   (4) $8,000   (5) $10,000

Sheppard SD-3 Row-crop (1948–1957)
(1) $1,750   (2) $3,000   (3) $4,000   (4) $6,250   (5) $8,250

Sheppard SDG-3 Grove (1950–1956)
(1) $2,250   (2) $3,500   (3) $5,000   (4) $8,000   (5) $11,500

Sheppard SDO-3 Orchard (1950–1956)
(1) $2,750 (2) $4,000 (3) $5,500 (4) $8,500 (5) $12,250

Sheppard SDI-3 Industrial (1950–1956)
(1) $ 2,250 (2) $4,250 (3) $5,500 (4) $7,500 (5) $9,750

Sheppard SDHI-3 Heavy-duty Industrial (1950–1956)
(1) $ 2,750 (2) $4,750 (3) $6,000 (4) $8,000 (5) $10,500

Sheppard SD-4 (1955–1957)
(1) $2,000 (2) $4,250 (3) $6,250 (4) $8,250 (5) $11,750

Sheppard SCTC-4 (torque converter, 1955–1957)
(1) $2,500 (2) $4,500 (3) $7,500 (4) $11,250 (5) $15,000

Square Turn Tractor Company, Norfolk, Nebraska
Square Turn Tractor 18-30 (rerated 18-35, 1918–1921)
(1) $12,000 (2) $23,000 (3) $30,000 (4) $38,000 (5) $45,000

Star Tractor Company, Findlay, Ohio
Star 5-10 (1918)
(1) $3,500 (2) $5,000 (3) $7,200 (4) $9,000 (5) $11,000

Stearns Motor Manufacturing Company, Ludington, Michigan
Stearns Model Q 15-35 (1919–1920)
(1) $7,250 (2) $11,000 (3) $14,000 (4) $16,500 (5) $21,000

Sterling Machine and Stamping Company, Wellington, Ohio

Wellington Model F 12-22 (1920)
(1) $4,500 (2) $6,200 (3) $9,000 (4) $11,000 (5) $14,000

Wellington Model B 16-30 (1920)
(1) $4,800 (2) $6,700 (3) $9,500 (4) $11,750 (5) $15,000

Stinson Tractor Company, Minneapolis, Minnesota
Stinson 18-36 (three known to exist, 1917–1922)
(1) $6,500 (2) $12,000 (3) $15,500 (4) $18,500 (5) $24,000

Thieman Harvester Company, Albert City, Iowa
In 1932, Thieman designed a tractor kit to appeal to farmers with little money. These thrifty little steel-wheeled tractors had Ford Model A engines. By 1938, Thieman streamlined the old overhead steering model version with a steering shaft below the hood and a nifty vertical-bar grille. Some hard-to-find versions have the optional factory rubber rear tires, and rare early models have a single front steel wheel. These tractors have gone from being completely overlooked to highly cherished collectibles in only a few years.

Theiman (steel rear wheels, rubber front, open drive chain, overhead steering, ca. 1930)

(1) $900 (2) $1,700 (3) $2,250 (4) $3,000 (5) $4,100

The Thieman was an economy-type tractor that used an automobile engine in the drivetrain to save costs. There was a time when used Thieman tractors were considered barely worth parking in a hedgerow. Today collector interest is reviving these wonderful pieces of tractor history and the values are climbing.

Theiman (steel front and rear wheels, open drive chain, overhead steering, ca. 1930)
(1) $1,500   (2) $2,400   (3) $3,000   (4) $3,800   (5) $5,000

Theiman (steel rear wheels, rubber front, enclosed drive chain, overhead steering, ca. 1930)
(1) $900   (2) $1,700   (3) $2,250   (4) $3,000   (5) $4,100

Theiman (steel rear wheels, rubber front, streamlined, grille, ca. 1940)
(1) $1,800   (2) $2,700   (3) $3,400   (4) $4,300   (5) $5,500

Theiman (factory rubber tires, streamlined, grille, ca. 1940)
(1) $1,900   (2) $2,800   (3) $3,500   (4) $4,450   (5) $5,700

Tioga Manufacturing Company, Philadelphia, Pennsylvania
Tioga Tractor (1920-1931)
(1) $5,750   (2) $8,750   (3) $11,000   (4) $13,250   (5) $16,500

Toro Motor Company, Minneapolis, Minnesota
Toro Motor Cultivator (3 wheels, 1920-1927)
(1) $3,250   (2) $4,750   (3) $6,000   (4) $7,250   (5) $9,000

Toro Model 10 and 12 (4 wheels, 1920-1927)
(1) $3,500   (2) $5,500   (3) $7,000   (4) $8,500   (5) $11,000

Townsend Manufacturing Company, Janesville, Wisconsin
Bower City 10-20 (1915-1918)
(1) $9,000   (2) $13,000   (3) $20,000   (4) $25,000   (5) $30,000

Bower City 12-25 (1918-1919)
(1) $10,000   (2) $14,000   (3) $22,000   (4) $27,000   (5) $32,000

Townsend 15-30 (1919-1924)
(1) $8,000   (2) $12,000   (3) $18,000   (4) $22,000   (5) $28,000

Townsend 20-40 (1923–1931)
(1) $13,000   (2) $20,000   (3) $28,000   (4) $33,000 (5) $40,000

Townsend 25-50 (1924–1931)
(1) $15,000   (2) $22,000   (3) $30,000   (4) $37,000 (5) $45,000

Townsend 30-60 (1924–1931)
(1) $20,000   (2) $32,000   (3) $40,000   (4) $50,000 (5) $64,000

Townsend 12-20 (1924–1931)
(1) $10,000   (2) $16,000   (3) $21,000   (4) $25,000 (5) $30,000

Traylor Engineering Company, Cornwells, Pennsylvania
Traylor 6-12 (1920–1928)
(1) $5,000   (2) $7,500   (3) $9,000   (4) $10,500 (5) $13,000

Turner Manufacturing Company, Port Washington, Wisconsin
Simplicity 12-20 (1915–1920)
(1) $8,500   (2) $12,000   (3) $16,000   (4) $20,000 (5) $24,000

Simplicity 14-25 (1919–1920)
(1) $10,000 (2) $15,000   (3) $20,000   (4) $24,000 (5) $28,000

United Tractor Corporation, New York, New York
Mohawk 8-16 (1921)
(1) $6,000   (2) $8,000   (3) $10,000   (4) $12,000 (5) $14,000

U. S. Tractor and Machinery Company, Menasha, Wisconsin
Uncle Sam 12-20 (1918–1922)
(1) $11,000 (2) $16,000   (3) $20,000   (4) $24,500 (5) $30,000

Uncle Sam 20-30 (1918–1921)
(1) $13,000   (2) $18,500   (3) $24,000   (4) $28,000 (5) $34,000

Velie Motors Corporation, Moline, Illinois
Biltwell 12-24 (1916–1920)
(1) $14,000   (2) $21,000   (3) $27,000   (4) $32,000 (5) $38,000

Montgomery Ward, Chicago, Illinois
Model HR Row-crop (made by the Custom Tractor Mfg. Co., 1947–1953)
(1) $800   (2) $1,500   (3) $2,000   (4) $3,000   (5) $8,000

Model HW Wide-front (made by the Custom Tractor Mfg. Co., 1947–1953)
(1) $1,000   (2) $1,700   (3) $2,250   (4) $3,500   (5) $8,000

Model E Row-crop (made by the Custom Tractor Mfg. Co., 1947–1953)
(1) $1,000   (2) $1,700   (3) $2,200   (4) $3,200   (5) $8,000

Montgomery Wards sold tractors made by different companies throughout the years. This 1949 Wards Twin-row was actually a B. F. Avery tractor with the Wards' logo on the hood. The values of these B. F. Avery tractors tends to be quite modest, but collector interest is on the rise.

Model E Wide-front (made by the Custom Tractor Mfg. Co., 1947–1953)
(1) $1,300   (2) $2,000   (3) $2,800   (4) $4,000   (5) $9,000

Twin Row (1939–1942)
(1) $400   (2) $800   (3) $1,500   (4) $3,800   (5) $4,500

Utility Tractor (conversion kit used various automobile chassis, ca. 1930)
(1) $175   (2) $400   (3) $975   (4) $1,600   (5) $2,700

Waterloo Company, Ontario, Canada

Waterloo built about 1,000 tractors during three years of production. The values of these tractors will likely increase over the next few years as there is a tremendous surge of interest in these "lesser known classics," the phrase that the late Ed Spiess helped make famous.

Waterloo Bronco (12-horsepower Wisconsin engine, 1948–1950)
(1) $1,200   (2) $2,100   (3) $2,800   (4) $3,600   (5) $4,800

Waterloo Gasoline Engine Company, Waterloo, Iowa

Waterloo Boy One-Man Tractor (25 horsepower, 1912–1913)
(1) $28,000   (2) $45,000   (3) $58,000   (4) $72,000   (5) $90,000

Waterloo Boy (15 horsepower, 1912–1913)
(1) $18,000   (2) $29,000   (3) $38,000   (4) $45,000   (5) $55,000

Waterloo Boy R 12-24 (rerated 12-25, 1914–1916)
(1) $14,000   (2) $21,000   (3) $23,000   (4) $32,500   (5) $45,000

Waterloo Boy California Special 12-25 (single front wheel, ca. 1915–1919)
(1) $15,000   (2) $22,500   (3) $25,000   (4) $35,000   (5) $45,000

John Deere eventually
bought out the
Waterloo Gasoline
Engine Co. The
powerful interest from
John Deere
collectors keeps the
demand for these
Waterloo Boy tractors
at an all-time high.

Waterloo Boy N 12-25 (1917–1924)
(1) $12,750   (2) $18,750   (3) $20,500   (4) $30,000 (5) $37,500

Wetmore Tractor Company, Sioux City, Iowa
Wetmore 12-25 (1919–1931)
(1) $8,000   (2) $13,500   (3) $17,000   (4) $20,000 (5) $24,000

Wharton Motors Company, Dallas, Texas
Wharton 3WD 12-22 (1920–1923)
(1) $10,000 (2) $16,000   (3) $20,000   (4) $24,000 (5) $30,000

Wharton FWD 20-40 (1920)
(1) $12,000 (2) $19,000   (3) $24,000   (4) $28,000 (5) $35,000

Wheat Tiller and Tractor Company
(see Hession Tiller and Tractor Company)

Whitney Tractor Company, Cleveland, Ohio
Whitney 9-18 (1918–1920)
(1) $11,000 (2) $18,000   (3) $23,000   (4) $28,000 (5) $34,000

Wichita Tractor Company, Wichita, Kansas
Midwest 8-16 (1918–1920)
(1) $12,000 (2) $18,500   (3) $24,000   (4) $29,000 (5) $36,000

Wisconsin Farm Tractor Company, Sauk City, Wisconsin
Wisconsin 16-32, 20-35, 22-40 (all models similar, 1917–1923)
(1) $9,000   (2) $14,000   (3) $18,000   (4) $21,000 (5) $25,000

Wizard Tractor Corporation, Los Angeles, California
Wizard 4-Pull 20-35 (1925–1930)
(1) $8,000   (2) $11,500   (3) $14,000   (4) $17,000 (5) $21,000

CHAPTER 2

CRAWLER TRACTORS

Acme Harvesting Machine Company, Peoria, Illinois
Acme 12-20 Tracklayer (half-track, 1918–1919)
(1) $18,000 (2) $26,000   (3) $33,000   (4) $40,000 (5) $51,000

Allis-Chalmers, Milwaukee, Wisconsin
In February 1928, Allis-Chalmers bought the Monarch Tractor Company for $500,000. Monarch was well known for its large chain-drive crawlers, but the Monarch designs were becoming outdated when Allis-Chalmers took over. By the early 1930s, Allis-Chalmers upgraded the Monarchs by replacing the archaic steering wheel with gear-driven final drives and steering levers. In 1934 the company offered an optional Hesselman-type oil engine on its bigger crawlers. This spark-ignition diesel is much less common than the gasoline versions and causes increased demand. The interest in crawler collecting is beginning to increase, and the Monarch and early Allis-Chalmers models are quite collectable. The costs of crawler restorations are generally very steep. Crawlers with extremely nice undercarriages and strong engines will bring high dollars.

Monarch 50 (1928–1931)
(1) $8,000 (2) $12,000   (3) $15,000   (4) $18,000(5) $20,000

Monarch 75 (1928–1931)
(1) $8,000 (2) $12,000   (3) $16,000   (4) $20,000(5) $27,000

Monarch 35 (1928–1933)
(1) $1,500 (2) $2,400   (3) $4,800   (4) $7,000 (5) $12,000

Model K Crawler (steering wheel, 1933–1935)
(1) $1,000 (2) $1,250   (3) $3,000   (4) $6,000 (5) $10,000

Model K Crawler (steering levers, 1935–1943)
(1) $800   (2) $2,500   (3) $5,500   (4) $7,000   (5) $9,000

Model KO Crawler (diesel fuel, 1934–1943)
(1) $2,250 (2) $5,500   (3) $8,200   (4) $10,500 (5) $14,500

Model L Crawler (1931–1942)
(1) $750   (2) $3,000   (3) $7,000   (4) $11,000 (5) $15,000

Allis-Chalmers used the engine from its popular Model U farm tractor to build the little Model M crawler. Weighing 6,620 pounds, this compact crawler pulled 5,576 pounds during its Nebraska test. The M was built from 1932 to 1942 with an engine size increase during 1936. Allis-Chalmers has boomed as a collectible tractor in the past four and five years, augmenting interest in the crawlers along with it.

Model LO Crawler (diesel fuel, 1934–1942)
(1) $2,250   (2) $7,000   (3) $9,000   (4) $14,000   (5) $22,000

Model LD (General Motors Diesel, 1939)
(1) $6,500   (2) $12,000   (3) $19,000   (4) $27,000   (5) $35,000

Model M Crawler (1932–1942)
(1) $500   (2) $1,850   (3) $3,000   (4) $6,000   (5) $8,500

Model M Orchard (high seat and low seat, 1932–1942)
(1) $4,500   (2) $8,000   (3) $10,000   (4) $12,000   (5) $14,000

Model S (1937–1942)
(1) $2,500   (2) $5,000   (3) $7,000   (4) $10,000   (5) $15,000

Model SO (diesel fuel, 1937–1942)
(1) $5,000   (2) $7,000   (3) $9,000   (4) $14,000   (5) $20,000

Model HD-7 (General Motors diesel, 1940–1950)
(1) $1,500   (2) $3,500   (3) $4,055   (4) $5,000   (5) $7,750

Model HD-10 (General Motors diesel, 1940–1950)
(1) $1,700   (2) $4,000   (3) $5,000   (4) $6,250   (5) $8,500

Model HD-14 (General Motors diesel, 1939–1947)
(1) $2,400   (2) $4,500   (3) $5,750   (4) $7,500   (5) $9,750

Model HD-5 (General Motors diesel, 1946–1955)
(1) $1,600   (2) $3,000   (3) $4,800   (4) $6,000   (5) $8,250

Model HD-19 (General Motors diesel, 1947–1950)
(1) $2,700   (2) $4,700   (3) $6,250   (4) $8,000   (5) $10,500

Model HD-9 (General Motors diesel, 1950–1955)
(1) $1,800   (2) $4,250   (3) $5,500   (4) $6,500   (5) $9,000

Model HD-15 (General Motors diesel, 1950–1955)
(1) $1,950   (2) $4,400   (3) $5,750   (4) $6,800   (5) $9,450

Model HD-20 (General Motors diesel, 1951–1954)
(1) $2,900   (2) $4,900   (3) $6,750   (4) $8,500 (5) $11,000

Model HD-21 Series A (diesel, 1954–1969)
(1) $3,000   (2) $5,100   (3) $7,000   (4) $9,250 (5) $13,000

Model HD-16 Series A (diesel, 1955–1970)
(1) $2,200   (2) $4,600   (3) $5,950   (4) $7,000 (5) $10,000

Model HD-11 Series A (diesel, 1955–1970)
(1) $2,200   (2) $4,400   (3) $5,650   (4) $6,750 (5) $9,750

Model HD-6 (diesel, 1955–1974)
(1) $1,650   (2) $3,200   (3) $5,000   (4) $6,200 (5) $8,450

Model H-3 (gasoline, 1960–1967)
(1) $1,400   (2) $2,700   (3) $4,250   (4) $5,500 (5) $7,250

Model HD-3 (diesel, 1960–1968)
(1) $1,100   (2) $2,500   (3) $4,100   (4) $5,500 (5) $7,250

American Tractor Corporation, Churubusco, Indiana

The Terratrac crawlers produced from 1950 to 1957 by American Tractor were well-built machines. In 1957, J. I. Case bought the company and continued a similar line. Early Case crawlers often have Terratrac inscribed parts on them. Several models were built with low production: the Model 200h had only 80 copies built, the M-2 had only 32. Up until now, the demand for Terratrac crawlers has not been strong, but because of their smaller size and low production, one should expect their values to increase in the next few years.

Terratrac GT-25 (gasoline, 1950–1953)
(1) $800   (2) $2,050   (3) $2,550   (4) $3,400 (5) $5,950

Terratrac GT-30 (gasoline, 1951–1954)
(1) $700   (2) $2,150   (3) $2,550   (4) $3,400 (5) $5,950

Terratrac GT-34 (gasoline, 1951–1954)
(1) $800   (2) $2,050   (3) $2,725   (4) $3,575 (5) $6,125

Terratrac DT-34 (diesel, 1952–1954)
(1) $1,000   (2) $2,550   (3) $3,225   (4) $4,100 (5) $6,625

Terratrac M-2 (gasoline, 1952–1953)
(1) $800   (2) $2,150   (3) $2,550   (4) $3,400 (5) $5,950

Terratrac GT-32 (gasoline, 1953–1954)
(1) $800   (2) $2,150   (3) $2,550   (4) $3,400 (5) $5,750

Terratrac GT-28 (gasoline, 1953–1954)
(1) $800   (2) $2,150   (3) $2,550   (4) $3,400 (5) $5,750

Terratrac M-3h (gasoline, 1953–1956)
(1) $1,000   (2) $2,200   (3) $2,875   (4) $3,750   (5) $6,300

Terratrac 200h (gasoline, 1954–1955)
(1) $800   (2) $2,150   (3) $2,550   (4) $3,400   (5) $5,750

Terratrac 300 (gasoline, 1954–1955)
(1) $900   (2) $2,200   (3) $2,725   (4) $3,575   (5) $5,950

Terratrac 400 (gasoline, 1954–1955)
(1) $1,200   (2) $3,050   (3) $3,575   (4) $4,425   (5) $6,800

Terratrac 400 (diesel, 1955)
(1) $1,300   (2) $3,225   (3) $3,750   (4) $4,750   (5) $7,150

Terratrac 500 (gasoline, 1954–1955)
(1) $1,300   (2) $3,225   (3) $3,750   (4) $4,750   (5) $7,150

Terratrac 500 (diesel, 1954–1955)
(1) $1,500   (2) $3,575   (3) $4,075   (4) $5,100   (5) $7,475

Terratrac 256h (gasoline, 1955–1956)
(1) $900   (2) $2,200   (3) $2,725   (4) $3,575   (5) $5,950

Terratrac 356h (gasoline, 1955–1956)
(1) $1,000   (2) $2,375   (3) $2,900   (4) $3,750   (5) $6,125

Terratrac 456 (gasoline, 1955–1956)
(1) $1,300   (2) $3,225   (3) $3,750   (4) $4,600   (5) $6,975

Terratrac 456 (diesel, 1955–1957)
(1) $1,400   (2) $3,400   (3) $3,900   (4) $4,925   (5) $7,300

Terratrac 556 (gasoline, 1955–1957)
(1) $1,400   (2) $3,400   (3) $3,900   (4) $4,925   (5) $7,300

Terratrac 556 (diesel, 1955–1957)
(1) $1,600   (2) $3,750   (3) $4,250   (4) $5,275   (5) $7,650

Terratrac 656 (gasoline, 1955–1957)
(1) $1,400   (2) $3,575   (3) $4,600   (4) $5,600   (5) $8,000

Terratrac 656 (diesel, 1955–1957)
(1) $1,700   (2) $4,075   (3) $5,100   (4) $6,300   (5) $8,500

F. C. Austin Company, Chicago, Illinois
Austin Multipedal 18-35 (1916–1917)
(1) $10,000   (2) $18,000   (3) $28,000   (4) $35,000   (5) $50,000

Austin Multipedal 12-20 (1917–1918)
(1) $5,500   (2) $8,000   (3) $17,000   (4) $22,000   (5) $30,000

Austin 20-40 (1919–1920)
(1) $9,000   (2) $12,000   (3) $19,000   (4) $25,000   (5) $40,000

Auto-Track-Tractor Syndicate, San Francisco, California
Auto-Track 30-50 (1921–1924)
(1) $10,000   (2) $15,000   (3) $19,000   (4) $23,000 (5) $30,000

Avery Company, Peoria, Illinois
Track Runner (half-track, 1923–1924)
(1) $8,500   (2) $10,000   (3) $13,000   (4) $15,000 (5) $20,000

Badley Tractor Company, Portland, Oregon
Angleworm 10 (1936)
(1) $7,000   (2) $11,500   (3) $14,000   (4) $16,000 (5) $20,000

Bates Machine and Tractor Company, Joliet, Illinois
Model D 12-20 (half-track, rerated 15-22, 1918–1920)
(1) $4,000   (2) $10,000   (3) $15,000   (4) $18,000 (5) $25,000

Model F 18-25 (half-track, 1921–1937)
(1) $4,000   (2) $10,000   (3) $15,000   (4) $18,000 (5) $25,000

Model G 25-35 (half-track, 1921–1928)
(1) $4,000   (2) $10,000   (3) $15,000   (4) $18,000 (5) $25,000

Bates 25 (1924–1928)
(1) $8,000   (2) $12,500   (3) $17,000   (4) $20,000 (5) $30,000

Bates 30 (1926–1928)
(1) $22,000   (2) $30,000   (3) $34,000   (4) $40,000 (5) $45,000

Bates 40 (1924–1929)
(1) $8,000   (2) $14,000   (3) $19,000   (4) $23,500 (5) $35,000

Model 40 Diesel (1937)
(1) $20,000   (2) $26,000   (3) $29,000   (4) $33,000 (5) $40,000

Bates 80 (1929–1937)
(1) $23,000   (2) $32,000   (3) $42,000   (4) $50,000 (5) $60,000

Bean Spray Pump Company, San Jose, California
Bean Track-Pull 6-10 (1915–1921)
(1) $2,600   (2) $4,750   (3) $7,500   (4) $9,000 (5) $13,000

Bean Track-Pull 8-16 (1920–1921)
(1) $2,750   (2) $4,900   (3) $7,750   (4) $9,250 (5) $13,000

Bear Tractors Incorporated, New York, New York
Bear 25-35 (1923–1925)
(1) $6,000   (2) $13,000   (3) $19,000   (4) $23,500 (5) $30,000

C. L. Best Traction Company, San Leandro, California
Best 75 (1913–1919)
(1) $21,000   (2) $29,000   (3) $50,000   (4) $90,000 (5) $125,000

This 1913 Best Model 30 Humpback crawler is part of the Heidrick collection. Values are somewhat difficult to establish on these rare crawlers as the cost of restoration is enormous and the numbers are so limited. One could spend in the five-digit range to restore such a machine suitably.

Best 30 Horsepower Muley (1920–1925)
(1) $11,250   (2) $15,000   (3) $18,750   (4) $27,500   (5) $38,000

Best 8-16 Pony (ca. 1920)
(1) $4,800   (2) $11,250   (3) $18,250   (4) $23,250   (5) $28,250

This 14-ton monster is a Best Model 40. Standing 10 feet tall, it is capable of running down the road at a top speed of 2-3/8 miles per hour while it guzzles fuel from its 80-gallon tank. Large crawlers like this are superstars at tractor shows and are coveted by many a collector.

Best 40 (1919–1925)
(1) $10,000   (2) $21,750   (3) $28,750   (4) $31,250   (5) $37,500

Best 60 (1919–1925)
(1) $12,500   (2) $20,000   (3) $26,000   (4) $30,000   (5) $35,000

Best Tracklayer 25 (1920–1925)
(1) $10,000   (2) $17,000   (3) $22,500   (4) $27,500   (5) $32,500

This Best 75 was rated to pull 8 to 12 14-inch plows and could cover 20 to 30 acres in a day. Restoration of such a machine is not for someone on a small budget. Few collectors have the capability or the resources it takes to restore such an immense crawler.

Blewett Tractor Company, Tacoma, Washington
Webfoot 28-53 (single tiller wheel, 1920–1921)
(1) $15,000   (2) $32,000   (3) $40,000   (4) $45,000 (5) $60,000

Webfoot 25-40 (1921)
(1) $7,000   (2) $14,000   (3) $18,000   (4) $20,000 (5) $26,000

Buckeye Manufacturing Company, Anderson, Indiana
Chain Tread 16-32 (1917–1919)
(1) $10,000   (2) $15,500   (3) $19,000   (4) $24,000 (5) $30,000

Trundaar 20-35 (1917–1923)
(1) $10,000   (2) $17,000   (3) $22,000   (4) $26,500 (5) $35,000

Trundaar 25-40 (1920–1923)
(1) $10,000   (2) $17,000   (3) $22,000   (4) $26,500 (5) $35,000

Trundaar Model 10 (1920–1923)
(1) $10,000   (2) $17,000   (3) $22,000   (4) $26,500 (5) $35,000

Bullock Tractor Company, Chicago, Illinois
Creeping Grip 12-20 (1914–1920)
(1) $8,000   (2) $14,000   (3) $18,000   (4) $23,000 (5) $30,000

Creeping Grip 18-30 (1914–1920)
(1) $8,000   (2) $14,000   (3) $18,000   (4) $23,000 (5) $30,000

Caterpillar Tractor Company, Peoria, Illinois
Caterpillar 2-Ton (1926–1928)
(1) $1,000   (2) $2,000   (3) $4,500   (4) $7,750 (5) $9,250

Caterpillar 2-Ton Orchard (1926–1928)
(1) $1,500   (2) $2,750   (3) $5,750   (4) $9,000 (5) $12,500

Caterpillar 5-Ton (1926–1927)
(1) $3,500   (2) $5,000   (3) $7,500   (4) $9,900 (5) $13,750

Caterpillar 10-Ton (1926)
(1) $4,000   (2) $9,000   (3) $14,500   (4) $18,500 (5) $21,250

Caterpillar 10 (1928–1932)
(1) $1,000   (2) $3,000   (3) $4,500   (4) $5,500 (5) $6,750

Caterpillar 10 Wide (1928–1932)
(1) $1,500   (2) $3,500   (3) $4,750   (4) $7,500 (5) $9,000

Caterpillar 10 Orchard (1928–1932)
(1) $5,250   (2) $6,500   (3) $8,000   (4) $10,000 (5) $13,750

Caterpillar 10 High-clearance (1928–1932)
(1) $3,250   (2) $5,250   (3) $7,500   (4) $9,000 (5) $11,250

Caterpillar 15PV (1929–1932)
(1) $1,250   (2) $2,500   (3) $3,500   (4) $5,000 (5) $6,500

171

The Caterpillar Thirty was a popular crawler that was carried over from the Best Model Thirty. The gray paint on early Model Thirty crawlers was replaced with yellow on December 7, 1931.

Caterpillar 15PV Orchard (1929–1932)
(1) $1,650 (2) $3,250 (3) $4,250 (4) $5,750 (5) $6,750

Caterpillar 15 7C (also called Small 15, 1932–1933)
(1) $3,750 (2) $5,500 (3) $7,500 (4) $8,500 (5) $12,500

Caterpillar 15 7C Orchard (also called Small 15 Orchard, 1932–1933)
(1) $4,250 (2) $6,700 (3) $9,000 (4) $10,500 (5) $12,750

Caterpillar 15 7C High-clearance (also called Small 15 High-clearance, 1932–1933)
(1) $6,750 (2) $8,500 (3) $10,500 (4) $12,500 (5) $15,750

Caterpillar 20L and PL (1927–1931)
(1) $925 (2) $2,500 (3) $4,000 (4) $5,500 (5) $7,250

Caterpillar 20L and PL Wide-tread (1927–1931)
(1) $1,250 (2) $2,750 (3) $4,250 (4) $6,000 (5) $8,000

Caterpillar 20L and PL Orchard (1927–1931)
(1) $800 (2) $2,600 (3) $4,250 (4) $5,750 (5) $7,250

Caterpillar 20 8C (also called Small 20, 1932–1934)
(1) $1,750 (2) $4,000 (3) $6,000 (4) $7,000 (5) $9,000

Caterpillar 20 8C Orchard (1932–1934)
(1) $4,000 (2) $4,500 (3) $5,000 (4) $5,900 (5) $7,000

Caterpillar 22 (1934–1939)
(1) $600 (2) $1,000 (3) $2,850 (4) $4,500 (5) $5,500

Caterpillar 22 Orchard (1934–1939)
(1) $550 (2) $1,200 (3) $3,500 (4) $4,500 (5) $5,500

Caterpillar 22 High-clearance Wide (1934–1939)
(1) $8,250 (2) $9,000 (3) $12,500 (4) $14,000 (5) $16,500

Caterpillar 25 (1931–1933)
(1) $3,500 (2) $4,800 (3) $6,500 (4) $7,500 (5) $9,750

Caterpillar 25 Orchard (1931-1933)
(1) $3,250   (2) $5,000   (3) $7,000   (4) $8,500 (5) $10,000

Caterpillar 28 (1933-1935)
(1) $1,900   (2) $3,500   (3) $4,750   (4) $6,250   (5) $7,500

Caterpillar 28 Orchard (1933-1935)
(1) $2,250   (2) $2,800   (3) $4,000   (4) $6,000   (5) $8,500

Caterpillar 30S and PS (1925-1932)
(1) $1,500   (2) $3,000   (3) $4,500   (4) $6,000   (5) $7,250

The Caterpillar Sixty was a gasoline-powered machine that sold 18,948 copies from 1925 to 1931. The diesel version sold only 157 units and was built from 1931-1932. A restored gasoline version sold for $21,000 at the Keith Clark Auction in 2000.

Caterpillar 30S and PS Orchard (1925-1932)
(1) $3,250   (2) $4,750   (3) $6,000   (4) $8,500 (5) $11,750

Caterpillar 30 6G (1935-1942)
(1) $1,600   (2) $2,500   (3) $4,500   (4) $6,500   (5) $8,250

This 1932 Caterpillar Sixty Five has a rare butane fuel option. Only 521 gasoline models were built while the butane numbers are unknown. Variations such as orchard, high-clearance, and LPG fuel models tend to increase the value of crawlers, but perhaps a bit less percentage-wise than with wheel tractors.

Caterpillar 30 6G Orchard (1935-1942)
(1) $3,000   (2) $4,000   (3) $5,750   (4) $8,000 (5) $11,000

Caterpillar 30 R4 (1935-1942)
(1) $900   (2) $1,950   (3) $3,500   (4) $5,000   (5) $6,250

Caterpillar 30 R4 Orchard (1935–1942)
(1) $2,375   (2) $3,250   (3) $4,500   (4) $6,000   (5) $7,500

Caterpillar 35 (gasoline, 1932–1934)
(1) $1,500   (2) $3,800   (3) $5,000   (4) $6,000   (5) $7,750

Caterpillar 35 (diesel, 1933–1934)
(1) $1,125   (2) $2,500   (3) $4,000   (4) $5,250   (5) $6,500

Caterpillar 35 Wide (diesel, 1932–1934)
(1) $1,400   (2) $3,000   (3) $4,500   (4) $5,500   (5) $7,000

Caterpillar 35 Orchard (1932–1934)
(1) $3,000   (2) $5,000   (3) $8,500   (4) $12,500   (5) $14,500

Caterpillar 40 (gasoline, 1934–1936)
(1) $5,000   (2) $8,000   (3) $10,500   (4) $14,500   (5) $19,500

Caterpillar produced only 46 D-5 9M-Series crawlers. Built between July 12 and July 19 of 1939 as a D-4 chassis with a D-6 R-Series Engine, this crawler is in high demand by Caterpillar collectors. With the horrendous costs of restoring crawlers, one can expect a collector to concentrate on a rare model like this before putting his effort and money into a high-production model.

Caterpillar 40 (diesel, 1934–1936)
(1) $1,400   (2) $2,000   (3) $4,000   (4) $6,000   (5) $7,000

Caterpillar 40 Wide (diesel, 1934–1936)
(1) $1,850   (2) $3,000   (3) $4,500   (4) $6,500   (5) $8,000

Caterpillar 40 Orchard (1934–1936)
(1) $4,000   (2) $8,500   (3) $10,000   (4) $12,500 (5) $15,500

Caterpillar 50 (gasoline, 1931–1937)
(1) $4,000   (2) $7,500   (3) $9,000   (4) $14,000 (5) $17,500

Caterpillar 50 (diesel, 1933–1936)
(1) $2,100   (2) $3,000   (3) $4,500   (4) $7,000   (5) $8,500

Caterpillar 50 Wide (diesel, 1933–1936)
(1) $2,350   (2) $3,000   (3) $5,000   (4) $7,500   (5) $9,750

Caterpillar 60 (gasoline, 1925–1931)
(1) $4,250   (2) $7,000   (3) $10,500   (4) $16,500 (5) $20,500

Caterpillar 60 (diesel, 1925–1931)
(1) $7,500   (2) $9,500   (3) $20,000   (4) $29,000 (5) $38,000

Caterpillar 65 (gasoline, 1932–1934)
(1) $10,000 (2) $12,500 (3) $18,000   (4) $20,000 (5) $22,500

Caterpillar 65 (diesel, 1931–1932)
(1) $12,000 (2) $18,000 (3) $22,000   (4) $26,500 (5) $30,000

Caterpillar 70 (gasoline, 1933–1937)
(1) $6,000   (2) $12,000 (3) $18,000   (4) $22,000 (5) $25,000

Caterpillar 70 (diesel, 1933–1937)
(1) $11,000 (2) $16,500 (3) $20,000   (4) $24,000 (5) $27,000

Caterpillar 75 (diesel, 1933–1935)
(1) $2,000   (2) $4,000   (3) $6,000   (4) $8,000 (5) $10,000

Caterpillar R-2 5E (3-speed, 1934–1937)
(1) $1,500   (2) $2,500   (3) $3,000   (4) $5,000 (5) $7,000

Caterpillar R-2 J series (5-speed, 1938–1942)
(1) $1,500   (2) $1,800   (3) $2,000   (4) $3,000 (5) $5,000

Caterpillar D-2 J series (5-speed, 1938–1947)
(1) $1,500   (2) $2,500   (3) $4,000   (4) $5,000 (5) $6,500

Caterpillar R-2 J series Orchard (1938–1942)
(1) $1,500   (2) $2,250   (3) $4,300   (4) $5,200 (5) $6,500

Caterpillar R-3 (1934–1935)
(1) $7,500   (2) $9,500   (3) $12,000   (4) $22,000 (5) $25,000

Caterpillar R-4 (1935–1944)
(1) $2,000   (2) $3,000   (3) $4,000   (4) $5,500 (5) $6,850

Caterpillar R-4 Orchard (1935–1944)
(1) $900   (2) $1,500   (3) $3,000   (4) $4,500 (5) $6,000

Caterpillar RD-4 and early D4 (1936–1939)
(1) $800   (2) $1,500   (3) $3,000   (4) $4,500 (5) $6,000

Caterpillar D-4 U series (1947–1959)
(1) $900   (2) $1,500   (3) $3,500   (4) $5,000 (5) $6,500

Caterpillar R-5 (gasoline, 1934–1940)
(1) $3,000   (2) $3,500   (3) $6,000   (4) $7,500 (5) $8,500

Caterpillar D-5 9M series (diesel, 1939)
(1) $8,500   (2) $10,000 (3) $14,000   (4) $18,000 (5) $20,000

Caterpillar R-6 (gasoline, 1941)
(1) $30,000 (2) $40,000 (3) $45,000   (4) $48,000 (5) $50,000

The Cletrac crawlers are some of the most popular collectible crawlers, second only to Caterpillar. This 1920 Model F Hi-Drive 9-16 crawler could bring over $10,000 if its owner decided to sell it. Roland White, the same man who founded the White Motors Corp. and started his fortune from the White sewing machines, founded Cleveland Tractor Company.

Caterpillar RD-6 (3-cylinder, 1935–1942)
(1) $900   (2) $2,200   (3) $4,250   (4) $5,500   (5) $7,750

Caterpillar D-6 (6-cylinder, 1941–1947)
(1) $1,000   (2) $2,000   (3) $4,250   (4) $5,750   (5) $7,500

Caterpillar RD-7 (1935–1940)
(1) $1,500   (2) $2,500   (3) $4,500   (4) $6,500   (5) $8,250

Caterpillar D-7 7M series (1940–1944)
(1) $1,500   (2) $2,250   (3) $4,250   (4) $5,500   (5) $7,500

Caterpillar RD-8 (1935–1941)
(1) $2,250   (2) $3,800   (3) $5,000   (4) $6,900   (5) $10,000

Caterpillar D-8 8R series (1941–1945)
(1) $1,250   (2) $2,200   (3) $4,500   (4) $6,250   (5) $9,250

Clark Equipment Company, Detroit, Michigan

The tiny Clarkaire crawlers were built during World War II with a track gauge of about three feet so they could be dropped by parachute and used to repair airstrips and clear out small areas. Many collectors are attracted to the Clarkaire crawlers because of their small size and military history.

Clarkaire (military, 1941–1946)
(1) $500   (2) $2,000   (3) $3,500   (4) $6,000   (5) $8,000

Cleveland Tractor Company, Cleveland, Ohio

With a differential-type steering assembly, the Cletrac was among the best-selling crawlers of its day. Most other crawlers used individual steering clutches and brakes to stop power to each track for turning. The Cletracs had a planetary-gear differential with individual brakes that reduced the speed for turning without total interruption of power to either track. The advantage of this type of steering coupled with its extremely durable construction made the Cletrac very popular. Well known for its excellent weight-to-horsepower ratio, the Cletrac was desirable for orchard work and other farming tasks. In 1945 the Oliver Tractor Company acquired the Cleveland Tractor enterprise.

Cletrac R (1916–1917)
(1) $2,400   (2) $5,250   (3) $8,800   (4) $12,375 (5) $18,750

Cletrac H (1917–1919)
(1) $2,000   (2) $3,750   (3) $5,500   (4) $7,500 (5) $11,250

Cletrac W (1919–1932)
(1) $1,500   (2) $2,100   (3) $3,750   (4) $6,000 (5) $11,000

Cletrac F (1920–1932)
(1) $1,600   (2) $3,000   (3) $6,000   (4) $9,000 (5) $13,500

Cletrac 20K (1925–1932)
(1) $800   (2) $1,500   (3) $3,750   (4) $6,000   (5) $9,000

Cletrac 30A (1926–1928)
(1) $1,500   (2) $3,750   (3) $6,925   (4) $10,125 (5) $15,000

Cletrac 30B (1929–1930)
(1) $1,500   (2) $3,750   (3) $6,925   (4) $10,125 (5) $15,000

Cletrac 40 (1928–1931)
(1) $1,500   (2) $3,750   (3) $6,925   (4) $10,125 (5) $15,000

Cletrac 55-40 (1931–1932)
(1) $1,500   (2) $3,750   (3) $6,925   (4) $10,125 (5) $15,000

Cletrac 55 (1932–1936)
(1) $1,800   (2) $4,500   (3) $6,925   (4) $10,125 (5) $15,000

Cletrac 100 (1927–1930)
(1) $6,000   (2) $15,000   (3) $32,500   (4) $50,000 (5) $75,000

The Cletrac Model 20K was a popular crawler built from 1925 until 1932. 10,107 copies of this crawler were produced. Cletrac is a popular crawler among collectors, followed only by Caterpillar as the most popular brand in the hobby.

Cletrac 15 (1931–1933)
(1) $1,200   (2) $2,250   (3) $4,875   (4) $7,500   (5) $11,250

Cletrac 20C (1933–1936)
(1) $1,200   (2) $2,250   (3) $4,875   (4) $7,500   (5) $11,250

Cletrac ED-38 (1938–1939)
(1) $900   (2) $1,500   (3) $3,750   (4) $6,000   (5) $9,000

Cletrac HG (1939–1951)
(1) $900   (2) $1,500   (3) $3,750   (4) $6,000   (5) $9,000

Cletrac ED-42 (1938–1941)
(1) $900   (2) $1,500   (3) $3,750   (4) $6,000   (5) $9,000

Cletrac ED-2-38 (1937–1938)
(1) $900   (2) $1,500   (3) $3,750   (4) $6,000   (5) $9,000

Cletrac ED-2-42 (1938–1941)
(1) $900   (2) $1,500   (3) $3,750   (4) $6,000   (5) $9,000

Cletrac EHD-2 (1938–1941)
(1) $1,200   (2) $3,000   (3) $5,250   (4) $7,500 (5) $11,250

Cletrac EN (1934–1939)
(1) $1,200   (2) $3,000   (3) $6,000   (4) $9,000 (5) $13,500

Cletrac E-38 Nonstreamlined (1934–1936)
(1) $1,200   (2) $3,000   (3) $5,250   (4) $7,500 (5) $11,250

Cletrac E-38 Streamlined (1936–1938)
(1) $1,000   (2) $1,875   (3) $3,950   (4) $6,000   (5) $9,000

Cletrac E-42 (1938–1942)
(1) $1,000   (2) $1,875   (3) $3,950   (4) $6,000   (5) $9,000

Cletrac EHG (1937–1941)
(1) $1,000   (2) $1,875   (3) $3,950   (4) $6,000   (5) $9,000

Cletrac AG (1936–1942)
(1) $1,200   (2) $3,000   (3) $4,875   (4) $6,750 (5) $10,500

Cletrac AD (1937–1959)
(1) $1,200   (2) $3,000   (3) $4,875   (4) $6,750 (5) $10,500

Cletrac AD-2 (1937–1940)
(1) $1,200   (2) $3,000   (3) $5,250   (4) $7,500   (5) $11,250

Cletrac 25 (1931–1935)
(1) $1,500   (2) $3,750   (3) $6,950   (4) $10,100 (5) $15,000

Cletrac BG (1937–1945)
(1) $1,500   (2) $3,750   (3) $5,625   (4) $7,500 (5) $11,250

Cletrac 30 (gasoline, 1937–1945)
(1) $1,650 (2) $3,750 (3) $7,675 (4) $11,250 (5) $16,500

Cletrac BD (1935–1956)
(1) $1,200 (2) $3,000 (3) $5,250 (4) $7,500 (5) $11,250

Cletrac BD-2 (1937–1938)
(1) $1,800 (2) $4,500 (3) $8,650 (4) $12,750 (5) $18,750

Cletrac 35 and CG (1931–1942)
(1) $1,500 (2) $3,750 (3) $6,950 (4) $10,100 (5) $15,000

Cletrac 35D (diesel, 1934–1935)
(1) $1,500 (2) $3,750 (3) $8,250 (4) $12,750 (5) $18,750

Cletrac 40 (diesel, 1934–1937)
(1) $1,500 (2) $3,750 (3) $8,250 (4) $12,750 (5) $18,750

Cletrac DG (1936–1956)
(1) $1,000 (2) $2,250 (3) $4,550 (4) $7,500 (5) $11,250

Cletrac DD and 35 (diesel, 1934–1958)
(1) $1,800 (2) $4,000 (3) $6,750 (4) $9,000 (5) $13,500

Cletrac FG and 80 (gasoline, 1930–1943)
(1) $3,000 (2) $7,500 (3) $18,750 (4) $35,000 (5) $55,000

Cletrac FD (1938–1945)
(1) $3,000 (2) $7,500 (3) $13,850 (4) $20,250 (5) $35,000

Cletrac FDLC (1941–1944)
(1) $3,000 (2) $7,500 (3) $13,850 (4) $20,250 (5) $35,000

Cletrac MG-1 (1941–1943)
(1) $1,800 (2) $4,500 (3) $8,650 (4) $12,750 (5) $18,750

Cletrac FDE (1945–1952)
(1) $3,000 (2) $7,500 (3) $13,850 (4) $20,250 (5) $35,000

Cletrac AG-6 (1944–1957)
(1) $1,200 (2) $3,000 (3) $4,500 (4) $6,000 (5) $9,000

Cletrac BGS (1945–1948)
(1) $1,000 (2) $2,250 (3) $4,875 (4) $7,500 (5) $11,250

Cletrac HGR-68 (rubber tracks, ca. 1940)
(1) $3,200 (2) $8,000 (3) $15,500 (4) $23,000 (5) $35,000

Dayton-Dick Company
(renamed Dayton-Dowd Co.), Quincy, Illinois
Leader 25-40 (half-track, 1916–1918)
(1) $18,000 (2) $27,000 (3) $35,000 (4) $41,500 (5) $50,000

Leader C 25-40 (half-track, 1919)
(1) $18,000   (2) $27,000   (3) $35,000   (4) $41,500   (5) $50,000

Leader D 25-40 (half-track, 1920)
(1) $18,000   (2) $27,000   (3) $35,000   (4) $41,500   (5) $50,000

Leader C 18-36 (half-track, 1919–1920)
(1) $18,000   (2) $27,000   (3) $35,000   (4) $41,500   (5) $50,000

Leader GU 16-32 (full-track, 1921–1923)
(1) $12,000   (2) $20,000   (3) $28,000   (4) $34,000   (5) $40,000

Deere and Co., Moline, Illinois

John Deere built 1,675 BO Lindeman crawlers. Most were used in the western part of the country for orchard work. These BO tractors were converted into crawlers from 1939 to 1947 by Lindeman's Yakima, Washington, plant. Nicely restored models can sell for over $10,000.

John Deere BO Lindeman (1939–1947)
(1) $2,500   (2) $3,000   (3) $4,500   (4) $8,500   (5) $12,000

John Deere MC (1949–1952)
(1) $800   (2) $2,200   (3) $3,500   (4) $6,500   (5) $10,000

John Deere 40C (gasoline, 3 rollers, 1953–1956)
(1) $1,300   (2) $2,800   (3) $4,000   (4) $7,000   (5) $10,500

John Deere 40C (gasoline, 4 rollers, 1953–1956)
(1) $800   (2) $2,200   (3) $3,500   (4) $6,500   (5) $10,000

John Deere 40C (all-fuel, 4 rollers, 1953–1956)
(1) $1,800   (2) $3,200   (3) $4,500   (4) $7,500   (5) $11,000

John Deere 40C (gasoline, 5 rollers, 1953–1956)
(1) $800   (2) $2,200   (3) $3,500   (4) $6,500   (5) $10,000

John Deere 40C (all-fuel, 5 rollers, 1953–1956)
(1) $1,800   (2) $3,200   (3) $4,500   (4) $7,500   (5) $11,000

John Deere 420C (gasoline, 4 rollers, 1956–1958)
(1) $800   (2) $2,200   (3) $3,500   (4) $6,500   (5) $10,000

John Deere 420C (all-fuel, 4 rollers, 1956–1958)
(1) $2,300   (2) $3,700   (3) $5,000   (4) $8,000   (5) $11,500

The MC was the first crawler built entirely by John Deere. The success of the aftermarket crawler conversions from the BO tractor models led the John Deere Company to buy out the Lindeman operations. About 10,509 MCs were built from 1949 to 1952. The strength of the John Deere two-cylinder tractors as collectibles puts the MC on the wish list of more and more collectors each year.

John Deere 420C (gasoline, 5 rollers, 1956–1958)
(1) $1,000   (2) $2,500   (3) $3,800   (4) $7,000 (5) $11,000

John Deere 420C (all-fuel, 5 rollers, 1956–1958)
(1) $2,500   (2) $4,000   (3) $5,300   (4) $8,500 (5) $12,500

John Deere 430C (gasoline, 4 rollers, 1958–1960)
(1) $1,200   (2) $3,000   (3) $4,500   (4) $8,000 (5) $12,000

John Deere 430C (all-fuel, 4 rollers, 1958–1960)
(1) $3,200   (2) $5,000   (3) $6,500   (4) $10,000 (5) $14,000

John Deere 430C (gasoline, 5 rollers, 1958–1960)
(1) $1,200   (2) $3,000   (3) $4,500   (4) $8,000 (5) $12,000

John Deere 430C (all-fuel, 5 rollers, 1958–1960)
(1) $3,200   (2) $5,000   (3) $6,500   (4) $10,000 (5) $14,000

John Deere 430C (LPG, 1958–1960)
(1) $5,000   (2) $10,000   (3) $16,000   (4) $20,000(5) $25,000

Model 440 CI (1958–1960)
(1) $1,500   (2) $2,000   (3) $4,500   (4) $6,500   (5) $9,000

Model 440 CID (1958–1960)
(1) $1,500   (2) $2,000   (3) $4,500   (4) $6,000   (5) $8,000

The selling price of a Model 40C John Deere crawler in 1946 was $2,500. Even though nearly 17,000 of these crawlers were built, a nicely restored model can fetch about four times the original selling price.

Eimco Corporation, Salt Lake City, Utah

Eimco Model 103 (1959-1964)
(1) $800   (2) $2,500   (3) $5,500   (4) $7,000   (5) $9,000

Eimco Model 105 (1953-1961)
(1) $800   (2) $2,500   (3) $5,500   (4) $7,000   (5) $9,000

Eimco Model 165 (1961-1964)
(1) $900   (2) $2,700   (3) $5,800   (4) $7,500   (5) $9,500

Eimco Model 106 (1958-1964)
(1) $1,200   (2) $3,000   (3) $6,000   (4) $8,000   (5) $10,000

Electric Wheel Company, Quincy, Illinois

Allwork 25-35 (5-ton, 1925-1928)
(1) $6,000   (2) $12,000   (3) $17,000   (4) $22,000   (5) $29,000

Allwork 80 (1926-1928)
(1) $10,000   (2) $16,500   (3) $22,000   (4) $27,000   (5) $34,500

Franklin Tractor Company, Greenville, Ohio

Franklin Flexible 15-30 (1919-1920)
(1) $15,000   (2) $21,000   (3) $25,000   (4) $28,500   (5) $35,000

General Tractor Company, Seattle, Washington

Westrak Crawler (ca. 1948)
(1) $1,200   (2) $3,250   (3) $5,500   (4) $8,000   (5) $12,000

Holt Tractor Company, Stockton, California

The Holt 45 Model B used a pair of front wheels for steering. Apparently, this is one of only two Model 45s that were built this way.

Holt 60 Horsepower (ca. 1912)
(1) $20,000   (2) $48,000   (3) $70,000   (4) $98,000   (5) $120,000

Holt Baby Caterpillar (ca. 1914)
(1) $15,000   (2) $26,000   (3) $34,000   (4) $40,000   (5) $50,000

Holt Junior (ca. 1916)
(1) $12,000   (2) $23,000   (3) $30,000   (4) $36,500   (5) $45,000

Holt 25-45 (1916-1919)
(1) $20,000   (2) $38,000   (3) $52,000   (4) $64,000   (5) $80,000

A Holt 75 is a show-stopper. A Model 75 sold at the Oscar's Dreamland Auction in 1998 for $120,000. Values for such a machine are tremendously dear as are the restoration expenses.

Holt 50-75 (1916–1919)
(1) $20,000   (2) $48,000   (3) $70,000   (4) $98,000   (5) $120,000

Holt 70-120 (1916–1919)
(1) $25,000   (2) $53,000   (3) $75,000   (4) $100,000   (5) $130,000

Holt 5-Ton (1919–1925)
(1) $3,500   (2) $7,500   (3) $9,800   (4) $12,000   (5) $15,000

Holt 10-Ton (1919–1925)
(1) $12,500   (2) $20,000   (3) $28,500   (4) $35,500   (5) $45,000

Holt 2-Ton (1923–1925)
(1) $1,800   (2) $3,400   (3) $6,500   (4) $9,800   (5) $13,500

International Harvester Company, Chicago, Illinois

This International Harvester T-6 crawler used the same engine as the popular Model M farm tractor. Only a limited amount of collector interest is aimed toward the T-series crawlers, but the tide is changing. Seldom does a T-6 get restored as exquisitely as the one pictured here.

Tractractor 10-20 (1930–1931)
(1) $1,000   (2) $2,500   (3) $5,000   (4) $7,500   (5) $10,000

Tractractor T-20 (1931–1939)
(1) $1,000   (2) $2,000   (3) $3,750   (4) $6,000   (5) $8,000

Tractractor T-35 (gasoline, 1936–1939)
(1) $1,000   (2) $2,000   (3) $3,750   (4) $6,000   (5) $8,000

Tractractor TD-35 (diesel, 1936–1939)
(1) $1,000   (2) $2,000   (3) $3,750   (4) $6,000   (5) $8,000

At present time, the International T-9 crawler is barely considered a collectable. The value for such a machine is based perhaps more on practical use than collector appeal. One can expect this to change in the near future as collecting crawlers is becoming more commonplace. This T-9 has a seldom-seen Trackson Crane.

Tractractor T-40 (gasoline, 1932–1939)
(1) $1,000 (2) $2,000 (3) $3,750 (4) $6,000 (5) $8,000

Tractractor TD-40 (diesel, 1932–1939)
(1) $1,000 (2) $2,000 (3) $3,750 (4) $6,000 (5) $8,000

International T-6 (gasoline, 1939–1969)
(1) $1,000 (2) $2,200 (3) $3,500 (4) $4,200 (5) $6,000

International TD-6 (diesel, 1940–1969)
(1) $670 (2) $1,675 (3) $3,350 (4) $4,000 (5) $6,000

International T-9 (gasoline, 1940–1956)
(1) $1,340 (2) $2,680 (3) $4,025 (4) $6,200 (5) $9,000

International TD-9 (diesel, 1940–1956)
(1) $1,000 (2) $2,000 (3) $4,025 (4) $6,200 (5) $9,000

International T-14 (gasoline, 1940–1956)
(1) $1,000 (2) $1,675 (3) $2,680 (4) $3,600 (5) $6,000

International TD-14 (diesel, 1940–1956)
(1) $700 (2) $1,200 (3) $2,500 (4) $3,600 (5) $6,000

International TD-18 (diesel, 1938–1949)
(1) $1,200 (2) $2,200 (3) $4,200 (4) $6,750 (5) $9,500

International TD-24 (diesel, 1947–1959)
(1) $1,800 (2) $4,250 (3) $6,500 (4) $8,800 (5) $10,500

J-T Tractor Company, Cleveland, Ohio
J-T 16-30 (Erd engine, 1918–1919)
(1) $8,000 (2) $13,000 (3) $17,000 (4) $21,000 (5) $28,000

J-T 40 (Chief engine, 1920–1921)
(1) $7,500 (2) $12,500 (3) $16,250 (4) $20,000 (5) $26,000

J-T 25-40 (Climax engine, 1925–1929)
(1) $10,000 (2) $15,000 (3) $19,000 (4) $23,000 (5) $30,000

Keystone Iron and Steel Works, Los Angeles, California
Keystone 30 (1921–1923)
(1) $10,000 (2) $15,000 (3) $19,000 (4) $23,000 (5) $30,000

Mead-Morrison Manufacturing Company, East Boston, Massachusetts
Mead-Morrison 55 (1924–1930)
(1) $10,000 (2) $15,000 (3) $19,000 (4) $23,000 (5) $30,000

Minneapolis-Moline Company, Minneapolis, Minnesota
2-Star Crawler (1958)
(1) $800 (2) $1,100 (3) $3,000 (4) $4,500 (5) $7,000

Motrac (gasoline, 1960–1961)
(1) $800 (2) $1,100 (3) $3,000 (4) $4,500 (5) $7,000

Motrac (diesel, 1960–1961)
(1) $750 (2) $1,000 (3) $2,800 (4) $4,000 (5) $7,000

Monarch Tractor Corporation, Watertown, Wisconsin
Lightfoot 6-10 (1916–1918)
(1) $8,000 (2) $12,000 (3) $16,000 (4) $20,000 (5) $25,000

Model M Neverslip 12-20 (1916–1923)
(1) $8,000 (2) $12,000 (3) $16,000 (4) $20,000 (5) $25,000

Model N Neverslip 18-30 (rerated 20-30, 1919–1925)
(1) $8,000 (2) $12,000 (3) $16,000 (4) $20,000 (5) $25,000

Model D 6-60 (1924–1926)
(1) $6,000 (2) $8,000 (3) $12,000 (4) $15,000 (5) $18,000

Model C 25-35 (1925–1926)
(1) $6,000 (2) $8,000 (3) $12,000 (4) $15,000 (5) $18,000

Model E 4-40 (1923–1925)
(1) $6,000 (2) $8,000 (3) $12,000 (4) $15,000 (5) $18,000

Model F 10-ton (1926–1928)
(1) $8,000 (2) $12,000 (3) $16,000 (4) $20,000 (5) $27,000

Model G 5-ton (1926–1927)
(1) $6,000 (2) $8,000 (3) $12,000 (4) $15,000 (5) $18,000

Model H 6-ton (1927–1928)
(1) $8,000 (2) $12,000 (3) $15,000 (4) $18,000 (5) 20,000

Monarch 35 (1928–1933)
(1) $1,500   (2) $2,400   (3) $4,800   (4) $7,000 (5) $12,000

Monarch 50 (1928–1931)
(1) $8,000   (2) $12,000   (3) $15,000   (4) $18,000 (5) $20,000

Monarch 75 (1928–1931)
(1) $8,000   (2) $12,000   (3) $16,000   (4) $20,000 (5) $27,000

Monarch 80-50 (ca. 1925)
(1) $20,000   (2) $24,000   (3) $30,000   (4) $36,000 (5) $40,000

Oliver Corporation (see Cleveland Tractor Company for early models), Chicago, Illinois
Oliver OC-3 (1951–1957)
(1) $400   (2) $1,000   (3) $2,000   (4) $3,500 (5) $5,250

Oliver OC-4 (1956–1958)
(1) $750   (2) $1,500   (3) $2,500   (4) $4,000 (5) $6,000

Oliver OC-4-3G (1958–1965)
(1) $750   (2) $1,500   (3) $2,500   (4) $4,000 (5) $6,000

Oliver OC-4-3D (1957–1965)
(1) $750   (2) $1,500   (3) $2,500   (4) $4,000 (5) $6,000

Oliver OC-6G (1953–1960)
(1) $800   (2) $1,800   (3) $3,000   (4) $5,000 (5) $7,500

Oliver OC-6 42-inch (1953–1960)
(1) $800   (2) $1,800   (3) $3,000   (4) $5,000 (5) $7,500

Oliver OC-6 31-inch (1953–1960)
(1) $1,000   (2) $2,000   (3) $3,500   (4) $6,000 (5) $9,000

Oliver OC-6 High-clearance (1953–1960)
(1) $2,000   (2) $4,000   (3) $6,000   (4) $9,000 (5) $13,500

Oliver OC-6D (1953–1960)
(1) $800   (2) $1,800   (3) $3,000   (4) $5,000 (5) $7,500

Oliver OC-9 (1959–1964)
(1) $1,000   (2) $2,000   (3) $4,500   (4) $8,000 (5) $12,000

Oliver OC-12G (1955–1960)
(1) $750   (2) $1,500   (3) $2,500   (4) $3,500 (5) $5,250

Oliver OC-12D (1954–1961)
(1) $750   (2) $1,500   (3) $2,500   (4) $3,500 (5) $5,250

Oliver OC-15 (1956–1961)
(1) $1,000   (2) $2,000   (3) $3,500   (4) $5,000 (5) $7,500

Oliver OC-18 (1952–1960)
(1) $1,000   (2) $2,000   (3) $4,500   (4) $8,000 (5) $12,000

Oliver OC-46 (1962–1965)
(1) $500   (2) $1,200   (3) $2,500   (4) $3,500 (5) $5,250

Oliver OC-96 (1959–1965)
(1) $1,000   (2) $2,000   (3) $4,500   (4) $8,000 (5) $12,000

Oliver Tractor Company, Knoxville, Tennessee
Model A 15-30 (1919)
(1) $8,000   (2) $12,000   (3) $15,000   (4) $18,000 (5) $24,000

Model B 12-20 (1919)
(1) $6,500   (2) $10,000   (3) $12,500   (4) $15,000 (5) $20,000

Union Tool Corporation, Torrance, California
Sure-Grip 12-25 (1921–1922)
(1) $12,000   (2) $19,000   (3) $25,000   (4) $38,000 (5) $50,000

The only known example of the Union Tool Sure-Grip crawler belongs to the University of California at Davis. The front wheel is a free-riding support castor not unlike the pivoting wheels on a shopping cart. The strange-looking loops behind the seat protect the operator when backing up. Machines this rare often end up in museums after passing through private collections.

U.S. Tractor Sales Incorporated, Peoria, Illinois
USTRAC 10 (also built by Federal Machine and Welder Co., 1947–1950)
(1) $450   (2) $1,850   (3) $3,000   (4) $5,500 (5) $7,500

Yuba Manufacturing Company, Marysville, California
Yuba 12-20 (rerated 15-25, 1916–1931)
(1) $8,000   (2) $14,500   (3) $20,000   (4) $24,000 (5) $30,000

Yuba 18-35 (1916–1931)
(1) $8,000   (2) $14,500   (3) $20,000   (4) $24,000 (5) $30,000

Yuba 40-70 (1919)
(1) $8,000   (2) $14,500   (3) $20,000   (4) $24,000 (5) $30,000

MODEL CROSS REFERENCE

Allwork	Electric Wheel Co.
Angleworm (crawler)	Badley Tractor Co.
American	Russell and Co.
Ball Tread	Yuba Mfg. Co.
Bear	J. I. Case Plow Works
Beaver	Goold, Shapley and Muir Co.
Big Boss	Russell and Co.
Big Bull	Bull Tractor Co.
Big 4	Gas Traction Co.
Big 4	Emerson-Brantingham Implement Co.
Big Mo	Minneapolis-Moline Co.
Biltwell	Velie Motors Corp.
Blue J	Dart Truck and Tractor Co.
Bower City	Townsend Manufacturing Co.
Boyer Four	Huron Tractor Co.
Bradley	Sears-Roebuck Co.
Bronco	Waterloo Co. (Canada)
Canadian Special	Gray Tractor Co.
Capital	C. A. Dissinger and Bros. Co.
Caterpillar	Holt Tractor Co.
Chain Tread (crawler)	Buckeye Manufacturing Co.
Challenger	Massey-Harris Co.
Cletrac (crawler)	Cleveland Tractor Co.
Colt	Massey-Harris Co.
Creeping Grip (crawler)	Bullock Tractor Co.
Crop-Maker	Hart-Parr Co.
Cub	J. I. Case Plow Works and International Harvester
Cub Jr.	J. I. Case Plow Works
Dakota	G. W. Elliot and Son
DoAll	Advance-Rumely Thresher Co.
Du-All	Shaw Manufacturing Co.
Farmall	International Harvester Co.
Farmers Tractor	Huber Manufacturing Co.
Farmobile	William Galloway Co.
Fitch FWD	Four Drive Tractor Co.
5-Star	Minneapolis-Moline Co.
Flexible (crawler)	Franklin Tractor Co.
Flour City	Kinnard-Haines Co.
Fordson	Ford Motor Co.
Four-Plow	Kinnard-Haines Co.
4-Pull	Wizard Tractor Corp.
4-Star	Minneapolis-Moline Co.
GasPull	Advance-Rumely Thresher Co.
General	Cleveland Tractor Co.
Giant	Russell and Co.

G-O	General Ordnance Co.
Graham-Bradley	Graham-Paige Motors Co.
Heider	Rock Island Plow Co.
Ideal	Goold, Shapley and Muir Co.
Iron Horse	General Motors Corp.
Jet Star	Minneapolis-Moline Co.
Joy McVicker	McVicker Engineering Co.
Jumbo	Jumbo Steel Products
Junior	Kinnard-Haines Co., Nilson, Russell
Junior (crawler)	Holt Tractor Co.
Kay-Gee	Keck-Gonnerman Co.
Kerosene Annie	Advance-Rumely Thresher Co.
Kingwood	Knickerbocker Motors Inc.
Klear-View	Centaur Tractor Corp.
Leader	Dayton-Dick Co.,
	Leader Tractor Mfg. Co
Lightfoot (crawler)	Monarch Tractor Corp.
Light Four	Huber Manufacturing Co.
Lindeman (crawler)	Deere and Co.
Little Bear	L. A. Auto Tractor Co.
Little Boss	Russell and Co.
Little Bull	Bull Tractor Co.
Little Pet	Flinchbaugh Manufacturing Co.
Little Red Devil	Hart-Parr Co.
Macdonald	Cushman Motor Works
Master Four	Huber Manufacturing Co.
McCormick Deering	International Harvester Co.
Midwest	Wichita Tractor Co.
Mid-West	Agrimotor Tractor Co.
Modern Four	Huber Manufacturing Co.
Mogul	International Harvester Co.
Mohawk	United Tractors Corp.
Motrac	Minneapolis-Moline Co.
Muley (crawler)	C. L. Best Traction Co.
Multipedal (crawler)	F. C. Austin Co.
Mustang	Massey-Harris Co.
Neverslip (crawler)	Monarch Tractor Corp.
Oil King	Hart-Parr Co.
OilPull	Advance-Rumely Thresher Co.
Old Reliable	Hart-Parr Co.
OMC	Ostenberg Manufacturing Co.
Pacemaker	Massey-Harris Co.
Pacer	Massey-Harris Co.
Planet Jr.	S. L. Allen and Co.
Plow Boy	Interstate Tractor and Engine Co.
Plow Man	Interstate Tractor and Engine Co.
Plymouth	Fate-Root-Heath Co.
Pony	Massey-Harris Co. and
	Pioneer Tractor Mfg. Co.
Pony (crawler)	C. L. Best Traction Co.
Powerbilt	General Tractor Corp.
Power Horse	Harris Manufacturing Co.
Power-Horse	Eimco Corp.
Prairie Dog	Kansas City Hay Press Co.
Quadpull	Antigo Tractor Corp.

Quincy	Electric Wheel Co.
Rex	Leader Tractor Mfg. Co. (1920s)
Road King	Hart-Parr Co.
Ro-Trac	Avery Co.
Samson	General Motors Corp.
Senior	Nilson Tractor Co.
Shawnee	Shaw-Enochs Tractor Co.
Silver King	Fate-Root-Heath Co.
Simplicity	Turner Manufacturing Co.
Simpson	Jumbo Steel Products
Special	Pioneer Tractor Manufacturing Co.
Steel Clad	Denning Motor Implement Co.
Steel Hoof	Lambert Gas Engine Co.
Steel Mule	Bates Machine and Tractor Co.
Super	Oliver Corp. and International Harvester
Super Drive	Illinois Tractor Co.
Super Four	Huber Manufacturing Co.
Sure-Grip (crawler)	Union Tool Corp.
Terratrac (crawler)	American Tractor Corp.
Tilsoil	Farm Motors Co. (Canada)
Titan	International Harvester
Toehold	Advance-Rumely Thresher Co.
Tracklayer	C. L. Best Traction Co.
Track Runner (crawler)	Avery Co.
Tractair	Centaur and Le Roi
Tractractor (crawler)	International Harvester Co.
Trundaar (crawler)	Buckeye Manufacturing Co.
Twin City	Minneapolis-Moline and Minneapolis Steel
2-Star	Minneapolis-Moline Co.
Uncle Sam	U.S. Tractor and Machinery Co.
United	Allis-Chalmers Co.
Uni-Tractor	Minneapolis-Moline Co.
Universal	Minneapolis Threshing and Moline Plow Co.
Universal Farm Motor	American-Abell Engine and Thresher Co.
Vista	Minneapolis-Moline Co.
Wallis	Massey-Harris Co.
Waterloo Boy	Deere and Co. and Waterloo Gasoline Engine Co.
Weber	American Gas Engine Co.
Webfoot (crawler)	Blewett Tractor Co.
Wellington	Sterling Machine and Stamping Co.
Westrak (crawler)	General Tractor Co.
Wheat	Hession Tiller and Tractor Corp.
Yankee	American Tractor Corp.

GLOSSARY

all- fuel	Tractor uses gasoline as well as low-grade fuels
cane tractor	High-clearance tractor
crossmotor	Transverse engine, usually in reference to certain Case tractors
distillate	One type of low grade fuel
grove tractor	An orchard tractor, used around trees
high-clearance tractor	Variation of a common model that has greater height for special crops
high-crop	Same as a high-clearance tractor
I-head	Engine has valves in head (rocker arms)
industrial tractor	Model variation used for street work, factory chores, and other nonfarming duties
L-head	Engine has valves in block (flat head)
live axle	Axle driven directly by tractor differential
live hydraulics	Hydraulic pump not interrupted by master clutch
live PTO	PTO shaft not interrupted by master clutch
LPG	Liquefied petroleum gas
motor cultivator	Early type of light-framed tractor used exclusively for cultivating between crop rows
orchard model	Tractor with special shielding for tree branches
PTO	Power takeoff
rear tread	Rear width of tractor measured from wheel centers
rice tractor	Special standard tread tractor with rear tires that have very deep and widely spaced cleats and mud guards
road tractor	Designed for highway maintenance, heavier built wheels
row-crop tractor	Tractor has adjustable tread and adequate clearance for straddling crop rows
shuttle clutch	Unit changes direction of tractor in all gears
snap-coupler	Allis-Chalmers' quick-attach implement system
standard tread	Wide-front tractor without simple tread adjustments
streamlined	Modernized with a grille and aesthetically improved tin work
styled	Usually refers to modernized John Deere tractors with grilles and aesthetically improved tin work
thresherman's special	Deluxe version of Allis-Chalmers Model E that has extra horsepower, cab, and exhaust whistle
track gauge	Width of crawler from center to center of tracks
utility tractor	Tractor with lower stance than common models
wheatland	Fixed-tread tractor with wide tires and fenders

INDEX